The Complete Guide To

PURCHASING A CONDO, TOWNHOUSE, OR APARTMENT

What Smart Investors Need To Know— Explained Simply

Susan Smith Alvis

THE COMPLETE GUIDE TO PURCHASING A CONDO, TOWNHOUSE, OR APARTMENT
WHAT SMART INVESTORS NEED TO KNOW—EXPLAINED SIMPLY

Copyright © 2007 by Atlantic Publishing Group, Inc.
1405 SW 6th Ave. • Ocala, Florida 34471 • 800-814-1132 • 352-622-1875–Fax
Web site: www.atlantic-pub.com • E-mail: sales@atlantic-pub.com
SAN Number: 268-1250

ISBN-13: 978-1-60138-036-4   ISBN-10: 1-60138-036-4

Library of Congress Cataloging-in-Publication Data

Alvis, Susan Smith, 1969-
  The complete guide to purchasing a condo, townhouse, or apartment : what smart investors need to know explained simply / by Susan Smith Alvis.
        p. cm.
  Includes bibliographical references and index.
  ISBN-13: 978-1-60138-036-4 (alk. paper)
  ISBN-10: 1-60138-036-4 (alk. paper)
  1. House buying--United States. 2. Condominiums--United States. 3. Row houses--United States. 4. Apartments--United States. I. Title.

  HD255.A598 2007
  333.33'8--dc22

                        2007021986

EDITOR: Marie Lujanac • mlujanac817@yahoo.com
COVER DESIGN & ART DIRECTOR: Meg Buchner • megadesn@mchsi.com
INTERIOR LAYOUT DESIGN: Vickie Taylor • vtaylor@atlantic-pub.com

Printed in the United States

Printed on Recycled Paper

We recently lost our beloved pet "Bear," who was not only our best and dearest friend but also the "Vice President of Sunshine" here at Atlantic Publishing. He did not receive a salary but worked tirelessly 24 hours a day to please his parents. Bear was a rescue dog that turned around and showered myself, my wife Sherri, his grandparents Jean, Bob and Nancy and every person and animal he met (maybe not rabbits) with friendship and love. He made a lot of people smile every day.

We wanted you to know that a portion of the profits of this book will be donated to The Humane Society of the United States.

–Douglas & Sherri Brown

THE HUMANE SOCIETY
OF THE UNITED STATES ©

The human-animal bond is as old as human history. We cherish our animal companions for their unconditional affection and acceptance. We feel a thrill when we glimpse wild creatures in their natural habitat or in our own backyard.

Unfortunately, the human-animal bond has at times been weakened. Humans have exploited some animal species to the point of extinction.

The Humane Society of the United States makes a difference in the lives of animals here at home and worldwide. The HSUS is dedicated to creating a world where our relationship with animals is guided by compassion. We seek a truly humane society in which animals are respected for their intrinsic value, and where the human-animal bond is strong.

Want to help animals? We have plenty of suggestions. Adopt a pet from a local shelter, join The Humane Society and be a part of our work to help companion animals and wildlife. You will be funding our educational, legislative, investigative and outreach projects in the U.S. and across the globe.

Or perhaps you'd like to make a memorial donation in honor of a pet, friend or relative? You can through our Kindred Spirits program. And if you'd like to contribute in a more structured way, our Planned Giving Office has suggestions about estate planning, annuities, and even gifts of stock that avoid capital gains taxes.

Maybe you have land that you would like to preserve as a lasting habitat for wildlife. Our Wildlife Land Trust can help you. Perhaps the land you want to share is a backyard—that's enough. Our Urban Wildlife Sanctuary Program will show you how to create a habitat for your wild neighbors.

So you see, it's easy to help animals. And The HSUS is here to help.

The Humane Society of the United States
2100 L Street NW
Washington, DC 20037
202-452-1100
www.hsus.org

CONTENTS

DEDICATION..11

FOREWORD...13

PREFACE 15

CHAPTER 1: INTRODUCING SHARED
HOUSING...23
Apartments..27
Condos 28
Townhouses...33
Common Areas...34
Why Buy a Shared Housing Unit....................................36
What Being a Homeowner Means in Shared Housing 37
Pros and Cons: What to Expect......................................38
The Matter of Price 40

WHAT IS DIFFERENT AND WHAT STAYS
THE SAME..41
What Stays the Same 42
The Shared Housing Difference......................................44
Considerations to Ponder Before You Dive In................45

There is Too Much Activity 46

See if the Lifestyle is For You... 48

CHAPTER 3: PREPARATION AND PATIENCE: BOTH WILL SAVE YOU MONEY 49

Welcome to Life.. 50

Considering the Best Property for You 51

Questions To Ask Your Seller 52

Talk to Your Neighbors Before You Buy 55

Be as Curious as a Cat 55

Be Prepared.. 57

Be Patient... 57

CHAPTER 4: STEPS TO TAKE WHEN BUYING SHARED HOUSING 59

CHAPTER 5: IMPORTANT DOCUMENTS YOU NEED TO UNDERSTAND.. 61

Agreement of Purchase & Sale 61

Disclosure Statements 62

Homeowner's Insurance 62

Home Warranties.. 63

Sub-leasing Your Unit... 66

Closing Statement 67

CHAPTER 6: CAN YOU LIVE WITH RESTRICTIONS? 69

What You Should Know Before You Buy....................................... 69

Children Can Stay 70

Ordinances You May Need to Live By 71

Meet the Management or the Board.. 72

Ridiculous Restrictions: A Sign of Trouble 74

CHAPTER 7: WHY SHARED HOUSING IS A GREAT OPTION FOR EVERYONE (WELL, ALMOST).... 75

First-Time Homeowners 77
Downsizing 79
The Busy Person Loves Shared Housing.................................... 80
Outside Maintenance Be Gone 81
Perfect for Growing Families.. 82

CHAPTER 8: SHARED HOUSING EQUALS SHARED RESPONSIBILITIES 83

What You Own — You Maintain 85
The Homeowner's Association 85
Homeowner's Dues and What They Mean 88
Why Sit on the Board.. 89
Making or Breaking a Good Investment.................................... 90

CHAPTER 9: FINANCIAL CONCERNS & FINANCING YOUR PURCHASE 93

What You Can Afford 93
Financing Your Purchase Through a Lender.............................. 94
Creatively Financing Your New Home 96
Seller or Developer Financing 97
Your Payments Could Break You 98
Increases In Association Dues 99
When No One Wants the Assessment 100

CHAPTER 10: INVESTING IN SHARED HOUSING & THINGS YOU SHOULD KNOW 101

A New Way of Living 103
A Better Way of Investing... 105
Finding the Right Property.. 109

CHAPTER 11: IF YOU CAN LEASE FIRST—LEASE!..................................111

Shared Housing and the Trial Run.................................. 111
Why This is a better way to go 112
Things to Look for In a Lease.. 113
Things to Look for In a Rent-To-Own........................... 114
The Lease Option Contract You Want 115
The Smart Lease 116
Look at What Happens.. 117

CHAPTER 12: VACATION GETAWAYS.....................119

The Vacation Efficiency... 122
We Are Not Talking Timeshares 122
The Getaway You Deserve... 123
Buy a Getaway but Not Prime Property 124
More about vacation ownership................................... 125
The Real Reason People Buy Vacation Rentals............... 127

CHAPTER 13: BUYING & SELLING APARTMENT BUILDINGS..................................129

Finding Your Niche Market 130
Location — Above All Else 130
Manage Your Properties or They Will Manage You 131
Being Goal Oriented 132
Potential For Profit.. 132

CHAPTER 14: NEGOTIATIONS, PREPARATIONS, & OTHER LAST MINUTE THOUGHTS 133

Shopping for A Shared Housing Unit 134
Negotiations With the Seller 135
Securing the Financing and Buying Your Unit 137
Closing the deal... 138

The Big Moving Day 139

Being a Happy Homeowner 139

CHAPTER 15: THE PEOPLE YOU KNOW 141

More Information Concerning the Condominium Board 145

Attorneys are Our Friends — Well, Some of Them Are 146

Appraisers and Surveyors 147

Home Inspectors 147

Bankers and Other Lenders 147

Sellers and Buyers 148

CHAPTER 16: NEW DEVELOPMENTS 149

Buying Your New Unit 150

Being the First 150

Keep Your Best Interests in Focus 152

Stay Focused on What is Important 153

Another Observation 154

CONCLUSION 155

APPENDIX A 157

Questionnaire for Success in Shared Housing 157

Summary of the Above Questionnaire 160

Great Areas to Buy a Getaway 160

All the Furnishings You Need in Your Vacation Rental Home 163

APPENDIX B 165

Sample Condominium Bylaws or Rules 165

APPENDIX C 171

Sample Engineering Report 171

Summary of Inspection 174

APPENDIX D.. 175
Calculating Your Payment 175
Full Amortization Table Based on 30 Years.................... 177
Where the Final Summary is.. 192
For the Given Values...193
Where the Final Summary Is 201

REFERENCES 229

ABOUT THE AUTHOR...230

GLOSSARY..231

INDEX..285

DEDICATION

This book would not be possible if it were not for Angela Adams and everyone at Atlantic Publishing. I am grateful for the opportunity they gave me. It is uncommon for a publisher to put so much trust in the books of a new author, but Atlantic Publishing did just that.

This book is dedicated to my father, Bert Smith, who gave me the best childhood anyone could ever hope for and allowed me to grow up on a farm so beautiful it spoiled me for any other real estate. My brothers, sister, and I were truly blessed to have the privilege to grow up on Smith Place Road in Church Hill, Tennessee.

Thank you, everyone who contributed to this book with informative case studies and insight on real estate investments through shared housing complexes. I appreciate each of you beyond words and want you to know that without you this book would not have been possible.

To every client I had as a real estate agent, a huge thank you for teaching me what you knew. To my friends and builders, Tom and Mary, who were in the industry and had their lives cut short, build castles in heaven!

To my children, Matthew and Amber, thank you for allowing me to work when I needed to and for including me in your lives even as teenagers—you are awesome, and I love you both more than I could ever really explain.

Last, a big thank you to my husband, Brent, for always filling in when I need to be doing something else. You are one of a kind and everyone tells me I am lucky to have you—and I agree. None of these writing dreams would have been possible if you were not there to help with our two beautiful children and pick up where I leave off—you are something special.

FOREWORD

by Abe Deutsch

When a buyer faces a choice of a condominium, a townhouse, or an apartment, selecting one over another should be based on knowledge of the differences among them, trends in the local market, and comparable costs rather than an emotional reaction to the appearance.

Many buyers in my area of New York are savvy about the volatility of the three markets, I have found. Whenever overbuilding of one type of shared housing occurs or there is a twitch in the market, my customers and investors react accordingly. Author Susan Alvis is savvy about those big-city ups and downs, and confidently alerts her readers to signs of coming trends, which vary at any given time by city or area.

Helping a buyer weed out bad investments and hone in on a

favorable market, Susan Alvis also takes personal preferences into consideration in this book and helps a buyer evaluate, from her own experience, the amenities and annoyances of shared housing. Having read this book, a buyer can find just the right combination of qualities the same as buying that perfect suit. This book is tailor-made for prudent buyers who see the home, whether it is a condo, townhouse, or apartment, as an extension of their personality that enables them to achieve a lifestyle goal. The many pointers and tips in this book will certainly increase the number of smart buyers and happy owners of shared housing, as well as providing sellers with ideas for up-grades for higher profits.

Whether shared housing is available in your area depends on a favorable job market that attracts upwardly mobile 20 and 30 somethings or the natural attractions that lure empty-nesters and retirees to an area. Wherever there is a demand in the United States, a skilled entrepreneur will step in to meet that demand. Subsequent competition for tenants, or a buyer's market, puts out a variety of housing choices. That is where this book makes the difference for a prospective buyer to create a checklist of personal needs and wants in housing. The list can range from "party place" to "100 percent sound insulation" or from "easy airport access" to "wooded seclusion." There are as many idiosyncratic desires as there are people in this country, and Susan Alvis has compiled an eye-opening account of architectural and aesthetic differences that any buyer might overlook. In essence, she is offering insurance against buyer's remorse, a malady that, in my experience as a real estate agent, is very expensive to cure.

Westchester County, New York.
Member of NAR, NYSAR, WCBR,
WCBR Commercial & Investment Division.
Abe.Deutsch@century21.com
(cell) 914-980-8222 • (office) 914-946-9100
(fax) 914-422-1951

PREFACE

A record 42 million Americans live in shared housing. Condominiums, apartments, and townhouses are growing in popularity as the lazy man's way to invest, association products, the first-time home buyer's entry into ownership, and the choice way to downsize.

Planned unit developments (PUDs) are springing up where family farms used to be. In metropolitan areas, more concrete towers become home to many families, and more multi-family housing replaces large, comfortable, green yards. Picket fences and greenery are increasingly replaced by concrete and asphalt.

The bright side is the fact that these new developments bring a completely new world of upscale amenities, great floor plans, and an easier way of life. Multi-unit housing provides a lifestyle many only dreamed about.

These homes are a good way to invest. Once reserved only for wealthy property owners, now small investors can buy one or several units, find great financing, and create wealth. Anyone can own one of these units whether for their own housing needs or for rental income potential.

They are low-maintenance and hold their value. Best of all, when an investor chooses to buy multi-housing units in only one complex, management is simplified.

As a starter home, the association product is a way to put an affordable roof over your head with great amenities. These multi-unit complexes are diverse and, as with single dwelling homes, they offer a variety of styles, floor plans, square footage, and prices.

Several myths hang over the shared-housing market. The first one is about the value. People tend to believe condos, townhouses, and apartments will not hold their value.

The second is about the ownership of the individual unit. As a real estate agent in the 90s, I could not believe how many people actually questioned the ownership of condominiums, townhouses, and apartments. I remember the first time I heard one of these myths. I showed a condo in our area to a young couple with a baby. While going through the unit the couple looked around and I carried the baby while pointing out the finer features of the property, ending my spiel with "I am your realtor, also known as your babysitter." They seemed to like the unit, and I was sure I heard an offer coming.

After spending about an hour with the couple and their baby, I decided to ask for the sale. They agreed quickly and the woman went out to her car for her checkbook while Daddy took the baby for a stroll around the empty condo.

Upon returning from their walk, the baby began to cry uncontrollably. We tried to talk over his screams, and the couple tried to console him, but they decided they would wait to write an offer the next day. I agreed reluctantly but saw we were going nowhere fast with the baby demanding more attention. They assured me they wanted the condo, but left without signing the offer to purchase or leaving the check as a good faith deposit.

The next day, they came by to tell me they wanted to continue searching because even though they liked the condo, they knew it was not going to be for them. They said, "We talked to our parents about it, and why would we want to pay $90,000 for something we will never really own?" I laughed, but by the look on their face, I knew they were sincere.

Upon further probing, I understood their decision to keep looking. They believed if they purchased the condo, they would own it for as long as they lived but that once they were "dead and gone" the condo would simply vanish from their estate. Who they thought would claim ownership, I do not know—another myth of condo ownership. Condos have proven to be sound investments since their growth in popularity, primarily with twenty-something couples, both of whom work and have no time for home maintenance. The same holds true for townhouses.

Co-ops, however, have held steady but have not taken hold because of ownership differences. If property is a cooperative arrangement, title to all associated real estate is held by a corporation. Buyers purchase stock in the co-op corporation and are considered shareholders, not owners of real property. Each shareholder holds a lease to his unit that runs for the life of the corporation. Taxes are paid by the corporation. Any mortgages are normally held and paid by the corporation. All costs to operate the building are shared by shareholders. New cooperative shareholders must usually be approved by an administrative board. Cooperative ownership is not common in most states.

In a co-op, a tenant is a shareholder in the building itself. Management is patterned after Wall Street, and ownership is different from a condo or townhouse. In New York City, co-op housing holds steady, but elsewhere people want to own their home and feel that their money is in something tangible and salable. Condos and townhouses give owners pride in ownership. Co-ops confer pride, but is it pride of ownership? In co-op housing, it is possible for someone to buy shares in the building where they live, but it is really only stock in the building so that the owner of the stock has voting rights. There is one verity in co-op ownership: it allows discrimination, which an ethical person cannot condone.

Few new buildings are set up as a co-op, but the old co-ops are still viable housing options in some cities. They have shareholders and a board. The board determines who can and who cannot own shares in the complex or building. Many of them blatantly discriminate because they determine who will be part of their community. They do not care whether the individual lives in the complex. If the board does not want them to be there, they will keep them out of the important decision-making process by making sure they cannot have a share in building ownership.

In co-op ownership, the structure or complex is owned by the shareholders, meaning the fees and expenses of the building or complex are endured by the shareholders who have certain, limited tax advantages. From an investment standpoint, condos or townhouses far outdistance co-ops. However, if you like the idea of being your own landlord but without the profit, co-ops are probably a good match for you. It is a bad investment when there are better investments out there.

CASE STUDY: KIRK HANSEN

In San Diego there have been a lot of condo-conversions where an apartment bullding is converted into condominiums. Some are sold off as co-ops. In Co-op ownership you own a percentage of the whole building with exclusive use of your unit. In a sense, it is technically the same thing but co-ops are usually less desirable and have less desirable loan options.

Kirk Hansen
Century 21 Homes First
President
760-212-0062
Kirk.Hansen@Century21.com

In the 70s, housing changed dramatically. Housing complexes in large cities became condos. The concept caught on and before long, more condo complexes emerged even in some rural areas. Townhouses became more elaborate. Both had wide-ranging price tags from $70,000 to more than $10 million. Now they are a mainstay.

CASE STUDY

I have found that most people who are purchasing shared housing in New York City prefer condos. Historically, we have predominately more co-ops than we do condos and buyers are tired of the intrusiveness

CASE STUDY

of the co-op boards and the frequent board turn downs.

Eugenia Foxworth
Coldwell Banker Hunt Kennedy
NYS Licensed Realtor,
Certified International
Property Specialist
Eugenia.foxworth@cbhk.com

Shared housing is the term used for all the types of housing discussed in this book. Some people love the idea of living in a close-knit community with neighbors nearby. I loved "shared housing" when I was single. The lifestyle was great—many neighbors and 24/7 fun.

As a mother of two while we were building our house, I hated shared housing. It just did not work for us even on a short-term basis. Still, I have always loved the amenities of shared housing. They add value. There are many attributes that add value in shared housing, and in this book we will look at them along with many other aspects of living in a unit that you own in a shared building.

Apartment living has been considered a great choice for the individual or couple looking to downsize, while the condo-lifestyle was perfect for the first-time home buyer. In most areas, people bought condos and rented apartments. Now, individual apartment units are bought and sold, too. (Of course, entire buildings are also sound investment opportunities, and we will discuss them.)

These multi-unit living quarters have been misperceived as cramped and inconvenient but after the rise of towering apartment buildings with penthouse suites overlooking views in New York City, people started to like the idea of shared housing.

Why has purchasing a condo, townhouse, or apartment become so popular? We will look at various reasons that someone might choose to purchase a unit in one of these complexes versus purchasing a single dwelling. We are going to introduce you to a new way of life. A choice of home is a choice of lifestyle based on amenities rather than affordability. Convenience outranks affordability as the reason to live in a multi-family complex.

If you look around at where the condos and apartment buildings are located, you will notice many of them have great locations. They are near parks and shopping malls. Some are close to schools, churches, and grocery stores, or near large employers like industries and universities. As an example, in the Tunica/Robinsonville area of Mississippi, there are numerous shared housing units because they provide housing for the many casino employees in the area. Years ago, they solved an immediate need for housing in that particular location.

The beautiful, white sandy beaches in the Destin and Fort Walton Beach in Florida attracted people from all around the United States, and early on developers built condos. Since vacationing families' incomes varied, housing costs also varied to provide alternatives for anyone.

While some people move into condos or apartments for the affordability factor, others do so because they have no time for yard work or to keep up the home's exterior. Working adults love this advantage. They do not have to put garbage at the curb or weed flowerbeds. Someone else will do it in a complex with a homeowners association dedicated to keeping the complex in top shape. Shared housing ownership avoids the inconvenience of having to flip through the Yellow Pages to find contractors who may or may not correct the maintenance problem on your hands.

Throughout this book, we will look at shared housing and how it allows owners the time to do what they want. We will examine what you should look for when you are buying a unit in a complex of other units, and we are going to discuss home values and why an active homeowner's association is crucial in maintaining them. We will look at some things to consider when you are comparing homeowners associations and their established bylaws. We will see how a homeowners association can make or break your investment.

We will discuss facts about townhouses, condos, and apartments as investments and personal residences and introduce you to the residences many see as the only way to live if you want to enjoy life.

If you are uninterested in maintaining a home either as a first-time home buyer or if you are looking to downsize, this book was written for you.

1

INTRODUCING SHARED HOUSING

The decision to buy a home does not strike overnight and after you decide to buy, the real challenges set in. You will have choices of home types to accommodate your lifestyle: from single home dwellings to townhouses and apartments, the type of home you choose will expand or cramp your lifestyle.

Location is another important factor to consider when you decide to buy. Where you buy will be as important as what you buy because if you do not buy in a good area, the housing type you decide on will not matter. People want to be happy in their location. You could buy a million dollar castle, stick it in the middle of a large junk yard, and chances are no one would be happy with your housing choice.

The location and the type of housing you choose may rest on whether you can afford the housing type you want in the location preferred. In addition to affordability, amenities vary in some housing types but they are not normally found in single home dwellings. Some people prefer multi-unit housing because of the amenities. They may be the sole reason for buying in a particular complex.

There are homeowners who will never be happy with anything other than a single family home because they like their privacy and space far too much to forfeit them. Still, if you like the idea of neighbors, then amenities and low maintenance, multi-family living or shared housing may be perfect for you.

Multi-family homes usually mean apartment buildings with more than two units that enable the owner to live free by having the tenants cover the mortgage payments. An investor may hire an apartment manager to take care of the complex and offer the manager free living space and a small salary. This job is ideal for some retired couples.

Shared housing in the form of condos or townhouses is different from multi-family apartment housing. A property owner of an apartment building may provide water or electricity but no other amenities. Condos and townhouses offer a variety of activities.

The type of housing you choose depends on your likes and dislikes. You may choose an apartment or townhouse based on its location or style, or you may have a specific floor plan in mind.

You may find a housing environment is limited to one style or design. The advantages in shared housing complexes are not so much in the style as they are in the convenience of the floor plans and the amenities in the particular complex.

CASE STUDY: KIRK HANSEN

It seems as though people like to live in desirable neighborhoods for esteem and social reasons. They like to talk about what their community has to offer (such as a pool, hot tub, or gym) even if they never use them.

CASE STUDY: KIRK HANSEN

Kirk Hansen, President
Century 21 Homes First
760-212-0062
Kirk.Hansen@Century21.com

Decide on the amenities you would like to have and consider how much you are willing to pay for them. Have a price in mind before you start shopping for properties.

As a real estate agent in East Tennessee in the 90s, I sold far more single-family homes than I did any other home type. When homeowners bought single-family dwellings, they knew what they owned. They knew they would be able to do anything they wanted whenever they wanted to do it. They could paint, remodel, add-on, or tear the place down. They owned the house and they owned the property where the home was built. Some of these homes were in subdivisions, and the residents were required to follow subdivision restrictions when adding on a new room or putting in a swimming pool. A list of restrictions was given to home buyers so everyone knew their responsibilities to the others.

A single-family home is your own and you share nothing at all. Your yard and everything in it, whether it is a pool or a gazebo is also yours. You can decide what to do with the land you own and how to maintain it as long as it does not conflict with subdivision restrictions or break the law.

As the owner of a single-family dwelling, you have the responsibility of mowing, painting, trimming shrubs, planting trees, caring for the maintenance of the exterior walls, roofs, and doing everything else to keep the home in good repair. It is your responsibility to care for the maintenance of the structure and the land around it. All this work is the main reason that shared housing became so popular in the first place, but there are several reasons to consider shared housing. Consider what you GIVE UP living in a condo, for example.

- Yard work

- Building maintenance

- Free time not swimming in a community pool or playing tennis in a shared court and not taking care of the pool or court

- Higher heating and cooling bills

- Worries about your house whenever you leave town

- Possibly higher mortgage payments

There are a number of reasons the condo or apartment lifestyle will appeal to you, and after you see the fabulous floor plans and amenities now offered in these shared living units, you may decide this type of home ownership is for you!

CASE STUDY: EUGENIA FOXWORTH

Lifestyle is so important in New York City especially to entertainers and Wall Street brokers. The full-service luxury shared housing buildings that have indoor parking, a gym, health club, 24 hour attended lobby and concierge services are rather important throughout the boroughs. School districts are very  important to those who have children or are planning to start their family. If your child cannot get into one of the top private schools, you must be in a district that has one of the highest ratings. Therefore, I take my buyers to

CASE STUDY: EUGENIA FOXWORTH

the buildings that suit their lifestyle. Security is also a selling point especially if the building is in one on the "hot" areas that is still reasonably priced and is being gentrified.

Eugenia Foxworth
Coldwell Banker Hunt Kennedy
NYS Licensed Realtor,
Certified International Property Specialist
Eugenia.foxworth@cbhk.com

Here we define the kinds of shared housing in today's market.

APARTMENTS

Multi-family housing or apartment living can be a great way to pay for your own housing. If you own an apartment building, you are responsible for maintaining the grounds and the units in the buildings. There will be rents to collect and plumbing to repair. If you know how to do simple maintenance on the units and are physically capable of doing the work, apartment buildings can be a great investment.

If you do not want the headaches of taking care of buildings, an on-site manager is ideal especially if you own large complexes. Apartment managers sometimes work in exchange for free housing. They may have a "day job" but they oversee a housing complex as well, taking care of minor repairs and maintenance.

If you invest in multi-unit complexes, you will need liability insurance, as well as ground rules, restrictions, and leases for the tenants. Many investors use standard leases available online. However, if you want to protect your interests as an investor, you should obtain a legal document prepared by a qualified attorney. It is not as expensive as lawsuits.

Profit and manageability make apartment buildings attractive to investors. They like the bottom line at purchase. They understand they are easier to maintain and see the potential for income. Best of all, financing is easy. In larger cities, units that had been rented are sold as individual home space; some allow tenants a shot at ownership.

Apartments can be owned individually, but are usually smaller than a condo or townhouse and lack the amenities. Some are plain buildings with nothing grand or spectacular about their rooms or exterior. They have few perquisites for tenants. They are an affordable roof over your head.

There is a flip side. A high price tag raises the question, "Where's the rest of it?" in large cities. In New York, an apartment is a good investment. If you do not believe it, log on to a vacation rental site, do a search for common amenities, and see what it will cost you for a week. You will see what I mean! Investing in apartments in the city can be wise and it is doubtful the owners thought about any shared housing myths while they were accumulating these rentals. They know they have solid investments. Best of all, they know their units in desirable locations are going to rent easily.

Apartment buildings are an even better investment. Not only do apartments bring in monthly rents, but they also have good resale value: you can keep a building for a few years and sell it for a profit. You may need to do some updates. Either way, your money is hard at work for you—better than you working for it!

CONDOS

Condos share these distinctions. An individual owner holds title to the condominium unit only, not the land it sits on, so condos can be stacked on top of each other. All condo owners share title to common areas. Common areas include land, the exterior of buildings, hallways, roofs, swimming pools—any area used by all owners. Condominium owners pay property taxes on their individual units. A property owners' association usually manages the complex and collects fees from all condo owners to be able to maintain common areas.

Years ago, a remodeled apartment building might be converted to a condo. A proprietor who was ready to retire would make the necessary changes, incorporate bylaws, form a homeowners association, and a condo complex would take the place of an apartment building. The owner may have provided upgrades and financing for existing tenants or may have sold the units individually.

Condos, even if they had been apartments, are appealing to the homeowner looking for a lifestyle free of maintenance: the exterior is someone else's responsibility. As the condo owner, you own everything "inside" your unit from floor to ceiling. You are also in partnership with other condo owners in the exterior building including the roof, foundation, and structure. You are an ownership partner of the pool, tennis courts, riding areas, boat ramps, boat docks, and any other common areas. You are required to pay membership dues to the homeowners association for the maintenance of common areas such as mowing expenses, pool upkeep, clubhouse, and tennis courts.

While the association may be responsible for exterior repairs, it is still in the buyer's financial interest to be informed of exterior problems. For instance, a deteriorated roof could result in water damage to the interior of the condo; substandard entry stairs could result in an injury lawsuit against the individual condo owner, as well as against the homeowner's association; and faulty ground drainage problems could cause rot or mold to occur within the dwelling.

Considering the direct impact exterior problems can have on the interests of individual condominium owners, and in view of the fact that each owner shares in the collective costs of the association, an exterior inspection is a reasonable part of a thorough condominium inspection.

When you consider living in a condo that was once an apartment unit, remember to check on these items:

- Was the conversion simply cosmetic or thorough?

- How old is the building?

- What is the resale potential of the condo unit?

- Is it modern?

- Is the layout convenient both within the unit and within the complex?

- How new are the appliances?

- Are the bathrooms modern? (Remember that you are responsible for inside maintenance.)

Occasionally, condo homeowners associations charge a special assessment to handle needs such as a new roof or a new swimming pool. Most special assessments are in place for the improvement of the common areas or improvement of the exterior buildings of the units owned by the members. However, when buying a condo you should be aware of these special assessments because they are expensive enough to force owners to list their units for sale.

There are some pros and cons to becoming an owner of a condo. The pros are the obvious: you will not be responsible for the maintenance of your building because that is the responsibility of the homeowners association. Often you will find the price you pay for a condo relatively cheap compared to single-family dwellings because of the added value of amenities, which are affordable because they are shared.

CASE STUDY: BRUNO FRIIA

We really do not have to sell the idea of shared housing to potential buyers. Most of our customers are young professionals and students who are well aware of the advantages of community living, as well as snowbirds and vacationers from warmer climates. They know what they want. The amenities in the common areas make all the difference.

People expect to find a community room, pool, spa, and workout facilities. They seldom mention security although all units we have sold are pre-wired for security. The items that are in demand are high-speed wiring and up-to-the-minute kitchen designs, appliances, and décor. Even though we are a commercial real estate agency — the largest in Montana — about 10 percent of our income is derived from the shared housing market.

Bruno Friia
Lambros Real Estate
Western Montana

Look at the amenities you find at condos and it is easy to see why a homeowner looking for tennis courts, swimming pools, hot tubs, boat docks, riding facilities, and even putting greens would live there. As a condo owner, you can have more than you can afford because you are not paying for amenities; instead, several homeowners are paying for the perks.

High-end condo communities offer the best security systems available to any home owner, including personal hand-held emergency devices can activate alarm-sensors in your garage. Residents have a personal remote-control transmitter or a car transponder to enter garages and a computerized access-card for entry to common areas.

Intrusion alarms may be a standard feature, and ground floor homes may be outfitted with interior motion detectors and magnetic contacts on exterior doors and windows. There may be things that you would never think of or notice like extra bright lighting in the underground garages, and elevator lobby areas with glass windows that allow a clear view into parking areas.

There may be different fire-safety features in the community. Buildings may be designed to contain a fire should it occur, and each unit may have alarm panels. In addition stairwells and elevator shafts may be pressurized to receive a separate supply of fresh air to provide a safe and smoke free exit. Garbage chutes and lower garbage rooms can be outfitted with heat detectors, and there may be a sprinkler system that activates automatically should the need arise. Common hallways may have smoke-and-heat-sensors, a fire hose, and a direct contact firefighters' telephone.

There are some reasons not to live in a condo, just as there are in any other shared housing. While condo life lets you to feel safe with neighbors close enough to hear a loud scream, you give up privacy. You are always around other people—not appealing to a person who treasures quiet, independent times. Neighbors can be bothersome. You have to learn to set boundaries, especially if you have children and live where there are children looking for a playmate. It is a good idea to do your boundary-setting early on so others will respect your privacy. In multi-units, privacy issues are often a big deal so handling them appropriately is important.

The lifestyle is one of the reasons buyers purchase a condo. The community, the amenities, and the stability of the homeowners association are the reasons they choose a particular complex.

Understand, the maintenance fee covers the exterior building and the grounds including the yard work, painting, and roof repair. It is a given that you are required to maintain the interior space of your own home.

There is a myth regarding condo sales that they are hard to sell. They may have been — years ago. Now, with more people adjusting to the benefits of condo ownership, resale is not usually a concern, but it depends on the area, the reputation of the community, and the homeowners association.

TOWNHOUSES

Townhouse owners hold title to their units and the land beneath them, so townhouse units cannot be stacked on top of each other. As with condos, common areas are owned jointly by all townhouse owners. Townhouse owners pay property taxes on their individual units.

A property owners' association usually manages the townhouse complex and collects fees from all owners in order to maintain common areas. They are usually three-tiered or three-story homes with a garage on the entrance level and two additional floors of living space.

The biggest difference between townhouses and condos is ownership of ground space. Condo owners do not own the ground underneath their living area. Townhouse owners do own the ground where the townhouse is built. Townhouses can be freestanding or they can adjoin another townhouse. They can be in large clusters or they can be duplexes.

Like condo owners, townhouse owners have the luxury of being a shared owner in the amenities of the complex, such as a swimming pool or clubhouse. Most townhouses offer a patio or deck area, and some even have a courtyard or space outside your back door.

Townhouse restrictions are different from condo restrictions. The exterior maintenance of the building will be the responsibility of the homeowners association but some of the maintenance costs could be the homeowner's sole responsibility. It is important for you to know what is required of you as a homeowner in one of these homes.

If you like the community living of a condo or an apartment but find you prefer more privacy, townhouse ownership may be the answer for you because the units are occasionally freestanding or separated by carports and garages. Best of all, in most townhouses, you will not have a neighbor above or below you because of the floor plan. If noises bother you, a townhouse may offer tranquility.

COMMON AREAS

The common areas may be the reason a buyer finds shared housing agreeable. They are the "amenities" of the property. However, as common areas, the exterior of the buildings and the structures on the property (such as public restrooms in the pool area) are out of your control. You cannot alter common areas in any way. When you see something that needs improvement, you must take the matter up with the homeowners association. Doing so can be a double-edged sword. You cannot fix what is broken and probably would not want to do the work anyway, but if you have a slack homeowners board and want to fix something, you are not supposed to do it.

Common areas include hallways (and breezeways between units), elevators and stairwells, yards, gardens, driveways, parking spaces, lobbies, and meeting spaces such as clubhouses. Any other facilities that are under the care and direction of the homeowners association are common areas. Amenities contribute to the enjoyment of the homeowners.

Shared Amenities Homeowners May Enjoy	
• Pool areas	• Tennis courts
• Sports facilities such as basketball courts & volleyball areas	• Meeting areas such as clubhouses
• Bike and walking trails	• Park benches & playground areas
• Dog runs	

When you are looking for a place to live, I cannot stress to you how important it can be to read the bylaws or the manual for the definitions of amenities' uses. The manual will spell out the responsibilities of the association on behalf of all the homeowners. Does it handle trash removal? Operate and maintain recreational facilities such as a pool, tennis courts, jogging, and bike paths? Are all the roads within the community private and does the association maintain these as well? As the list of amenities and services goes up, so does the mandatory association fee. And, if you don't pay it, the association can place a lien on your house, charge late fees, demand that an entire year's fees be paid in advance if you are late several payments in a row, and prohibit you from using any of the amenities until the fees are paid.

WHY BUY A SHARED HOUSING UNIT

Look at the top reasons people find buying a home in multi-housing complexes works for them.

1. **Low Maintenance:** Life is busy for everyone. Some people do not mind yard work while other people loathe it. My husband is a great example of someone who should live in a shared housing environment. He does not necessarily mind the yard work, but he is married to his job. I hate yard work so unless he does it or hires someone to do it, let the weeds consume us! If you have an active family and a full-time job, you may feel as I do about home maintenance: who has time for it? Therefore, people who feel this way buy in housing complexes where such things are done for them. It is a win-win situation. They pay a monthly maintenance fee, and the homeowner's association hires someone to take care of the lawn, painting, and anything else. It is perfect for everyone.

2. **Security**: Security rates are high for those who choose shared housing. People want to go home and feel secure in their environment; they do not want to worry about a burglary. There is safety in numbers, and some of the housing complexes offer secure environments for tenants. Some even provide security systems, gated communities, and doormen or security guards — worth their weight in gold to owners of these buildings and complexes.

3. **Amenities:** Who would not want a swimming pool, tennis court, weight room, basketball court, and a playground for the children? The amenities found in many shared housing complexes are the reason people buy. The things we all want are affordable, and we do not have to maintain them!

4. **The Time Factor:** A multi-family housing environment allows people the freedom to come and go without having to worry about mowing the grass or painting the eaves.

5. **Affordability:** Shared units are more affordable to buy and they are more energy efficient — another savings. In some areas, people simply can afford to buy only a housing unit in a complex. When you add all the advantages combined with affordability, buying an apartment, condo, or townhouse makes sense.

6. **The Only Home Option Available:** In some areas, shared housing is the only thing available. In larger cities, a single-family dwelling may cost more than $500,000. In some areas nothing else is available even if you have the money. In some cities, high-rises are the only option.

Later in the book, we will look at why shared housing is absolutely the best option in vacation home ownership.

WHAT BEING A HOMEOWNER MEANS IN SHARED HOUSING

When you buy a shared housing unit, you are buying a lifestyle. You give up a certain amount of privacy, you are expected to attend meetings from time to time to discuss the upkeep of the building where you live, and you have to get used to noises of neighbors coming and going in the middle of the night, and other annoyances.

You have a responsibility to yourself and your family as a homeowner in shared housing to become an active member in the homeowners association. Understandably, if you own vacation units, you cannot be as active if the units are some distance from your primary home. Still, you want to be sure before you buy that there is an active association making the best living environment possible for the people who live there.

It is easy to become passive about ownership as a homeowner rather than a tenant in shared housing. If you are inattentive, you have no reason to become upset when things are not run the way you think they should be. Passive homeowners exist in every complex and those who choose to let someone else make all the decisions for them in regard to their home ownership have no room to complain when things do not go their way.

PROS AND CONS: WHAT TO EXPECT

There are pros and cons to any place you live. People who are new to a condo or an apartment become aware of the "Good-Morning Neighbor" scenario. If you are in a shared housing arrangement without the luxury of private garages or carports, you may be irritated.

Years ago, I lived directly above a retired couple with too much time on their hands. Whenever I came in from the grocery store, one or both would greet me with "What did you get?" as they peered into the open bags. One day as I was bringing in a bag with toilet paper in view over the top of the bag, my neighbor quickly asked me, "Did you run out of toilet paper?" I became so annoyed; I shopped only late at night so I could bring in my groceries without an inquisition.

You will discover some neighbors will be concerned with your business. Learn how to handle them appropriately. The biggest reason for owning a unit in a complex can be your neighbors and the biggest reason not to can also be your neighbors. Accepting the reality in shared housing environments will help you to be a good neighbor yourself.

Usually problems in the community occur when one person did not understand the rules or bylaws of the association before moving in. Urging prospects to review the bylaws before they buy a shared housing unit will curtail future problems.

Try not to involve the board in disputes with your neighbors. For example, if you have a fear of your neighbors' dog, take the time to talk to them about it. Explain to them that you are fearful of their dog that chases you every chance he gets. Tell them you would appreciate it if they kept him on a leash. If they do not comply, send them a letter before going to the board.

Go to a homeowner's association meeting to see the neighbors in action—how they get along and interact with each other.

A Little Tip

When you move into a new complex, set boundaries if you recognize something as a potential problem. For example, if you are a mom living in a complex full of children, and all the other mommies send their kids to your place anytime they need a little rest and relaxation, set down some ground rules. Do it in a nice way but let the neighbors know you have things to do after work. You may let them know that if you want their child, you will invite their child. Sometimes you have to be blunt.

One big strike against community living is the noise factor. If you are investing your money in a townhouse, apartment, or condo, find a home where privacy means upgraded soundproofing between the units. If you are unsure of the building structure, talk to the original developer of the complex who has that information.

THE MATTER OF PRICE

It is impossible to say what you should expect to pay for your home because the cost of living is so varied. In New York City, you might pay more than $1 million for a penthouse apartment, but in Johnson City, Tennessee, a condo with many of the same amenities and square footage would cost only $200,000. Some condos in some areas can be snatched up for $100,000 or less, while on the West Coast, you would not consider the dumps available at that price.

While I cannot give you a price to expect to pay for your home what I can do is tell you the importance of comparative market analysis. Assuming that eventually you will want to sell what you buy, you need a CMA so you are sure you are not paying too much. You need to be sure you can afford the association dues and that they are worth the price.

If you buy a gorgeous unit in a rundown building, you will not get your money back even if you are able to sell it. Always keep the future in mind when you buy.

Price is important, but value is king. Make sure you see value in your purchase. If you buy because of the amenities of a particular complex, make sure they are visible and meaningful to you. After all, the payments you make will be easier if you like what you are paying for.

2

WHAT IS DIFFERENT AND WHAT STAYS THE SAME

Remodeling is evident in homes converted into apartments or in apartments sold as condos. While the building's exterior may boast some improvements, most of the units have not changed. The floor plans, look, and feel of the unit are the same. The main difference is in the name: apartment or condo.

CASE STUDY: KIMBERLY JANES

There is some resistance, although minimal, to buying condos that were converted from apartments when sound proofing material has not been installed between units. They may be updated on the exterior and interior, but they do not meet today's standards for new condos as far as noise  reduction. However, the demand for shared housing keeps rising because they are attractive to single professionals who are taking on home ownership before marriage; to single parents with children; to empty nesters who want to be free of home maintenance; and to a large population of multi-generations living together who find shared housing is perfect. Apartment units that have not been remodeled as condos usually have structure

CASE STUDY: KIMBERLY JANES

issues: they lack the large lobbies, elevators, interior access to the units, private gymnasiums and concierges. Their big selling point may lie in their convenient location.

Kimberly Janes,
Realtor®
Seattle, Washington

WHAT STAYS THE SAME

When searching for a home, whether a single dwelling or a unit in a complex, you will have certain expectations. The following is a list of items to consider wherever you buy.

- Number of bedrooms
- Number of bathrooms
- Location
- Style
- Furnishings
- Kitchen space

- Good floor plan
- Convenience
- Outdoor space
- Restrictions
- Location

How close you are to schools, shopping, and your job? You will find that complexes are in great locations.

A floor plan with good use of living areas is important to most people regardless of the type of housing the person chooses.

A Little Tip

Even if you think you have found the exact unit you want to buy in a complex, consider looking at all the units for sale in the complex to give yourself more options so that you get the best plan to meet your needs. You may be surprised at the variety of floor plans in the units.

Buyers will be interested in what remains within the unit they are buying, more important when buying a vacation unit than when buying a primary home. Buyers expect to find vacation units already furnished because they do not have the added expense of buying furniture.

A Little Tip

Do not let something that you can add later be a deal breaker in a good deal. If you wanted a home with storm windows or a Jacuzzi, can you live without them? If not, move on, but if you recognize something missing as something you can add later, weigh its importance. Very often, you will find something perfect for you and your family only to let it slip away while you decide if you can live without something you could add on your own dime, relatively cheap, at a later date.

In addition, the outdoor space is important. Patios, decks, and courtyards can be important to the person who likes to see the sky. Some people prefer decks while others like a courtyard or patio, or even a greenhouse.

DID YOU KNOW?

Depending on what type of shared housing you choose to buy, your ownership may include the deck or patio. Be sure you know what you are buying!

Finally, wherever you live, you will probably have some building restrictions. For example, when owning a single dwelling, you may not be allowed to have a garage. If you are allowed to have one, you may need to build it a certain distance from the property line.

Restrictions are everywhere, but building restrictions will not matter after you buy in a development. However, if restrictions are not followed, you may need to reconsider whether you want to live there.

THE SHARED HOUSING DIFFERENCE

When you begin your search for a townhouse, apartment, or a condo, consider the following list before making a decision.

- **Too many restrictions.** Are there restrictions you know would prevent you from enjoying what you love? For example, the association may have a strict policy about playing loud music. If you cannot comply, reconsider before buying.

- **Are pets allowed?** If you cannot imagine life without Fido, you need to consider a place where he can live, too. Most homeowners associations will not budge on their issues regarding pets. The bylaws are enforceable.

- **Curb appeal.** How does the complex look to the naked eye? What will your guests see when they come to visit you? In single dwellings, you can fix an eyesore but in shared housing, most of the time what you see is what you get.

- **Homeowner's associations.** They are a real entity in most multi-unit living arrangements. What you think about the association and whether it is doing all it can to maintain the building and grounds are important. It is important to talk to the individual owners and get their take on the board.

- **Check the CMA.** What have the other units in the complex sold for recently? Are the units holding their value? If not, why? Have there been any improvements to the home ownership in the area?

As you can see, there are differences in the type of home you choose to buy. The steps you take to find the home you want are much the same, but the questions you should ask before buying are different.

CONSIDERATIONS TO PONDER BEFORE YOU DIVE IN

For many people, downsizing is the reason for moving from a single dwelling to an apartment. For some first-time homeowners, the idea of multi-family options presents a lifestyle they welcome. Others consider the conveniences important and still others find apartments more affordable. Whatever your reasons for choosing to live in a shared housing development, if you move in blindly, you will be miserable. Knowing what to expect will help you decide whether to buy.

In apartment living, you are free of maintenance, but what if maintenance is being ignored? There is an upside here. If you go into shared housing ownership as an active member of the housing community, you can ensure things are maintained by participating in the complex's homeowners association.

A Little Tip

If you can spare the time, you should make an effort to attend your homeowners association meetings and try to serve on the board once at least every two or three years so you have an active voice in your community.

Privacy may not be attainable in some areas. If you have children and you move into an area with children, you may have to establish some ground rules with their parents. You may find you have an elderly neighbor who is lonely and will drop by usually at the most inconvenient time.

A Little Tip

One of the best ways to avoid confrontation and manage your time in a shared housing community is to make time for the people who want to be included in your life as your neighbor, like children demanding your attention. If you have a neighbor child who wants your attention but you have no time, the child will take it anyway by doing something to provoke it. However, if you spend 10 or 15 minutes a day with the child, you can go about your day and finish what you need to do. In other words, give them the attention they crave or they will take it anyway.

While you cannot give a demanding neighbor that much time each day, you can allow them some time occasionally, especially if they are elderly. Cook a dish and take it to them or invite them to lunch. Be a good neighbor or be honest with yourself; you may not be the shared housing type. People who choose to live in multi-unit housing are there for the social interaction.

You may discover your lifestyle does not fit in the community you are considering. Multi-family housing is not perfect for everyone.

THERE IS TOO MUCH ACTIVITY

There will be complexes where you will fit in nicely with your neighbors. You will find you and your neighbors are compatible in work, lounging, and sleeping times. Then there are those complexes where your lifestyle is at odds with others.

When I was a freshman at Stephens College, I was assigned a dorm room on a floor full of juniors and seniors who were focused on their future. While these young ladies were great fun and super friends to have, the freshmen who lived in the dorm were aware that we were not in the "fun" dorm. Several of us moved out because we did not want to study. With the help of a friend and several fraternity boys down the street, several of us moved into a dorm where the party went on 24 hours a day. Much to my parents' dismay, I found where I fit at the time.

A couple of years later, I moved to East Tennessee State University and rented an apartment. While the apartment complex was full of upper classmen, there were some freshmen who, as I had done several years before, refused to respect any kind of curfew. While I still enjoyed my apartment, I cannot imagine people who work for a living would fit in with keg parties in between the buildings. It was tough for me to manage and I fit in with the bunch, but I could not have maintained a regular job or routine because it was too loud to sleep.

My point is that you will not fit in at every shared housing development. At 20, you might be ready for a party environment, but at 40 you may want a steadier pace. Therefore, you take the time to make a wise decision. Talk to your neighbors, ask direct questions of the current owners, and look around for yourself.

With so many apartments, townhouses, and condos all over the country, you will find where you need to be if you do your research. Drive by the area at odd hours. Sit in the parking lot and watch for activity. Take notes. Watch for heavy traffic times.

A Little Tip

If the place you want to buy is in a complex with 24 hour security, the guards are your best source of information. They will tell you everything you want to know about the area including what time is the noisiest and the kinds of problems they have experienced. Doormen also provide a wealth of information. If you want to know something, just ask and tip when you get answers!

While you are inside the unit you may want to purchase, have someone go outside and slam the door to a car and honk their horn. What do you hear from inside? When you seriously consider a particular home you have been shown, go to the unit after normal business day hours and stand on the balconies and patios. Do you hear the neighbors? Go inside and close the door. Now, what do you hear? Open a window and listen to every sound. Otherwise, you may discover problems too late.

SEE IF THE LIFESTYLE IS FOR YOU

Though it may sound extreme, one of the best ways to see if you like condo living is to live in one on a trial run. Take a trip and instead of staying in a hotel, try a condo or townhouse. Be a pretend homeowner for a few days. Watch how much activity is going on. Experience the whole community. Sit out on the deck and say hello to your "neighbors" when they wave. Grill out. Use the common areas. What do you think? Do you like the lifestyle?

The strongest suggestion I can make to someone who is considering shared housing for the first time is try before you buy. If you can buy on a lease option or a lease purchase agreement, do it. See whether the lifestyle is for you before you begin paying for something you may not like. While the lifestyle appeals to many people, others can never adapt to life close to others. There is nothing wrong with trying out shared housing before you experience it for the long haul.

PREPARATION AND PATIENCE: BOTH WILL SAVE YOU MONEY

When it comes to buying or selling a condo or townhouse, there is no one better to help you than a licensed real estate agent knowledgeable about the housing market in that locale. However, it is not necessary that one agent know all your business.

Watch out for the folks who run ads, "We buy houses." Some of these people are legitimate business investors who do buy houses, but many of them are only acting as real estate agents and have no license or expertise. Better to stick with a licensed agent.

In the shared housing market, a real estate agent can give you inside information on who developed the complex, the homeowners association, or upcoming assessments that may be the reason many units from the same complex are up for sale. An agent may be privy to this information, but you will not be unless you find an experienced agent you can trust or prepare to research on your own. An investor trying to broker the deal will take a cut of the money on the table but will offer little help to you.

CASE STUDY: KIMBERLY JANES

Here is a case where I intervened to get condos onto the market for the developer and saved each buyer $20,000 to $40,000. The builder constructed a 38 unit condo and hired an outside vendor to assist with pricing the units. Meanwhile, I did a comparative analysis with the competition in the area and

discovered that the units were overpriced for the area because of the lack of amenities. I compiled a 1,200 page report supporting my price decrease suggestion from $20,000 to $40,000 per unit depending on unit size and its location in the building. The builder was frustrated that they had paid an outside "expert" to compile their opening prices and had missed the mark by so much. My mortgage lending background and real estate experience allowed me to assess the situation and compile my data so that the builder decreased the prices according to my suggestion. The units started to sell. Currently, I search for land that can be subdivided and pass along the information to private investors who are looking to build single family homes.

Kimberly Janes,
Realtor®
Seattle, Washington

WELCOME TO LIFE

Have you ever noticed that retirees feel unburdened after they sell off the family home and move to a condo or apartment? Some of them say it is because they found a place full of recreational activities. When you begin your search for a condo, townhouse, or apartment, you can find any activity you want.

Shared housing communities are full of life's favorite activities.

Lake living is often at its finest if you find a condo complex that provides boat docks and ramps that someone else maintains. Some communities have swimming, tennis, and mini-golf for minimal fees to the residents.

If you buy into community housing, you are also buying a new way of life: you will have more time to enjoy the things you love and you will leave behind the things you are not fond of—like outside maintenance.

A Little Tip

If you are contemplating the move to a shared housing complex but you are not sure you will be able to adjust easily, list your goals. What do you like to do? Where do you like to go? Do you like being in a secure area? If you do, you may fit in perfectly in shared housing. What is it that drew you to look at shared housing in the beginning? Think about the things you would enjoy more if you had fewer responsibilities and consider the things you might miss in shared housing, privacy, for example. What matters to you?

Condos, townhouses, and apartment houses are often located near the things you lost touch with while you were occupied with single home ownership. You will rediscover parks, shopping malls, golf courses, and theaters when you join the shared housing lifestyle.

CONSIDERING THE BEST PROPERTY FOR YOU

After you begin to search for a condo, townhouse, or an apartment, you will see their differences. Some homeowners find they prefer the advantages of an apartment because of the door attendant and other staff on duty in large cities, while others prefer townhouses because they appreciate the privacy of the individual housing unit.

As you are looking for your home, you need to consider what amenities are most important to you both inside and outside the home. For example, if you entertain often and find your complex does not have a clubhouse, you may need to look elsewhere or look at a larger unit to be able to entertain at home.

If you have children, take into consideration what kind of environment your children will have at their doorstep. For example, if you are considering a complex in a college town, will the locale present a problem for your teenagers who may want to join college parties?

You also need to consider the schedules of those who live close. When do your neighbors go to work and when do they come home? Will they disrupt your good night's sleep because you work the night shift? If so, reconsider your options because if you cannot rest where you live, you will not enjoy living there.

Some of the suggestions seem a bit elementary, but if you do not take the time to discover all you can about where you are going to live, it can come back to haunt you later. One thing you want to consider is how everyone else likes the area by talking to your future neighbors.

If there is turnover in the area, take the initiative to find out why. It could be that the community is a target for crime. Is there an upcoming property assessment? Are there problems with busybodies in the neighborhood? If you note empty units, look for the reason. Find out why people are moving so you will not move, too, just as quickly as you moved in.

QUESTIONS TO ASK YOUR SELLER

Young buyers may be reluctant to ask a seller questions about why they are selling because they do not want to risk the seller's wrath. If you are going to make an investment in a home, you can ask anything that comes to mind. Ask anything you want to know. Below, you will find some questions to ask the seller before agree to buy.

- Why are you selling?

- Did you like living here? Why or why not?

- What did you like best about your particular unit?

- What did you like least?

- What did you like best about the community or complex?

- What did you like least?

- How is the homeowners association and do you think it needs improvement?

- How long have the members been on the board of the association?

- When was the last major assessment?

- Do you know of an upcoming assessment?

These are legitimate questions. Be wary of bad opinions of a neighbor because the neighbor could become your best friend. When I was in real estate, I sold condos at a lakeside community called Misty Waters. The first condo I sold in the complex was to a couple I liked. They came to me for several of their transactions. However, when I first met the gentleman, one half of the couple, he warned me about another man living in the complex who eventually turned out to be one of my best clients and someone I came to respect. I often thought after both men had passed away what a waste it was that they did not like each other, because they would certainly have enjoyed a friendship.

My point is that if I had listened to what one had to say about the other, I would have missed a great opportunity to work with one of the dearest people I have ever known in my lifetime. Do not let a sellers' likes or dislikes sway you. See if they have a reason they are moving based on facts rather than opinions.

When looking at shared housing, you need to find the property assessments. You will need to be direct about them. Find out when the next assessment will occur and how much it will be.

As a shared housing owner, you need to budget for the assessments. When you are trying to figure out what you can afford, budget for your dues. It is best to think in terms of the added fee as being part of your monthly payment. You will want to know the following in addition to the list above:

- Is there traffic through the area at night (or whenever you sleep)?

- Are there weekend parties and, if so, do they get out of hand?

- Is security a concern?

- Are there parking issues? What if someone takes your parking space? Is overflow parking available? If not, where are you supposed to park?

- If there is a major problem on the property, who is the first person you should, call 9-1-1 or the on-site security? Is anyone "in-charge"?

DID YOU KNOW?

*Many homeowner associations have the same acting president
year after year because the person is available to the homeowners.
Perhaps the president is a homeowner in the community who is
dedicated to its growth and profit in the units. Perhaps he or she is
retired and wants something to do. Regardless, when the right person
is in control, the directors are available to the homeowners to help
them with issues concerning the entire complex.*

TALK TO YOUR NEIGHBORS BEFORE YOU BUY

If you want to know something, ask the neighbors, the directors,
and anyone else who will talk to you. Understand, you are not
just buying a dwelling   you are buying your home. You want to
be comfortable and buy what you like and what you can afford.

While it is great to think that all sellers will tell you the truth, do
not be fooled by everything the seller tells you. When sellers are
desperate enough to sell, they will tell you anything you want to
hear. If that does not work, they will drop the price and tell you
how they hate to sell the place. Truth and money do not always
go together. Talk to those who do not have a vested interest in
whether you buy.

BE AS CURIOUS AS A CAT

Check out the by-laws, proposed by-laws, fees for maintenance
of outside areas. See if you are allowed to make improvements
in the condo's declaration of condominium document. See if the
by-laws are to your liking. Look into the financial health of the
condo by checking financial information listed under "reserve

fund" to see if it is set up to cover emergencies. Obtain a copy of the condo's current budget and study their financial statement so there will be no surprises. Get an Estoppel Certificate that will show whether the current owner owes fees or if any liens exist against the condo. Owners can be evicted for nonpayment of fees. Obtain a Certificate of Insurance showing how much the condo board has purchased to cover damages to the common areas. Get a statement of the percentage of occupancy of the condominium complex. This may alert you to potential problems if the occupancy rate is low. Obtain a statement that spells out the use of recreational facilities as well as a drawing or photo of the unit's interior and recreational facilities. Get a list of improvements, if any, the developer agrees to make. Get a statement that spells out the monthly or yearly maintenance fees you are expected to pay. Obtain a Certificate of Title for your condo unit. If you decide to use a real estate agent, use the best Buyers Agent in your area. Not only do you get better results, but they give you better counsel. They know the ropes. They are good resources of local information for insurance, inspections, legal counsel, and financing.

In today's marketplace, the prices of homes are outrageous, and if you are going to buy, go ahead, snoop! Drive by the complex at various hours in the day or night to see if all is well in the neighborhood. Pay attention to the number of lights you see at 1 a.m. Does it appear that everyone lives a quiet life or does the party just get cranking at 3 a.m.? What is going on at various times in the complex? Make a note of it. (Be sure to let a security guard, if there is one, know what you are doing driving around at all hours.)

After you have done your detective work and given the place your approval, you will feel better about buying. However, if you uncover some serious flaws in the complex you are considering but feel you can live with the flaws, you should use them as a bargaining chip in negotiations. For instance, if the unit you are considering is next to railroad tracks, this information is worth using to lower the price of the unit. Who wants to hear a train at midnight? However, the racket may not bother you if you can persuade the owner to drop the asking price a few thousand dollars.

BE PREPARED

As you begin your search for a shared housing unit, be prepared. Go into each unit you are considering with a list of questions. Ask for a copy of the bylaws of the complex, a list of phone contacts from the board of directors, the deed, and the survey. Play the smart consumer and put your hands on everything you intend to review. Keep a folder of information on the units you are interested in buying.

A condo that has a layout that is unusual for the complex should set off red flags in your mind. One buyer paid top price for a condo that had an enclosed balcony that was furnished as a home office. Some time later, the association management began strictly enforcing the rules. It was then that the buyer discovered that the balcony renovation was in violation of the rules which clearly stated that the only patio furniture was allowed on the decks. The lack of a home office diminished the value of the condo significantly, and when the buyer sold, she lost money.

BE PATIENT

Patience can play an important part in whether you buy the right unit. If you show patience, you will be able to make better housing choices and you will not be too quick to jump on the best sales pitch you hear. Learn to sleep on it and do not be eager to buy the first property you see or the first one an agent claims will get away if you do not buy today.

STEPS TO TAKE WHEN BUYING SHARED HOUSING

Your first step is to decide **where you want to live.**

What part of the city best suits your lifestyle? How far away is it from your work? Are there schools nearby? Where can you shop? These are questions any prospective homeowner must ask himself. "Where"?

You want a condo complex that offers the convenience and pleasure of living within an established neighborhood. All the amenities for a comfortable lifestyle should be close at hand, from shopping to green space, including public transit, entertainment, and more.

What Type of Home Do You Want to Live In?

After location, the next decision to make is about the kind of space you want to live in. There is a world of options to choose from, including high rise, low rise condos and townhomes. Think about the combination of rooms and living spaces that would best suit your needs. Do you need one bedroom, or two or more? What is the best type of layout for you? What direction do you want to face and how high up would you like to be? What types of amenities are you most interested in? A home is about more than square footage, and should reflect your tastes and values.

How Much Do You Want to Pay?

To answer this question, you will first need to determine how much you can afford based on the location and the type of home you want to live in. You will have to decide on an appropriate down payment as well as your mortgage-carrying ability, and do not forget dues you will pay for maintenance of common areas. You will need to add these numbers to all other loan expenses you might have as well as your total average monthly expenses. The sum of these numbers needs to be an amount that you can comfortably cover within your available financial resources.

Do Your Research

Check out various web sites, drive by locations and meet sales representatives. Learn about a builder's reputation through someone who actually lives in one of the buildings they have developed. Find out about the level of experience they have with the type of building you want to move into.

Prepare Your Offer

After you have made all the tough home buying choices, you will need to start the paper work. Because buying a home is such an emotional and exciting experience, it can be difficult to focus on contract details. We recommend that you work with a lawyer who specializes in condominium purchases to help you through this process.

5

IMPORTANT DOCUMENTS YOU NEED TO UNDERSTAND

It may not surprise you to discover the important documents you need are the same whether you buy a single dwelling home or a shared housing unit. The process of buying a home is work. It is time consuming and takes cooperation to make the transfer successful. There are home warranties and homeowner's insurance to buy. You need to understand how they can affect you as a shared housing owner. You will find the coverage you need in insurance and warranties is similar to the needs in a single family home.

AGREEMENT OF PURCHASE & SALE

The home purchasing process starts with signing the Agreement of Purchase and Sale. You need to review it carefully as it is a legally binding contract. Not only does it include the purchase price, it also includes terms and conditions that will apply to the transaction, a description of how the purchase will be financed; the closing date; the date possession will be delivered to the buyer; pre-delivery inspection, and other contingencies.

DISCLOSURE STATEMENTS

Disclosure Statements and Condo documentation (by-laws, rules and budget of the condominium corporation): The disclosure statement and documentation include all the important information about the condo you are purchasing. Read them very carefully.

HOMEOWNER'S INSURANCE

As a homeowner, you will have limits on the type of insurance you will be able to carry on a single unit in a complex. Most likely, it will be the equivalent of renter's insurance because the homeowners association bears the responsibility for insurance policies. Dues often increase as the premiums increase.

In an insurance policy on a single-family dwelling, the policy will cover loss due to theft, fire, and liability in the event someone is hurt while on your property. An association should have a policy covering the common ground and the exterior of the buildings. The insurance premium is usually included in the monthly maintenance fees.

While a homeowner covers their own personal assets such as jewelry and artwork through a policy similar to a renter's policy, it is advisable to look at the insurance policy the homeowners association has as well. See if flood damage or any other policy type should be required for you.

You need to talk to an attorney if the association does not have liability insurance to cover potential lawsuits. Ask how this situation could affect you as a homeowner in the association.

If the association does not have enough insurance to cover damage to the buildings or common areas in the event of flooding, fire, or any other unexpected occurrence, you may be able to secure a separate policy to cover your financial investment. Check with insurance companies and an attorney if you have questions. However, since the board of directors in your housing community put the insurance policies into effect, you should review them.

A Little Tip
You should always ask for a copy of the homeowners association insurance policies that are in effect so that you understand what is covered and when the due date falls so you can follow up to ensure your community never suffers a lapse in coverage. While this may seem to be someone else's responsibility, it is not. Let someone fall on ice on a sidewalk who is not a homeowner when there is a lapse in the policy, and you will quickly discover how this type of incident can affect all homeowners.

HOME WARRANTIES

Some people would never consider a home warranty if it were not offered to them through their real estate agent. Agents may offer a home warranty as a closing gift to a home buyer when the commission is large enough to handle the gift, while other agents offer their assistance in finding the best home warranty.

Occasionally, a seller will buy a home warranty to cover the house during the selling process, and it transfers to the new buyer—a good sales tool. The more you want to warrant, the higher the price you will pay for the warranty.

Warranty prices vary from $200 to $500. Deductibles are rarely more than $100. Consider the warranty your security blanket, good to have as a new homeowner because you may not have money to replace the heating and cooling system or a refrigerator.

Most of the home warranties I have seen cover the heating and cooling unit, plumbing, electrical, and all appliances. They are usually in effect for one year.

CASE STUDY: KIMBERLY JANES

I recommend to all my sellers that they offer the warranty in their listing—it is their way of being responsible for their home. I also recommend to my buyers to obtain a home warranty if there was not one provided, as their way of being responsible for their purchase decision. I have compared the  different vendors for my area and there is one in particular that I feel offers a better coverage than the others, and I share that with the client. It is been my experience that when I have paid for the warranty, the client didn't appreciate the gift or know the value (several hundred dollars) but when taking the same amount and applying in a gift card they can actually see and use the value for, they appreciate that more. It's like buying a high school graduate a $500 luggage set, who'd rather have a fat $500 check!

Kimberly Janes,
Realtor®
Seattle, Washington

A Little Tip

If you are a buyer who tries to get all you can from a seller, consider asking for a home warranty. You may just get one!

It is odd that when you talk to real estate agents about their personal feelings about a home warranty, you get mixed answers. Some will tell you their clients felt that home warranties were a waste of money, and others will tell you that the home warranty was a great thing to have for added protection. It boils down to hindsight: who needed their home warranty and who needed it within a year of closing on their new home.

CASE STUDY: EUGENIA FOXWORTH

I have never offered a home warranty as a closing gift. It is not something that we do in New York City. I give a two-hour gift certificate for a design specialist or interior designer as a closing gift to those who need this service. I do have professionals from financial institutions, mortgage companies, and insurance companies speak to the residents at gatherings that I organize in select buildings that I sell properties.

Eugenia Foxworth
Coldwell Banker Hunt Kennedy
NYS Licensed Realtor,
Certified International Property Specialist
Eugenia.foxworth@cbhk.com

You are buying peace of mind when you buy a home warranty. You cannot put a price on peace of mind. Try comparing the cost of the home warranty to the cost of a major appliance you cannot live without, and you will see the value in home warranties.

Your agent can recommend one of several companies to consider for your home warranty needs, or the title company you use may have some brochures to share with you about home warranties. Typical companies are National Home Protection, 2-10 Home Buyer's Warranty, and Home Warranty of America. There are others, and they vary by state and coverage.

CASE STUDY: BRUNO FRIIA

We always assist in finding the best home warranty for our buyers. We also take the time to educate potential buyers about the benefits of a home warranty in accordance with their property, but the developer offers the warranty.

Bruno Friia
Lambros Real Estate
Western Montana

CASE STUDY: KIRK HANSEN

Home warranties do not cost that much and are offered from a third party company. It is kind of like an insurance policy that you purchase. I think all selling agents should make sure that their buyer has one and, if not, purchase one for them. The cost is low and it could help avoid potential liability.

Kirk Hansen
Century 21 Homes First
President
760-212-0062
Kirk.Hansen@Century21.com

SUB-LEASING YOUR UNIT

When renting out a condo or another shared housing unit, you should take the time to go over the bylaws with the prospective tenants. Have them sign a document stating they will follow the bylaws enforced by the homeowners association. Most associations will not want the tenant to pay the membership dues or attending the homeowners' meetings. If your tenant has an interest in active participation in these meetings, check with the board for their policies.

Should you decide to buy a multi-family unit for investment and put a tenant in the unit, other homeowners may object, particularly if homeowners are in the majority. Check the bylaws.

Having the appropriate legal documentation can save you headaches in the future. You should have an attorney look over any lease you want a tenant sign, as well as the bylaws, rules, and regulations of the complex.

Many people use the generic leases online. If you are serious about being an investor, you should have a standard lease your attorney prepares for you because it will give you peace of mind.

CLOSING STATEMENT

In real estate dealings, you should get a closing statement before facing off with the buyer or the seller. Here are some of the costs for closing and transferring the title.

- Survey Costs

- Appraisal Costs

- Home Inspection Costs

- Mortgage Points

- Termite Inspections

- Loan Application Fees

- Attorney Closing Fees

- Deed Recording Fees

- Escrow Sum Listed

- Real Estate Agent Fees

Not understanding the closing statement can prove costly to you. You need to understand the fees and charges you incur and make certain your monthly payments are what you expected. Take the steps to ensure your fees are not going to make your monthly payments higher than you anticipated. If you do not understand something or if something is wrong on the closing statement, wait until everything is corrected before you close.

6

CAN YOU LIVE WITH RESTRICTIONS?

Avoiding restrictions can be a costly mistake. You should be aware of restrictions before you buy because they make carefree living impossible if they infringe on your rights as you see them.

One of the biggest complaints about shared housing arrangements is that homeowners do not follow restrictions. One way to put a stop to these complaints is to fine the miscreants.

WHAT YOU SHOULD KNOW BEFORE YOU BUY

Before you buy a condo, townhouse, or an apartment, you should take the time to review the restrictions and the bylaws of the homeowners association. They were put into place by either the developer of the complex or the original homeowner's association, and they are intended to benefit individual unit owners.

Potential buyers do not think about the bylaws when they begin to search for a unit in a complex. However, if you want to be a smart shopper, you will inform your real estate agent or the seller to bring along a copy of the bylaws to their first meeting with you. If possible, take home a copy to review. If you are looking at several homes, the bylaws will help you narrow the field.

Look at condo or townhouse bylaws online before you buy. See what is typical so that when you read the bylaws where you are considering buying, you will know what is considered normal.

CASE STUDY: KIRK HANSEN

Avoid buying if you know you are not going to be happy with the bylaws. You will be unable to demand a change in them, and you will never be content. Bylaws are seldom changed to please one homeowner, and typically when you begin to discuss the change of a written rule or regulation, no one will support it. It may be better for you to buy in an area where you are content with the managerial style without any "subject to change" issues.

Kirk Hansen
Century 21 Homes First
President
760-212-0062
Kirk.Hansen@Century21.com

You should know before you buy that a community with a governing body will want to enforce the restrictions and that they are usually followed. You will benefit by the bylaws' being enforced. If they are not, the property is usually losing value.

CHILDREN CAN STAY

Regardless of where you choose to live, you cannot be discriminated against because of children, race, or for any other reason. However, your landlord may ban pets so that some places you may want to live may not accept your pet.

Homeowner's associations have restrictions against pets. Do not attempt to move in with a pet if there are restrictions against them, and do not attempt to move in with a larger pet when the restrictions mandate only small pets under a set limit.

A Little Tip

Pets belong on leashes. Do not even consider walking around a complex with an unleashed animal. Of course, you love your pet, but others may be just waiting for an opportunity to send your beloved companion to the pound if you turn your head for a second!

Even in complexes where pets are allowed, there may be restrictions about where they can go. There are usually dog walks or other trails available but in most areas, and you will be required to clean up after your pet. If you find there is not a dog park or trail for your pet, take the time to notice where the other pet owners take their animal for walks. You want to be sure there is a "designated pet area" to avoid future problems.

ORDINANCES YOU MAY NEED TO LIVE BY

The bylaws of a condo or a townhouse board will be enforced. You will be provided with a copy of these bylaws when you move in and should see them before you buy as mentioned earlier. If you choose to ignore any of the bylaws, you will be fined and sued if you do not pay your fines.

The time may come when these restrictions will prevent you from living the lifestyle you want. It may be necessary to buck the system, but you will succeed only if you are already complying with the bylaws of the property and trying to prevent change in the complex.

The homeowners association is in place to keep a community worth living in, and the rules are in place to ensure everyone has a safe living environment that holds value and investment purpose. If residents can ignore the bylaws, all homeowners lose money on their investment because the value of their home units will go down. Should the association choose not to enforce rules set by the homeowners, someone must decide which rules should be followed and which ones ignored. The better places to live set the bylaws and follow them. They make no exceptions because if they begin making exceptions, residents feel they are not being treated fairly.

Restrictions are in place and bylaws exist to govern a number of people who invest in their homes.

You will notice that the bylaws listed in the Appendix address common areas, guests, parking lots, pets, and enforcement of the rules. The sample provides a guideline so that you will know what to expect from the board. The sample can be expanded.

MEET THE MANAGEMENT OR THE BOARD

In every condo, complex, or townhouse community, you will have a "go-to" person. That person is usually the president of the board of directors for the homeowners association. Anyone who wants to have an active voice on the board usually gets a turn. When a long-standing board is in place and everyone agrees that things are fine the way they are, board membership may not rotate.

When you are checking the bylaws of the homeowner's

association, also check your comfort level on how wisely the board allocates money for the improvement of the facilities. Monthly fees are not cheap.

Beware of the board that sits as judge and jury. They will screen applicants for ownership in the community. Their reasons are that they want to ensure the applicant can afford the dues, assessments, and other expenses. The board may want to check your credit report. If so, laugh, and move on. Your credit is none of the business of board members in any community no matter how nice it is.

I know of a specific subdivision using billboard advertising that was a running joke because it stated "Only a select few will be privileged enough to live within these walls." What a sly developer to appeal to the vanity of a "select few."

With so many developments popping up in desirable locations, you do not have to worry about being one of the "select few" who can enjoy living in an exclusive neighborhood. You will be able to find many of the units in your price range in a variety of communities. Many of them share the same floor plans and square footage. The difference lies in the amenities. You may decide you want to be one of the "select few" who is able to live in a planned unit development or a complex located on the golf course, or you may choose a complex with only a boat dock and swimming pool. Whatever is important to you should be your focus when you search for shared living.

If you are going to be living in the community, focus on what you like when you choose to buy, but if you know you are going to buy a unit for the sole purpose of renting it to someone else, focus on variety. The more activities and amenities the complex offers, the more appealing it will be to potential tenants. Of course, you could always run an ad in the paper, "Only a select few can rent from me," and watch how this marketing slogan works for you!

RIDICULOUS RESTRICTIONS: A SIGN OF TROUBLE

Many bylaws are ridiculous. Most homeowner's associations are standard but on occasion, you will find silly rules and regulations created by those few who have nothing better to do. It is hard to change rules — even ridiculous ones. Consider all the bylaws as set in stone from the beginning. If you find the rules too restrictive or unenforceable, you may need to reconsider your purchase. An association that tries to implement rules such as "no candles" is not dealing with reality. Such a rule cannot be enforced, and there is no predicting what other silly rule they may devise regarding, for instance, children, flags and flagpoles, holiday decorations, home businesses, landscaping, paint colors, and pets.

The first sign of trouble occurs when a board can reject someone as a resident. If you must be voted on to be accepted as an active member, beware of annoyances to come. Are they discriminating against a group of people? If the board must approve the owners, imagine what would happen if you wanted to lease your unit.

More homeowner's associations have a rule about who can have keys to homeowner units. I feel that there should be more opposition to this rule because you do not know who has access to those keys. Even if only some members of the board had access to the keys, should they be able to enter your home at any time?

7

WHY SHARED HOUSING IS A GREAT OPTION FOR EVERYONE (WELL, ALMOST)

F rom first-time homeowners to individuals ready to downsize, shared housing can be a good option for the homeowner who wants to be in a convenient location with great amenities. Well-planned developments consisting of condos, patio homes, townhouses, and other multi-family housing are in good locations with schools and shopping close to the complex.

Not everyone wants the American dream of the little cottage with a white picket fence on a picturesque yard. Now, when buyers are looking at a home, they start with the amenities and conveniences, and then they check its appearance.

Considered one of the best ways to buy affordable housing, the condo is often seen as the first-time home. In some areas, condos and townhouses are the best opportunity for affordable housing, but affordability is not the main enticement. The amenities and the lifestyle draw in the first-time home buyer.

After my husband and I moved to Kingsport in the Tri-Cities area of Tennessee, I was out showing real estate to a couple one afternoon and found a beautiful condo development. The condos were about 3,000 square feet with fine appointments. Kitchens had granite counter tops and the best custom cabinets. The units were all three-plus bedrooms and had a two-car garage. They were simply beautiful and the location was perfect. I went home and announced we were moving and was quickly reminded that our children would not have a yard to play in and we could not move again after one month in our new residence. Would you like to know how many times I threw this discussion up to my husband when he did not want to get off the couch to mow the acreage we bought for the children's play area?

Throughout this book, we discuss amenities you can expect, and they improve as you move to better locations and higher end developments. I have seen the lifestyle in a posh apartment building: doormen and room service. That is a "suite" deal! My guess is that soon the amenities offered the average family will improve as more complexes compete for sales.

Anyone can rent "suites" at hotels; they are not reserved for the affluent anymore. There are so many all-suite hotels now, it is evident society expects more value for their money. The same is true in homes. People want top of the line. If they are buying new, they want their units to have the best of everything from granite to marble and if they are buying old, there had better be some substantial upgrades. Otherwise, they can spend a little more and buy new.

Thank goodness consumers are finally demanding more bang for their buck because it is about time! With the new demands, fewer builders who do not know what they are doing will enter the home market because people demand more of them and guess what? It helps everyone when we expect to receive more for our money.

FIRST-TIME HOMEOWNERS

As a first-time homeowner, you will make your share of mistakes when it comes to trying to find your perfect residence. You may forget about the dues required by the homeowner's association; you may forget to take out homeowner's insurance until your lender calls to inform you that you forgot. You probably will not know what to expect and you will not know what to do. If you have an agent working with you, she will handle everything for you from the offer to purchase to the closing documents.

The first-time homeowner often makes critical mistakes when it comes to jumping on the first good deal. While buying your first home is exciting, consider a few things before you buy, such as what you like about the unit and those items that will remain in the unit you are buying. The following list is a list of reminders:

- Know what stays with the unit you are going to offer to purchase. Do the blinds and drapes stay? How about the ceiling fans and light fixtures?

- Do the appliances stay? Are they in good working order?

- Take note of any broken windows or locks and find out who is responsible for the repairs and make sure these things are repaired before you buy.

- Are there any repairs needed on the deck or exterior area of the particular unit you want to buy? If so, who is responsible for them and when will they take care of the problem areas?

- Did you notice whether there are washer and dryer hook-ups? If not, are there laundry facilities on the premises? If you have to use laundry areas on the property, are they maintained to your satisfaction? Is the area free of clutter and filth? Would you feel comfortable using the area?

- If there is a garage, does the door opener work and if not, will the current owner repair it before the closing date?

- Can the current homeowner give you an estimate of the monthly bills on the unit? For example, how much does it cost to cool or heat the unit?

- Is the heating and cooling unit in good working order?

- Turn on all the lights and check electrical outlets. Do they all work properly?

- How much do the taxes and insurance cost?

A Little Tip

Check your home warranty company about what is covered and make sure these things work before you buy. If they are not covered, it is the seller's responsibility to fix them before the transfer of title.

As a first time homeowner, it is easy to get caught up in the fact you finally own your own place. Try to keep a level head. Think about the investment potential of the place you are buying. Do your own comparative market analysis if you are not using a real estate agent. Go to the courthouse and look for complexes that are holding their value or have gone up in value. Make a wise investment decision and keep the profit potential in clear focus.

CASE STUDY: KIMBERLY JANES

When a young married couple bought a home 35 years ago, they raised their family in the home, set family traditions with grandchildren in the same home, and would die with that last known address, leaving their children to dissolve the property. Trends today indicate buyers buy and raise a family to a point in their first home, and usually around

CASE STUDY: KIMBERLY JANES

five to eight years later they sell to buy or build a larger home, which they typically reside in until the children are well on their own, at which point they then become today's empty nesters and highly desire a single story home or unit with two or three bedrooms.

Kimberly Janes,
Realtor®
Seattle, Washington

DOWNSIZING

Some of the condos and townhouses today would be considered anything but downsizing with an average of 5,000 square feet in townhomes and condos. The living space is roomy, and the new developments keep getting bigger and better.

There are still some cozy units on the market in most desirable areas that would qualify for downsizing. While first-time home buyer may consider a two- or three-bedroom, the person ready to downsize will look at one and two bedrooms are less expensive. Best of all, many of the complexes offer a large assortment of living spaces so that everyone can be accommodated based on the space they need.

In choosing a unit when you are downsizing, you may want to consider a single-level floor plan, considered more like patio homes than townhouses, but these floor plans and designs are also offered in townhouse communities to give some variety to those who need single-level living.

When people downsize, they often look for amenities such as bridge clubs, social events, activities at the club house, walking trails, and serene surroundings.

A Little Tip

As a buyer, when you are in the market for a new home, keep your eyes open for the couple looking to downsize because they are usually flexible on their price. They want a fair price, but they may accept less. The downsizing couple will often consider creative financing or contracts that need some seller assistance in the closing costs.

A complex with several aging couples and singles in the community is much better than looking toward assisted living or a true designated retirement community. The complexes designated for retirees are not always where your parents in their 50s will want to be especially if they are still in the work force. These individuals are not ready for a retirement community! Many of them are just beginning to live!

THE BUSY PERSON LOVES SHARED HOUSING

Do you work around the clock? If you do, you need to consider shared housing. Why work long days and come home to a yard to mow? Busy people seem to settle into the shared housing way of life better than most.

Active people enjoy shared housing arrangements because they can be on the move doing the things they love while leaving the work to someone else. They can swim without cleaning the pool or work out in the gym without worrying about maintaining the equipment. It is a terrific way to live for the active lifestyle.

DID YOU KNOW?

When you are looking to downsize, you are better off buying a two-bedroom versus a one-bedroom because they are much easier to sell later on. Even if you do not need an extra bedroom, there is not that much difference in price, but the average days on market

*vary greatly. Buy the two bedrooms unless it is much more economical
for you to buy the one bedroom. If it is an affordability issue, be sure
you have looked at all complexes before making a final decision.
Consider days on market as part of your comparative market analysis
because you may want to return the unit to the marketplace for sale.*

The idea of living in a shared housing complex is also perfect
for people who travel. They can leave town without lengthy
preparations and feel comfortable about locking everything up
for a couple of months. In most areas it is safe to do so and best
of all, the person who is traveling does not have to worry about
whether the exterior of their home is being maintained.

As a traveling homeowner, you will not worry unnecessarily
about theft while you are away. You feel that your investment is
safe, and everything you own inside the unit is secure   worth its
weight in gold!

A Little Tip

If you choose to live in a shared housing complex and you do travel
extensively, it is a good idea to leave your phone numbers with a trusted
neighbor or the president of the homeowners association should they
need to reach you. It is an added benefit of living in a complex as you
are downsizing and beginning to live life a little more.

OUTSIDE MAINTENANCE BE GONE

The maintenance fee you pay for your unit will ensure the
exterior of your home will be maintained. You will expect the
yard work to be done, but if it is not, can you do it? Well, yes and
no. You are not supposed to do it. Why would you want to do
it? Part of the fees you are paying every month are to keep the
grounds neat, and if they are not, find out what can be done to
keep up the value of your home.

A Little Tip

If you are paying your association dues and find nothing is being done in the complex to warrant them, it is time to speak out at the association meetings. The board of directors has an obligation to you and the community to keep the complex in good shape. If they are not fulfilling their obligations and the place is beginning to deteriorate, it is time to speak out. If you are paying dues, you need to ensure those dues are hard at work for you.

Preferably before you buy, you should be able to determine what areas you are responsible for maintaining. In some complexes, there is often a fine line between the responsibilities of the homeowner and the association. Be sure you understand who pays for the siding, roof, and deck repairs that are part of your exterior space. They are usually the responsibility of the homeowner's association and classified as common areas.

PERFECT FOR GROWING FAMILIES

Shared housing can be perfect for growing families if you have a floor plan that accommodates everyone.

How will everyone in your household like the idea? Most children will see only the amenities of the complex. Some complexes appeal to the youth in us with swimming pools, tennis courts, and racquetball courts, but make sure the unit is big enough. Your living space is still indoors not outdoors.

Shared housing can be a blessing in disguise for busy parents who can send their teenagers outside to find a game of basketball or to the tennis courts, but it can also be hectic having many teens and children around. Look at your lifestyle and consider what is important to you.

8

SHARED HOUSING EQUALS SHARED RESPONSIBILITIES

I have had the opportunity to observe two extraordinary homeowner's associations close up. One was in Hilton Head, South Carolina, at a large complex of condos with vacation homeowners, and the other was in Tri-Cities, Tennessee, where I was a real estate agent. The first reason these associations were remarkable is that homeowners were able to hold their homes' values in a development more than 20 years old, and the second was that several individuals worked hard.

Here are more reasons the two developments I mentioned worked well for everyone who owned in these complexes.

Homeowner's association members were active participants. Homeowners paid the dues, and the members did their part to ensure everyone enjoyed living in their community. In Hilton Head, the hands-on owners who lived in the complex beautified their living space. They set rules for the homeowners who rented to vacationing families, and they strictly enforced them.

When the board called meetings, most of the homeowners attended. Out-of-town homeowners reviewed the meeting minutes and voted in absentia.

The board had strong, active presidents in both locations who were hands-on and took the initiative to oversee everything that went on in the development. It was not uncommon to see them out on the property and while the newer homeowners had to get used to it, eventually everyone understood part of the board's responsibility was to make sure everything in the complex was in tiptop shape. A president of a homeowners association who takes the time to be seen and to see what is going on can keep havoc at bay.

Both associations kept the grounds of the property in great condition. The lawns were manicured and the landscaping was clean and neat. Both properties had visible groundskeepers at work five days a week.

Both properties enforced the rules. They made sure there were no loud noises coming from the units after 10 p.m., and if they found a problem, they quickly addressed it.

Both developments had designated parking for campers and boats keeping smaller parking areas free from oversized recreational vehicles.

Both complexes had active homeowners in their association dedicated to making the community nice for everyone.

The list could fill this chapter but these items stood out when I studied the developments. The development that had the stronger homeowners association was on the lake, and so the board had boat slips, docks, swimming pools, and tennis courts to govern. It was good to work there as a real estate agent because the community was welcoming, and I liked showing property there. I knew if someone bought in the community, they were buying a nice unit that would increase its value. I also knew they were buying into a lifestyle they would enjoy.

WHAT YOU OWN — YOU MAINTAIN

Homeowners who buy into a housing community of shared housing units often forget their responsibilities. It is easy to believe you take care of what you own and that ownership is within your four walls and possibly out on your deck or patio. Beyond that, you have no responsibility. However, you do own shares in a homeowners association and you have a responsibility with that ownership.

Before you buy any unit anywhere, you need to look at the board and the homeowners association. You want to be sure that the people in charge of the homeowners organization are pro-active. They want to be on the board, and they take pains to ensure the upkeep and improvement of the development. A passive board in a co-op community can allow home values to plummet. When you buy a condo, townhouse, or an apartment, your responsibility is to take care of what you own as well as the common areas. It is better to be pro-active in ensuring you are part of an active, thriving complex dedicated to holding and improving home values.

THE HOMEOWNER'S ASSOCIATION

There are two reasons I recommend attending a homeowners association meeting before you buy into a community of shared housing. First, you are able to see for yourself how they conduct business and how they reach decisions. Second, you will meet some of your potential neighbors.

CASE STUDY: JAY CROCKETT

There are many advantages to having a condo complex with a strong homeowner's association. You will find that condo complexes with strong associations are more attractive and more aesthetically pleasing to buyers. A condo owner can sell faster when a strong homeowner's association is at work because it will  see that all aspects of maintenance are done and will hire a ground maintenance crew to make sure all areas of the complex are properly maintained. All surface areas will be pressure washed and adequate money will be set aside for roofing, resurfacing, and painting. A good association will set parameters so that no homeowners modify their property to devalue that of another's in the complex. A buyer should always pick a complex that has a well-established homeowner association to that property values will escalate.

REALTY EXECUTIVES

Jay Crockett
Realtor
423-952-0226
Johnson City, Tennessee

The board is the government of the complex where you buy. They enforce rules, set guidelines, change the governing bylaws, and function like a business operating the day-to-day business of the complex. The board can make or break a community. If you do not think so, attend one of the meetings of a known complex where everyone is selling because of the lack of an intelligent governing body.

As a real estate agent, I was amused at the election of one officer for a seat on the board in one complex. He ran an active campaign to unseat the sitting president of the board. He posted announcements in the community to let people know he was running for the president's post on the board several months before the vote. Since then, I have seen many active campaigns start early and have found that they are common practice.

While many of the better communities do show a strong board in place, there are some that no one wants the responsibility of being on the board. It is time consuming and in today's society, who has the time to be a director for a condo complex? Not many. Still as a homeowner, you should take the initiative to step in and at least try out sitting on the board for a year or so before you decide not to take an active voice in your homeowners association. It can be rewarding and give you the opportunity to improve where you live.

A Little Tip

Most people have good intentions when they move into a complex or a multi-family housing complex. They plan to participate in the homeowners association meetings but after they attend one, they are not interested in going again, leaving their money in the hands of strangers. If you are going to buy in a housing complex, be an active homeowner and attend the meetings. Even if you are not neighborly, you have invested in a development that strangers manage. Why not ensure its appreciation?

If you attend a meeting of the homeowners and notice no one wants to sit on the board, take a closer look. Are there several homeowners in the community who make the directors' lives miserable with impossible expectations? If so, suggest they run for office and change things. Should you attend a meeting before you buy in a complex and find no one gets along well in these meetings, go somewhere else. There are too many housing choices in most areas to add disagreements to your future. It is not worth it and often these communities put too much focus on "he said she said" so they never accomplish anything in the meetings and much less in the community where they live.

CASE STUDY: KIMBERLY JANES

I have served on the board of directors of my own homeowner's association and have been involved in a lawsuit with my neighbor over a property line issue which escalated to restraining orders being issued on the other party. So, with that shared, the pros are that homeowners associations work so long  as the rules are enforced on all at all times. The cons are that you might get a weak association and the issue could be financially and emotionally all yours to deal with. Before you buy a property, meet all neighbors you will be sharing a corner with and anyone else who is home to talk to before you sign the purchase and sale. Homeowners associations only work as long as they uphold and enforce the rules.

Kimberly Janes,
Realtor®
Seattle, Washington

HOMEOWNER'S DUES AND WHAT THEY MEAN

When you are buying a new home in a complex full of other units, look at the bylaws of the communities you are considering. They will help you decide where you are best served to invest your money. They may determine which complex you prefer.

After you read the bylaws, consider the cost of the maintenance fees or membership dues. See where your homeowner's money will go. Here is where some of the money should be going:

- For building maintenance of all the exterior buildings in the complex, including siding, roofing, and sidewalks.

- Grounds maintenance by a lawn service or regular grounds keeper.

- Insurance premiums.

- Any amenities such as boat docks, swimming pools, and riding stables.

- Adequate dumpsters.

The board should always work within a budget. It will take months to get a housing complex back to strength after several years of bad management. When the homeowners' interests are not protected, all the homeowners suffer.

A Little Tip

If a board considers cutting the cost of maintenance fees, you need to ask questions and find out what would be lost. Will you lose your lawn service one day each week? Will the swimming pool only be open two months instead of three? What will the homeowners do without, and how will it affect your home value? When cuts are made in costs, amenities, or fees, something of value is lost. If that something is important to you, take a stand to protect your interests, lifestyle, and home value.

WHY SIT ON THE BOARD

People sit on the board in many of the complexes because they want to be proactive in gaining what they want for the community. Many will take a seat on the board long enough to get something they want accomplished and never run for another election again after their goal is completed. There is nothing wrong with that if it is for the betterment of the community, and if the entire homeowners vote and agree for the person to take an active voice on the board.

A Little Tip

What if you join the board and you make a difference in your community? Do you think it would be worth it if the home values increased because of your ideas? If you think you can make a difference, do it! Your help is probably needed and input from creative minds is often appreciated!

Many people have the time and the knowledge to run a successful homeowners association and they are the people who can raise your home values significantly if they take an active voice on the board. Often, investors in the complex who own several units will want to sit on the board in some capacity every term. Watch that the person does not control every aspect of the community. Such an investor can initiate assessments for amenities that will directly help him more than anyone else. For instance, he may have several units on the market, and he wants siding replaced on the building where his units are located. The entire community should benefit from assessments — not just one property owner.

MAKING OR BREAKING A GOOD INVESTMENT

One or two years with a slack board in place can ruin home values and tarnish the reputation of the community. You can see that doing your homework is important. Here are some requests for the directors and the association:

- Ask to see the bylaws of the complex and ask questions about anything you do not understand.

- Ask for the names and telephone numbers of the board members and call them with questions about the next anticipated assessment as well as when the last assessment took place.

- Determine whether the board has a particular agenda

that they are working toward at the time you are buying. What are their current short-term and long-term goals? Talk with some of the members — they will tell you.

- Find out about their meetings. When do the meetings take place? Who attends? What do they discuss? Do they send out newsletters of meeting minutes following the board meetings?

- After talking to the board, determine whether it protects the interests of all the homeowners or if it appears to be working only for the board members' own interests.

- Ask to see the operating budget.

- Does the board have reserves available? Is it obvious the board has used its money wisely?

- How do they collect past-due membership dues, and do they have a large majority of the homeowners running in arrears?

- How does the board handle the enforcement of the bylaws? How do they collect dues for the homeowners association? How do they conduct business day in and day out?

Finally, find out the opinion of the homeowners. Ask them if they feel that the board does a good job. Ask them why or why not. Find out how long the board has been in place. Do the same people tend to be in place year in and year out? If so, is this a good thing? It is hard to go into a new housing environment with an agenda for change. You will be the new kid on the block and if you have too many ideas for change, the board will spurn your opinions.

9

FINANCIAL CONCERNS & FINANCING YOUR PURCHASE

Most people finance their home purchases and in shared housing, you have to consider your monthly payment and your homeowner association dues when you are calculating what you can afford. As a homeowner in a shared housing environment, you also need to have a certain allotment put aside for assessments that may arise because they can be expensive and often happen without warning.

When considering a unit in a multi-family housing environment, you should find out the assessments the property has incurred in the past. Ask homeowners how much they were and how much lead-time they were given to pay them. Was the assessment added in with the monthly dues or were the homeowners required to come up with a lump sum? You cannot budget unless you have these answers.

WHAT YOU CAN AFFORD

Before you begin your search, calculate what you can pay for housing. You want to know what you are willing to pay out each month for housing. In my book *How to Buy Real Estate without a Down Payment*, we discussed in detail housing costs and how to calculate what you can afford. I recommended that you calculate 25 percent maximum, but some lenders will tell you to allow up to one-third of your income for housing. Spending that much on housing can imperil your home.

Twenty-five percent of your total gross is still a little much if you have debts so you have to calculate your debt-to-income ratio more precisely than simply looking at a certain percent of the gross being allowed for housing. To know what you can afford, it is important to look at your entire debt picture. Start by contacting one of the major credit reporting agencies listed in the Appendix to get a copy of your credit report. Go through the report and determine whether everything on it is true. If you find discrepancies on the report, begin to clean up the inaccurate data by contacting the creditor reporting the false information and asking for it to be removed as soon as possible.

If your credit report is a mess, it is better for you to wait to buy something until you clean up everything on it. You will be able to secure a much better interest rate if you take the initiative to clean up your debts and your credit report before buying.

FINANCING YOUR PURCHASE THROUGH A LENDER

As with any home purchase, you can finance your condo, apartment, or townhouse the same way you would any other home purchase. There is a myth that it is harder to obtain financing from a lender if the borrower is purchasing a home in a multi-family environment. This perception has changed considerably with the advent of planned unit developments.

The myth that banks frown on shared housing loans has been debunked. With so many large multi-unit buildings, lenders are eager to invest, making it easier for the shared housing home buyer to obtain financing. Your lender will want to know about the homeowners association.

- Is their investment is secure.

- The assessments and condition of the property.

The lender depends on the homeowners association to look after their interests as much as you do. It is crucial that the homeowners association meets the lender's approval.

The lender will want to see proof of liability and fire insurance at closing as well as the association's policies on the complex. Some lenders will want to know whether firewalls were used in construction.

A Little Tip

It is great to be loyal. I love loyalty. However, if you cannot secure a good deal at your bank, go somewhere else. If you have been sending a bank your business for years, but they are unable to offer you a decent loan package, there are other banks and lenders out there.

New developments often have a unique feature to lure home buyers, such as the lender's financing individual home spaces sold to help the builder move the units quickly, an advantage if you borrow from the bank already familiar with the development. Also, the developer may buy down the interest rate to allow buyers with good credit an extra incentive to borrow money from the builder's lender of choice.

A bank or mortgage company should treat your application as they would any of your others, and if they do not, ask why.

Maybe they know something about the particular development you do not know or you cannot see. Always ask why you have been turned down.

CREATIVELY FINANCING YOUR NEW HOME

When it comes to creatively financing your purchase, I could take to my soapbox in a New York minute. I love lease options on these homes. In Chapter 10, we will discuss leases but for now, let us look at the more common ways to find creative financing for your new home purchase.

A Little Tip
You may make the best deal with the sellers of the property. They may offer you a lease option or a subject-to deal you cannot refuse. However, in these deals, make sure you always have an attorney look over the agreement before you move the first piece of furniture!

Talk to the developer or the seller. There are several reasons for going through the seller or developer for financing. The first is not being able to obtain financing you want through a traditional lender. The second is that you may be an investor most interested in obtaining as many non-traditional loans as possible for properties you buy. If you are able to obtain financing from the seller, you should be able to save money on your closing costs. The seller will carry the note through a purchase money mortgage, and the parties involved will decide the terms of the note. The seller or developer may not wish to carry the note for more than ten years. Five years is common. Discuss your seller's goals and your goals and see what you can do to find one of the best notes you can have—a purchase money mortgage.

Rent-to-own. Some developers and sellers will look at renting a unit to you until you are able to buy with a certain part of the rent going toward the purchase, if not all of it. Ideally, rent-to-own home buyers will rent until the unit is paid for, and the seller will simply sign over the title of the property. It is uncommon to see rent-to-owns on new developments but if a builder is having trouble moving the units, he or she might consider rent-to-own contracts.

Private lender through equity sharing. Outside lending is available from investors who will want only an arrangement so that you pay them interest, or they may require equity sharing. If you are going to be sharing equity in the property with an investor, make sure the interest rate is low. Equity sharing can be a win-win situation if the interest rate is far below the prime rate and if expenses for improvements are shared. If a private lender is only interested in providing money for your purchase, do not mention equity sharing. Home values will be on the rise at some point. Why share with someone if you do not have to?

Other creative measures to consider in financing your home purchase can be a combination of traditional lending and seller financing through second mortgages, assumable mortgages, wraparound mortgages, overlapping mortgages, and options.

Sometimes you have to work harder to secure the home loan you can afford by using different options for getting a loan.

SELLER OR DEVELOPER FINANCING

If you find a unit you like in a newer development and notice the units are not moving, understand you may be in a unique position. A developer needs to put someone into his new complex as quickly as possible and may be flexible with the first buyer. He may offer some assistance either through his own lender of choice or by handling the financing.

Should you decide to talk to the developer or the seller about seller assisted financing, you want the seller to feel as if the financing benefits him most while providing you with the best financing options. Begin by checking out the interest rates lenders are offering in your area. See who is offering the best rates and look for the best terms. Try to get the seller to finance to you at the going prime rate or less.

Consider your terms carefully. First, you want to have the loan amortized over a period of 30 years if possible with a balloon payment in five years. Here is an example. You find a new condo at the asking price of $165,000. You talk the seller into financing the property for $160,000, explaining to him he will make up the difference in the sales price in the interest money he earns. You ask the seller to amortize the payment for you over a period of 30 years at 7.25 percent to place your payment at $1,091.48. At the end of five years you balloon the payment and finance with a bank, and the seller walks away happy with the interest money he earned and the balance you owe at the end of the five years. Everyone is happy.

YOUR PAYMENTS COULD BREAK YOU

As you calculate the amount you can afford when purchasing a condo or townhouse, you have to add in your monthly homeowners association dues. One thing you can be certain of is that if you live in a condo complex and are not paying your dues, everyone will know it. Those dues are needed to pay for things that benefit every homeowner, and if one person falls behind on the dues, everyone will feel it in those complexes where the money is needed.

As you calculate the amount you feel comfortable paying, settle on one amount you will be able to pay each month. Let us say you come up with $800 a month. As you begin to look around at condos, you see most of the dues at the complexes you are considering run around $150 per month. That is $1,800 per year. You now know you cannot purchase anything in any of these complexes that will place your monthly payment at more than $650 per month. Your limit is $800 per month. Assessments can exceed the $10,000 mark so that you may want to buy less than you can afford to save money for assessments. If homeowners are expected to come up with the money pronto, they begin to sell in these communities.

INCREASES IN ASSOCIATION DUES

There is something every homeowner in shared housing environments dreads. They are called the special assessments. Depending on how well the board has managed the funds in the past and how much reserves or savings the homeowner's association has, special assessments may be few and far between. However, if the reserves are low and everything goes at one time, there can be one expensive assessment requested of homeowners at one time.

Special assessments may be needed to replace sidewalks and roofs. Siding can be expensive and all of it is usually replaced at the same time. Swimming pools need new liners, and gym equipment wears out. High one-time expenses can be avoided if the board has budgeted well.

A Little Tip

You want to avoid the experience of a friend of mine whose association recently told her that to pay for roof repairs to the entire complex she and all owners in her development would have to hand over $650 in addition to her $120 monthly condo association fees and her mortgage.

Occasionally, if an anticipated assessment is in the works, the board may opt to raise dues temporarily. They should explain they are trying to avoid an assessment, and homeowners appreciate the warning.

When the homeowner's association raises dues, analyze the reason for the increase. What is the benefit of increased dues? If you have questions about the raise in the dues, you should immediately bring them to the attention of the board without challenging their authority. Membership dues need to be increased occasionally, but as a homeowner you should be able to judge whether they are necessary. Natural occurrences may necessitate special assessments so that being prepared is crucial.

If you have attended meetings occasionally, you have power in some of these decisions. You do not want to be a member of the community who only comes out to address your concern over membership dues, but rather an active participant throughout the year.

WHEN NO ONE WANTS THE ASSESSMENT

Some assessments can be avoided if the community works together. You can encourage community action if an assessment seems to be looming. For example, if you live in an area struck by a natural disaster, it would be much better to arrange for the clean up yourself rather than encourage all homeowners to pitch in and pay for the clean up. Elbow grease and a little muscle can save money.

10

INVESTING IN SHARED HOUSING & THINGS YOU SHOULD KNOW

————

When you move into a shared housing development, you quickly get the meaning of "shared" not as it refers to multi-family housing necessarily but as it applies to the concept of sharing common areas such as the swimming pool, tennis courts, and clubhouse. If you or someone in the complex does not take care of the complex and the amenities, everyone is affected.

The "shared" aspect is often forgotten and sadly, it may anger homeowners. Common consideration for the common areas can make the lifestyle you find in shared housing a pleasure, but if neighbors refuse to be neighborly by being careless with the common areas, it can provide for undesirable living conditions.

With your neighbors in mind, as well as the current unit you are considering, go over the following list. Answer the questions to assess the complex and be certain you are making the right decision. If you are thinking about buying a shared housing unit as an investment, use the following items to help you when you sell your unit.

- Are you moving into a community known for its high profile members? Do you need to be interviewed before the board will agree you can become a member of the homeowners association? If so, beware. If you buy into such a community, you may not be able to rent to anyone you choose. While this type of interview process is not called discrimination, it should be. It is best to avoid such a place.

- How exactly does the association function? Will one owner have more voting shares if they own more units? It is likely. If an investor does own many of the homes in a housing development, is it a problem or does the investor strive to improve the community?

- Be sure you are comfortable with the location. Most large shared housing complexes are close to shopping, schools. When buying any home for your family or for an investment, you should be sure you are in a location that others would find accommodating, too. Otherwise, it will be hard to sell in the future.

- Is the unit you are considering priced comparably to other units for sale in the complex? If not, why? Does the unit you want to buy have better upgrades or more square footage? If it is priced higher than other units listed for sale in the complex, find out why and make sure the price difference is warranted.

- Look at the maintenance fee at any condo, townhouse, or apartment complex you may consider buying. How much is it? Compare it to the fees of other homeowners associations. See if the dues are worth what you pay. See what the dues cover. How hard at work will your money be? Make sure the homeowners are getting what they pay for before you buy.

- Look at the lifestyles of the people in the complex. If you are ready for retirement and you notice your potential neighbors are college students ready for the next party, think it over. Consider whether you will fit in the neighborhood. It may be hard to think of not fitting in somewhere but if your lifestyle is different from those around you, you have a problem. For example, if you work day shift and your neighbors around you are rolling out of bed around the time you come home from work, it is one thing, but if those same neighbors are gearing up for an all-night party, it can become a real hassle for you.

- Look at the things that could become important. Do you have a place for outside storage? Do you have an area where you can put a grill? Do you have adequate parking for yourself and at least one other car?

Be smart and do your homework before you buy. Are there several units in the same complex for sale at the same time? If so, ask the owners who have them for sale why they are trying to sell? Is an assessment coming up soon? If so, is it so pricey that homeowners are trying to get out of paying it? Are there underlying problems you cannot see? Know why people are moving from the area. It could be that an area plant is closing or it could be a number of burglaries.

A NEW WAY OF LIVING

People are in for a culture shock when they first move into shared-housing if they have never lived in that environment. First, they feel that everyone can hear them walking, and sometimes they can. Second, they seem to hear people coming and going at all hours of the day and night, and they are. Third, they feel as if someone is telling them how to live and what they can or cannot have, and they are.

If it is difficult for you to get used to, try to overlook the little things because shared housing can be a great way to live. It is a lifestyle to be savored if you are an active person on the go.

You will need answers to some of the following questions before you move. These questions address lifestyle choices that are important to some people.

- **Can you have pets?** If so, is there a weight limit on the size of your pet? If so, what is it? Are there designated dog runs or doggie rules when you take your dog for a walk? What are they?

- **Is parking a big deal?** It will be if you work on cars as a pastime hobby. Most people do not want the neighbor to have a clunker parked outside so be sure you understand the restrictions on cars and working on cars in the neighborhood.

- **Do you have a RV or a boat?** If so, where will you park it? Most complexes have an area for the tenants to store their boat or their camper. Find out what the rules are. It never hurts to sneak a peek at the bylaws before you buy in any community.

- **Does your teenager's band practice at your house?** If so, you need to know that shared housing is probably not going to welcome loud music. Check out rules about noise before you buy. A strict noise ordinance may be in effect.

There may be a way for you to accommodate the band with sound barriers in today's condos with basements and garages. However, you still want to check the bylaws to ensure everyone is happy with your living choices.

There are several other lifestyle items you may think of as you go along. If you want to know something, ask!

A BETTER WAY OF INVESTING

Seven out of ten millionaires made their money in real estate investments. If you are looking for a safe investment that yields high returns, obviously real estate is an area of investment that steadily rises, particularly in areas where employment is steady. Owning an empty single-family home that may be vacant for a few months periodically is a poor investment compared to a shared housing building where one vacant unit does not mean 100 percent loss of income; money is still coming in. Should you hesitate at the thought of devoting time to being a landlord, what do you do? Invest in condos.

And, of course, you do not have to be a landlord simply because you have invested in rental properties. Most of the time, condos operate on automatic pilot so that you will put in about 20 hours a year for each unit. That is because you will be in partnership with the homeowners association which takes care of all exterior maintenance and some interior work as well.

You will find that well-run condos, that is, those with strong homeowners associations, will not attract trouble-making tenants who tend to avoid living condition where rules are enforced, and they will not be able to get away with their antics. With a weak association, vacancies increase and property values stagnate.

However, an unruly situation can be corrected by enforcing daily accelerating fines to make an investment worthwhile. Turnaround projects can yield thousands in quick returns.

CASE STUDY: EUGENIA FOXWORTH

Every building is different. I have had every experience working with homeowners associations that you can possibly think of and then some! A strong homeowner's association generally has the best maintained buildings and the most prestigious privately owned gated communities.

However, one of the weakest homeowner's associations that I encountered was in Manhattan where the previous board president was on a fixed income and lacked the perspective needed for the job. Five years later, he was voted out but it was too late. It was at this time that the homeowner's found out that he was not reporting the building's problems as they occurred. The building's maintenance costs doubled per shareholder because of the negligence.

Eugenia Foxworth
Coldwell Banker Hunt Kennedy
NYS Licensed Realtor,
Certified International
Property Specialist
Eugenia.foxworth@cbhk.com

As with any other real estate investment, location is just about everything. You will want a convenient location of the complex avoiding areas that are shared housing "cities"—those with no other type of housing in the entire area—because of population density problems. Ideally, your investment should have contrasting, but pleasant, surroundings such as single-family homes, an urban setting, or recreational area such as a lake or park. Look for units near good schools with easy access to freeways or mass transit so that your tenants can find employment nearby.

Location of the unit itself can be important as well. While the complex may offer mountain or beach views, the unit itself may be devalued because it offers only a fine view of a parking lot or highway. And, on the subject of parking lots, is the parking layout convenient? If there is a parking garage, how much time does it take to exit?

Are the common areas accessible by foot? If not, is there adequate parking at the meeting site or at the pool?

When you buy a condominium, you hire a home inspector to find conditions that directly affect the function and safety of your immediate living area. Make sure you have acquired an official inspection clearance to check the soundness of construction. It may be the most important protection you can take for the security of your investment. An inspector can tell you what is around, above, beneath and behind the complex you are about to put your money toward so that you can avoid sinking money into it at later time — unexpectedly. Just imagine the expense if you were responsible for removing asbestos from your walls and ceiling.

For nationwide information on properties, check out **dataquick.com** on the Internet. The site offers vital information on 87 million properties in the United States with phone numbers. If you have honed in on a particular area, use the Internet to check with Chambers of Commerce, police (crime information), and schools of merit. Start by locating the market with the greatest yield and the properties within that market that have the greatest potential. You can acquire these properties with little or no personal capital and negotiate the purchase. If you lack the courage to follow through on this plan, find a fellow investor or mentor who will team with you, such as a physician, a Certified Public Accountant, or a proven real estate investor.

When it comes to investing, owning a condo, apartment, or a townhouse can be one of the best ways to invest for three reasons. First, if you are planning to purchase several units in a given area, you can confine your investment units to one complex. Second, if you are not handy with roofing and siding, shared housing is perfect because your upkeep will be minimal, and finally, you can always count on your neighbors to call you screaming "Evict!" if the tenants are getting raucous. You will also discover it is easier to evict tenants from shared housing because most of the time you will have witnesses that the tenants are not caring for the property as they should.

While investors have to look at their profit potential, there are several reasons they would want to start investing in complexes. If an investor plans to have a multitude of units, it makes sense to invest in condos because they will be able to keep their own work load down when they need to collect rents and conduct maintenance. They can also accumulate another voting share in the homeowners association each time they purchase another unit. Doing so can improve the look of the complex, heightening their own home values.

Another reason investors consider multi-family housing with recreational facilities and common areas is that these units are easy to rent out. Tenants like clubhouse rentals, swimming pools, and tennis courts. This is an attractive leasing point the investor can "play up" and ultimately it can help keep the units rented for a steady income flow. Single-family houses cannot compete with condos, for instance, for cash flow and for avoiding cash-flow "shock" from major (exterior) repairs such as roofs.

CASE STUDY: EUGENIA FOXWORTH

The financial strength of a building can be an asset or a liability when selling a property. The amount of money that is in the building's escrow fund, the amount of the outstanding mortgage, tax write offs, maintenance/costs of condos can be a strong selling point for a complex.

Eugenia Foxworth
Coldwell Banker Hunt Kennedy
NYS Licensed Realtor,
Certified International
Property Specialist
Eugenia.foxworth@cbhk.com

FINDING THE RIGHT PROPERTY

Setting out on your search for the perfect property to buy is never easy. First, you have to decide what your plans are for the property and how much you are willing to pay for it. When buying a unit to rent out, consider the amenities that will draw tenants to you. They will rent from you if they feel you offer them something they cannot find in a single dwelling home. Tenants will want three things when they come to the investor who owns a multi-family unit: a good floor plan, great amenities, a pool, a playground, and a convenient location.

If you are buying a shared housing unit as a rental income investment property, the investment unit needs to be able to pay for itself so you must consider your payment (if any) and the maintenance fee. Ideally, the unit should pay for itself and pad your pocket. For example, if your payment is $300 and the maintenance fee is $200, ideally you would like to charge your tenants at least $600 so you can realize some cash in hand for the unit. The basic idea is that you will never pay your own mortgage on a rental unit; your tenants will, and they will be paying the maintenance fee as well.

A word of caution. You bought the unit in the complex and your name is the one that homeowners recognize. Therefore, you should pay the maintenance fee. Set a rental rate that includes the maintenance fee. It is not the responsibility of the tenant to pay the fee to the homeowner's association and most of the time, if you do not include it in the rental rate, you will pay it. When you set your rental fee in the lease, make sure you explain the rent includes the maintenance fee but as the true homeowner, you will pay it to the board.

11

IF YOU CAN LEASE FIRST—LEASE!

———

One of the best creative financing measures is to take out a lease option as discussed in Chapter Eight. However, there are other reasons to consider a lease option besides financial convenience. You can lease option or rent-to-own as a trial run! Granted, not every seller will give you the option of leasing or renting to own, but if you can try out the complex before you invest in it—why not do it?

SHARED HOUSING AND THE TRIAL RUN

My husband and I used a lease option for a condo, but we decided not to buy. The lease option saved us money because if we had bought the condo without a trial run, we would have sold it immediately. That is when I learned the best way to buy anything in the condo market was to try it out first.

There are many reasons to use the lease option for financing your shared housing unit. It can be a way for you to finance your home by using the lease time to save money for a down payment to buy points and get a better interest rate. However, the best reason to choose this option is to give yourself time to try before you buy.

You will not know everything there is to know about a community or a complex until you have the opportunity to live there. The "try before you buy" enables you to live there and experience the community.

If you cannot get an owner to lease to you on a lease option, ask for a lease- or rent-to-own aspect. See if the owner will lease to you first before you commit to buying.

WHY THIS IS A BETTER WAY TO GO

If you plan to rent out the space, watch for a clause in the contract prohibiting you from renting the home to someone else while you are in the process of buying.

The object of a lease option or a rent-to-own (outside of the financing factor) is to try out your new home. If you are able to experience life as a resident, you will begin to notice if activities like pool side parties are an every day affair. You will also notice noisy neighbors, yapping pups, and endless traffic. You can see how a lease gives you a way out if you find you do not like where you are living.

Lease options can be costly if you do not exercise your right to buy so I am not suggesting that you go out and take out a lease option contract or try out a rent-to-own if you are not serious about buying because you will spend money on moving and deposits. However, in shared housing, the lease is a perfect way to observe the complex where you intend to live. Consider it an insurance policy.

DID YOU KNOW?

Lease options and lease purchases are confusing. Many buyers think they are the same, but they are different. A lease option is a

lease with an option to buy at some point, if desired. A lease purchase is a lease-to-buy with lease payments going toward the purchase. It is also called a lease-to-own or rent-to-own contract.

If you will be living in the unit yourself, there are concessions you will not be willing to make, but if you are buying for investment purposes, there may be a few things you can simply overlook.

THINGS TO LOOK FOR IN A LEASE

Since I have been involved in lease options before, I know first hand how great—and how awful—they can be. First, a seller who does not want to lease the unit will probably ask for a high non-refundable deposit. In a "trial run" on a condo or any other shared housing unit, do not pay a huge deposit. If I am serious about buying, I will offer $1,000 to the seller as a deposit.

Do not expect a seller to like a $1,000 binder. Expect a counteroffer when you go in at a $1,000. A good rule of thumb to use when you lock yourself into a lease option is never to offer more than half of the amount of your anticipated closing costs as a deposit. More investors are trying to lease option their homes and units on a 10 percent down or nothing concept. I would run the other way. Here are several tips for when you are buying on a lease option contract:

- You never want to put down a large deposit you may end up walking away from.

- Make sure much of your monthly lease payment is applied toward the purchase of the unit. Do not rent it without a set amount going toward the purchase.

- The contract should contain a written agreement about dues. Who pays them during the lease period?

- If you are going to lease option, try to lease the unit for at least one year so you are able to go through all four seasons at your new home.

When working out the terms of a lease option, you need to keep your goals and the goals of the seller in focus. For example, if the seller tells you he is happy to work with you on a lease option but needs to keep the terms to around nine months, work with him if he is working with you! Try to make it a pleasant experience for everyone involved.

THINGS TO LOOK FOR IN A RENT-TO-OWN

Rent-to-own is one way to finance what you buy creatively. It is easy to understand. You and the seller agree upon set terms in the rent-to-own contract, and you rent the unit by the month. After all payments have been made, the seller signs the title over to you, and you are an owner with a paid-in-full investment.

You want to have an airtight contract with the seller because there are a number of things that can go wrong with rent-to-owns. The main problem with the rent-to-own contract is that people can rent for a few years thinking they are making a good investment only to find out at the end of the rent-to-own term, the property is covered in liens—a worst case scenario.

Renting-to-own in shared housing is most attractive but carries the most risk. If a builder or developer is willing to contract for a rent-to-own on his new project, he is in serious trouble: the units are not selling. If the project is not a success, you need to know what will happen to the money you pay in a rent-to-own scenario. Could the bank eventually foreclose and take the development? If so, you will probably be left out in the cold. Understand the terms of the rent-to-own contract and make it air tight to secure your investment.

Before you lock yourself into a rent-to-own, ask whether the seller will consider a lease option on the property, but if a rent-to-own seems to be the only way to go, talk to a real estate attorney to protect your interest. One problem with rent-to-owns is that the seller who rents the property to a potential buyer will control the contracts and the entire transaction, making it impossible for the buyer to have redress in the event of a problem.

THE LEASE OPTION CONTRACT YOU WANT

The lease option contract I want as a buyer, I would never want as a seller. Double-edged sword? Yes, indeed. When it comes to lease options as a buyer, I make sure I can always walk away. When I was in real estate, I wanted to be sure my buyers could always walk away, too, even if it meant I lost the commission. They usually bought from me again so that I suffered no loss. The following will help you decide the best way to compose your offer to purchase contract when you want to buy on a lease option.

- You want to put as little down as possible to make the sellers feel comfortable with the down payment because they will keep your deposit, should you default.

- You want more than half of the monthly payment going toward the purchase, and so ask for all the payment to be applied toward the purchase in hopes at least half will be.

- If it is an investment property, you should try to secure a lease option with a term of at least three years.

- You stipulate in the lease option what is to remain with the unit from the beginning. Write the contract as if you were buying because your intent is to buy. Even though it is usually understood that all appliances remain with the unit, put it in writing. If it is not in writing, it will not hold up under scrutiny.

Always make your real estate agent, if you use one, and the seller think you are offering your best deal. I was in the business and if you think real estate agents do not talk to sellers about buyers, you are mistaken. Approach all your contracts with your final deal in mind. If a seller wants to negotiate, the ball is back in your court and you can make your final offer, reluctantly, of course.

THE SMART LEASE

Some people use lease options only long enough to organize their finances. However, the best ways to use them will save you money over the long term. Look at the following example and you will understand why a lease option can offer you more when financing your purchase.

You offer to purchase a condo for $150,000 and you ask the seller to finance for you for five years. You explain that you will need to have the loan amortized over 30 years but want the note to balloon at the end of the five years. See chart in Appendix D for reference.

If you notice in the chart mentioned above at the end of each year, the totals indicate how much interest you paid during the year. At the end of five years, on $150,000 you will have paid $49,187.39. This amount is interest alone — thrown away. In the example above you are paying out $972.90 per month, meaning well over 80 percent of the money you are paying out is interest.

This is where a lease option used wisely can prove valuable to finance your real estate purchase creatively. Take the above purchase price of $150,000 and offer your seller a lease option. You tell the seller you want to offer him a $5,000 non-refundable retainer for the condo. You want to lease option the unit instead of seller finance and have every intention of buying the condo.

You tell the seller you want to lease option the condo for a period of three years (more if you can get him to go along with the idea) and at the end of the three years, you will either pay it off or you will finance it through a traditional lender. Here is what you offer:

- You offer the seller $150,000 for the unit.

- You offer him a $5,000 deposit and stipulate it is non-refundable should you choose not to go through with the purchase.

- You owe $145,000.

- Tell the owner you will pay $950 per month and you would like one half (more if you can get him to agree) to go toward the purchase price of the condo.

LOOK AT WHAT HAPPENS

In the first example above where the seller is financing the unit, you will still owe $140,813.56 at the end of five years. At the end of three years, in a lease option agreement you will owe $127,900. Now, if you are able to get the seller to go along with the five-year term, you will be in much better shape. If you ask the seller to carry you on a lease option for five years with 50 percent of the lease going toward the purchase, at the end of the five years, you will owe only a total of $121,500 on your condo. Best of all, you have not thrown away that much on interest money.

You may be able to convince a seller who needs to move the unit to apply even more of the monthly payment toward the purchase. The more you can apply toward the purchase, the better off you will be. In the last example, when leasing a condo for three years with half the money applied toward the purchase, you would go to closing with your initial $5,000 investment plus the additional 50 percent you are allowed out of your monthly payment each month. Doing so means you would take to closing a total of $22,100 or 15 percent of the purchase price. That down payment would help you secure a much better interest rate for the loan.

CASE STUDY: ANONYMOUS INVESTOR, TN

As an investor, I never buy any other way than subject-to or by using lease options. I am one of those "We buy houses" people whom Susan warns about in this book, but I buy on subject-to and lease options, and buyers and sellers find their way to me to use the same way to buy their properties. It works and it is one of the reasons I own so many properties. You have to do what works for you. I think everyone has in mind the best way to buy, but there is not one good way to buy or sell. I gauge it all by the money: how much money is going to be in my bank account at the end of the day? In lease options and subject-to deals, I can tell you one thing—you will have substantial savings.

Another reason to lease is to discover what you like and do not like about the property before you buy or invest. There is nothing like being on-site to become aware of noises from plumbing, neighbors, or planes. You will have a grand opportunity for the "wind" in windows to find you, as well as neighborhood smells: outdoor cooking, a nearby paper plant, or sewage treatment plant. After a couple of showers, you will know the recovery time for the water heater and the water pressure changes in the morning and evening. You will know whether the unit's heat and air are even throughout and the convenience of using the kitchen or home office. Before long, you will know whether the toilets, fireplaces, doors, and gates are operating efficiently and whether you are alone or sharing your space with pests, insect and otherwise.

You may have second thoughts about investing in a particular complex if dogs and children are allowed, particularly if there is a weak homeowners association.

VACATION GETAWAYS

W ho does not love to travel? Who does not love to get away? Just knowing you have a place to go when you need a break gives you satisfaction. When looking around at the possibility of home ownership in a vacation area, consider the things you want in a lifetime of vacations. When I go to Mississippi, I know I am going to shop and gamble. A home in Mississippi would be a big waste of money for me, but a condo is a different story.

Consider what you want from a vacation home when you begin to look for one. What do you like to do? Do you like to surf? Do you own a boat? If so, you may prefer a simple little townhouse on a lake near your home as opposed to a condo on Atlantic Beach. As a rental investment, if you are close to your vacation getaway you can oversee the day-to-day business of renting the unit.

I cannot imagine owning a vacation getaway home that would require me to do maintenance. That is not a vacation. For me, that is a nightmare. My stepdad used to have a gorgeous home in Titusville, Florida, and when I was there with him and my mother he was always working. He did the gardening, worked around the pool, and cleaned up everything. It did not look like a vacation to me, but he may have enjoyed his getaway from one yard to another.

Many people prefer to visit new places rather than being confined to one vacation destination. Others, even if they can afford a vacation home, will not take the plunge because it is too much work. If you are one of those people, maybe you will feel different by the end of this chapter. Investing in a vacation getaway can be profitable if done carefully. A home on the golf course in Hilton Head's Palmetto Dunes may be for you, but if you want low maintenance, you may prefer to look at the condos at Villamare or Windsor Place in South Carolina.

Seaside homes are expensive and the work that goes with them is costly too. For a fraction of the price, people can afford a seaside condo or a townhouse overlooking a run on the slopes. Maintenance is easy because someone else does it.

When you buy in a complex or a townhouse community, there are residents who live there year round. While they do not want the responsibility of looking out for your investment, they will probably let you know if something goes wrong with one of your vacation tenants. If you buy a vacation rental in an area where there are many vacation units on the market, chances are you will place your home with a rental management company so that they handle another headache for you. Vacation home ownership is easy.

Should you think that only the wealthy can afford a vacation getaway, let me direct you to the **VRBO.com** Web site, one of the largest assortments of vacation rentals online today. Many of the vacation homeowners live near the rentals and bought them at a bargain, upgraded them into a vacation retreat, and began to rent to interested parties. Others bought their vacation dream home and realized it would be easier to afford if they shared their home with vacationers in the area and collected rental income in the process.

Thanks to creative financing and other options, vacation homeowners have found buying their getaway home is affordable and profitable when they rent it to other vacationing families. Choosing their tenants wisely solves the issue of maintaining a high quality vacation rental.

At the beginning of this chapter, I told you about my stepdad who owned a beautiful home in Titusville, Florida. Well, he sold it. Now, when he vacations in Florida, he goes to his condo in Titusville down the street from the house he owned. Guess what? He does not work on vacation anymore. There is not that much to do when the homeowners association does everything for you.

When it comes to vacation home rentals, purchasing a condo or townhouse makes sense because you will not be a local owner. Even if you are, have someone else take care of the maintenance for you.

In vacation getaways, emphasis on the "getaway," try to find a condo or townhouse with an active homeowner's association. The biggest cost you have to consider in affluent vacation areas is the assessments. However, if you are in the right location, you should not have any problem affording them if you are renting your vacation getaway to other people on a weekly basis.

There are great vacation getaway areas with high rental traffic. Coastal areas are the busiest, and the number of the high rises on the ocean is testament to the fact that tourists still like beach front properties. Some of the rentals on the ocean easily bring in $50,000 every year after association dues have been paid. As you can see, a condo, townhouse, or apartment in the right place can be a good investment depending on what you pay for your cash-generating rental.

THE VACATION EFFICIENCY

In Chapter One, we talked about apartments that have been converted into condos or flats. There is another conversion taking the real estate world by storm and the hotel rooms that have been converted into efficiencies and sold as oceanfront or ocean-oriented sun suites. These remodeled hotel rooms are being snatched up fast and sold as small units. With just under 500 square feet, some earn more than $100,000 in a seaside town.

The efficiencies or sun suites are small, limiting the number of people who will want to rent your unit. However, if you are looking for a lifetime of vacations, they can be ideal because you can remodel your space into a nice suite, and the rental potential is great in beach areas and other touristy areas.

Something else for you to consider when you are looking at the sun suites or the upgraded hotel rooms refurbished as efficiencies is the fact that just as if you bought a condo, there will be a homeowners association in place to help improve the property. You will also have the opportunity to gut the interior and do what you will to make it a great living area for your family. These efficiencies can be pet friendly and decorated to bring in families who will want to stay with you every year.

WE ARE NOT TALKING TIMESHARES

I am not a big fan of timeshares. I feel that most timeshares are a bad investment. There are some exceptions and most of those exceptions fall on the resale market.

One of the best ways you can own vacation rental property is through an investment club and we are not talking timeshare weeks in the mountains. See the following example:

CASE STUDY: ANONYMOUS INVESTOR, SC

An investment club buys properties in three vacation areas: an oceanfront home in Hilton Head, South Carolina, an apartment in New York City, and a Colorado chalet. Since there are 13 owners, each owner gets four weeks every year at each of the three properties. They can trade between themselves, they can rent their  weeks, or they can simply forfeit their weeks. Overall, they have 12 vacation weeks a year so for the most part, they probably will not be able to use the weeks they own. However, this savvy group of investors employs a rental company in each area to handle the rentals for them and when the investor forfeits his or her week. The agent rents it for them and sends them the cash for their week. It works out nicely because even though there are 13 owner-investors, they know each other. They know they can get along well enough to manage their maintenance fees and if needed, they can trade vacation weeks to accommodate everyone in the investment group. Best of all, they have bought a lifetime of vacations in a growing investment. If owners want out, there is always someone to replace them so the timeshare works. It is the new way to invest, because it is not a timeshare but shared ownership among investment partners.

Selling points to use for your vacations is another type of timeshare growing in popularity in the vacation rental market. It allows you to have a lifetime of vacations in a wide variety of areas. You can use your vacation club points for houseboat rentals, campgrounds, lakefront, oceanfront, and even mountain vacations. Even the traditional timeshare allows you to trade your weeks with other timeshare owners.

THE GETAWAY YOU DESERVE

When you begin to look at buying a condo, townhouse, or an apartment as a vacation getaway, there are some things you will need to consider. If you plan to rent the unit out to ensure it pays for itself, there are things to consider.

Before you buy a vacation getaway, look at the Appendix for a list of areas with great vacation getaway potential. It lists areas where you can make a good profit either by hanging onto the investment or by renting it out.

When searching for a vacation getaway, the homeowners association is important because you will be depending on it to keep your vacation home presentable on the outside. A strong association is a great advantage to the off-site owner.

The association will consider your views and you will vote on issues that affect your home away from home, but you will have to accept the fact that the hands-on owners are the people who decide the fate of the complex, meaning you need to buy where there are strong leaders on the board.

BUY A GETAWAY BUT NOT PRIME PROPERTY

Most people who consider a vacation getaway begin their search in the most desirable location of the area. For instance, you decide to buy a beach condo, where do you look? Probably your favorite beach destination. However, the affordability of the oceanfront itself in any area puts homes out of reach for the average family. If you are earning $60,000 a year, you cannot afford a condo in Malibu, but you can afford a condo two blocks off the Atlantic in Myrtle Beach, South Carolina.

If you decide to buy in a complex where pets are allowed, you can offer the traveler with pet in tow something unique by providing a pet-friendly place for vacationers with pets. Pet owners will jump at a home that allows pets, even if they may have to pay a little more.

My family and I went to Tybee Island, Georgia, on a whim at the last minute on a July weekend. What we ended up with was darling. It had two bedrooms, one bathroom, and a great room with a super kitchen/den combination. It allowed pets and had an outside fenced area. The location of the property was two streets from the ocean so you could not see the beach unless of course, you stood in the road on your tiptoes. Still, it was great.

While we were in Tybee, we picked up a Homes Magazine and checked on the prices of oceanfront properties and the ocean-oriented properties. On Tybee, you are hard pressed to find anything under $200,000 off the beach and anything under $500,000 on the beach. However, we noticed something about the homes listed for sale: most of them were low maintenance homes. If they were single home dwellings, the use of gravel drives and concrete patios prevented the owners from the worry of having a home to care for miles away from their primary resident. Condos were even lower maintenance.

MORE ABOUT VACATION OWNERSHIP

When buying a vacation rental unit in a development or a complex full of townhouses, condos, or even patio homes, think low maintenance. Even though you will not be doing the maintenance yourself, you want to save money on dues and minimize special assessments that can be high in vacation communities. In properties near the ocean, one of the things people do not think about is the salt-water damage to the wooden parts of buildings on the ocean.

When purchasing a vacation rental, find out when the last assessment was and how much it was. Ask if the association has any reserves and if so, how much, and what portion of the fees go into reserves every month so that you can determine whether the community takes care of its finances.

You will want to talk to as many of the homeowners as possible. How many of the homeowners are hands-on and how many are renting out their vacation units. Find out the location of the directors. If you are buying in a community where every director lives out of town, you cannot assume things are handled properly on-site all the time.

The best vacation rental unit you can hope to have is where several hands-on owners are living in the complex, keeping an eye on their investment. Talk to some of these owners for a realistic look at how things are run at the complex. Ask some of these questions.

- Who takes care of property maintenance? Who takes care of building repairs and updates? Who takes care of the grounds?

- Is there someone on-site managing the units in the rental program? If so, who is it?

- Which rental agency do most of the homeowners use to manage their vacation rental property? If there are several, get the names and numbers of a few of them.

- Do any of the homeowners recommend anyone in particular for housekeeping after each vacationing family leaves the unit?

- How do the hands-on homeowners handle disturbances? Is there a procedure?

- Do they know many booked units there are during the vacation season?

You will be able to find out most of this information from a property manager or a real estate agent handling rentals in the community, but information from other homeowners will be more accurate.

Vacation homeowners may take their rental properties into their own hands. They set up rentals and maintain the property. They derive more income for themselves. You can see examples on the Internet. Places such as **VRBO.com** and **VacationRentals.com** provide a service for their clients helping them avoid paying out large rental agency fees — for a price.

A rental agency can help you in many ways: answering tenants' questions and solving problems with the property — and you collect the income with few problems — a luxury many rental homeowners cannot afford. If you are looking at rental home ownership for profit, you will want to pocket as much of the income as possible.

A hands-on property manager is essential if you are going to rent the units you own in a vacation resort area. You will pay them a flat fee or a per-job fee.

THE REAL REASON PEOPLE BUY VACATION RENTALS

Vacation homeowners find pleasure in owning a rental property in the right area. They provide a great income and a place to call your own when you are on vacation. Sure, there will be work in any rental you own but owning a vacation home rental can be rewarding. Marilyn Erickson of Sedona, Arizona had this to say:

CASE STUDY: MARILYN AND KEN ERICKSON

Vacation rentals have been a good source of income for us. We bought properties when they were priced low, and we do all the renting ourselves. We have an 800 number and a good Web site and that is all there is to it. Each of our three properties needs access to a reliable service person. We need to have a good cleaning crew at each property. We need to be available by phone to these properties so that if there is a problem, we can be reached. The cleaning crew is the key.

It has been pleasant. The properties have all gone up in value. The income is substantial and we have three beautiful vacation properties to visit each year. There will always be things to do, but that is part of the fun. We link our site with other vacation rental sites and we pay so much per year to be on the major vacation rental sites.

It is important to respond quickly to the inquiries. We use many form letters that respond to different situations on various properties. We make the form letters as personal and complete as possible. Nice, chatty form letters are crucial in the vacation rental business. They save time and can be personalized for each response.

Keep the properties in good repair at all times. Vacation rentals, if purchased at a good price, can be profitable and pay well. We have had tremendous success.

Marilyn and Ken Erickson
www.fabulousvacation.com

If you are going to buy homes or rental units as vacation rentals, having people available to take care of the unit or home when you are not around is crucial. They will be the people who make your vacation rental business a success.

13

BUYING & SELLING APARTMENT BUILDINGS

When choosing properties to buy for investments, one of the reasons condos and townhouses have often been called the lazy man's way to invest is because they are low maintenance for the landlord. However, single units in complexes can be high maintenance. When the property owner also owns of all the units in the building, things change. Being a proprietor of numerous units in an apartment building can be taxing.

The most obvious change is in cash flow. Owners of apartment buildings understand cash flow. They know apartment building ownership is a way to manage several income-producing units. Sometimes, the cash flow is steady with long-term tenants who pay their rent like clockwork. Other times, the landlord wonders if the payments are worth the effort: tenants will not pay and when they do, they pay late. They have loud parties and do not keep their unit in good shape. They call when their drain is clogged or they hear noises from the other neighbors. In short, they are nuisances. In spite of these problems, owning apartment buildings usually leads to wealth.

Many invest in real estate and properties that cater to low income families. The reason is simple: it is because the U.S. government provides some assistance. These apartment buildings will continue to make the rich even richer while providing housing to families who need it.

FINDING YOUR NICHE MARKET

You have to find your comfort zone. Find the types of apartment buildings you want to own. Consider where you want to own these buildings. What kind of income do you want to generate for yourself and your family from those buildings? Before you jump in and buy, you need to research.

- Think about the location.

- Look at the average rents in the area.

- Think about manageable properties.

- Look for empowerment zones.

- Think about your own goals for the property.

- Look at the potential for profit.

Below we will discuss each of the above mentioned points.

LOCATION — ABOVE ALL ELSE

Location is crucial if investors want to keep the property leased. When you begin to locate properties for investment, you will want to consider two things. You want the location to be close to your home and you want a good location so you can rent it out.

If you are trying to buy properties to rent quickly, you want to buy in areas that attract the blue-collar workforce. Look for apartment buildings near shopping areas or parks where people are eager to make honest livings and pay their bills on time. You do not want to go into the slums just because you found a deal and then cross your fingers that it will pay off.

Instead, find bargains where children and families are safe. Find income producing properties in areas where the families who live there take pride in their neighborhood. Look for areas with clean streets and nice buildings. Find an apartment building located in a good school district.

MANAGE YOUR PROPERTIES OR THEY WILL MANAGE YOU

When you start out as an investor, the smartest thing you can do is keep your investments close to home while you learn how to invest and what to look for in income producing properties hard to do as a long-distance landlord.

Start out by investing in smaller complexes. Find a good deal on a duplex or look for a building with only four to six units. A good occupancy rate will tell you what it means to be a landlord, and you can branch out into other areas of investing.

CASE STUDY: KAY WHITE

As a real estate agent, I have the opportunity to show many different properties. Apartment buildings rarely come up for sale if they are earning money. Since there are not that many of them on the market, it is probably safe to say that property owners are making a good  income and have no reason to sell. When there are apartment buildings on the market, someone snatches them up quickly.

Kay White, Realtor
kwhite5048@earthlink.net
www.tricityareaproperties.com

BEING GOAL ORIENTED

Make sure you treat the business of owning investment units seriously from the start. Keep adequate records. Maintain good communication with your tenants and have people on call to take care of their needs immediately if you do not plan to do so yourself.

Think about the future of the apartments you own. What are your goals for them? Do you have room to grow? If so, how will you expand? Will you add another building?

What can you do to increase the interest in your units while decreasing the turnover rate you experience? Can you market the apartment complex or community in a better light to generate more interest? If so, begin doing it as you can. Having goals for the properties you own can help you become more desirable as a landlord and as an investor while increasing your profits.

POTENTIAL FOR PROFIT

After you begin building, buying, selling, and trading in apartment buildings, your potential for profit will be evident. You will see the profits and not just from the tenant rents coming in every month but also in your potential for selling the property in the future.

If you have steady rents coming in and are maintaining a high occupancy rate when you sell the building, it will attract potential buyers. A profit awaits you when you sell the complex. High tenant rents and low turnover will add to your profit potential when you decide to sell.

NEGOTIATIONS, PREPARATIONS, & OTHER LAST MINUTE THOUGHTS

If I had a guide to follow when I moved into my first multi-family complex, I would have enjoyed living there much more than I did. If someone had offered me a set of rules to follow or guidelines to consider, I would have known what to expect. Instead, as a country girl in the middle of a community of close-knit neighbors, I only wanted my privacy.

There is much to consider when you move into a shared housing development. Everything you do is under a watchful eye from the moment you move in because people want to see who you are. They may be merely curious. Do not be quick to judge their intentions.

If you have children, they will probably make friends first, and then you will meet their parents. Children have a way of making sure their parents get to know everyone they know.

From the moment you arrive in your new housing development,

you can decide what you want that environment to be.

This chapter will take you through the home buying process from start to finish.

SHOPPING FOR A SHARED HOUSING UNIT

When you set out to buy a shared housing unit, you need to consider what you are most interested in buying. Are you more interested in a condo or a townhouse? Do you prefer an apartment? If you do, are you interested in buying a building where you can let the other units in the complex pay for your housing while you begin your investment and housing needs at the same time?

Make a list of everything you want in a home. Do not think about it from a single-dwelling or a shared-housing unit perspective. Instead, think about the things you would like to have: how many bedrooms, what kind of kitchen, and how much square footage. List them in the order of importance.

After you make your "I want" list, consider what type of floor plan you like. Do you want single-level living or do you like the idea of having a multi-level house? Consider whether you want a patio, a deck, a garage? Know what it is you are looking for before you set out to find it.

Next, decide if you need to work with a real estate agent. Below are the top four reasons to do so:

- If you are new to an area and have no idea where to begin to look, an agent can direct you to a good complex that will match your lifestyle.

- For the person short on time, an agent can find what you need and set up showings for you.

- If you have never bought a home before, using an agent is advisable.

- In multi-family housing, an agent can help you study the bylaws and determine where to put your investment dollars. An agent is privy to information that can save you money, such as assessments and CMA reports.

When you begin shopping for a shared housing unit in a planned unit development, take time to think about amenities that are important to you. How do you spend your leisure hours? Do you swim? Play tennis? Golf, jog, or hike? What do you do for fun? Do you have many visitors? Does the property have ample parking? Is there a clubhouse to handle your larger gatherings? Make a list of the things you want in amenities because they are the real value when weighing shared housing against single-family dwellings.

NEGOTIATIONS WITH THE SELLER

Before you begin negotiations with the seller, you should take a good look around the complex. Find out what other people are saying about the complex. As mentioned earlier in the book, be a snoop. We suggested that you attend a meeting of the homeowners association before making an offer to purchase. After you have the field narrowed down to three units you are interested in buying, compare bylaws and the homeowners associations. Ask about any foreseeable special assessments and consider them before you buy.

After you choose your unit and before you make a legal offer to purchase, there are several steps you need to take. Find out as much information as you can from the courthouse: whether there are liens on the property and how much the current owner paid for the property. Get a CMA on the property from your real estate agent if you have one. If not, check the courthouse records or check online for comparable sales.

After you have all the information together, see what you can afford and what you are willing to pay for this particular property. After you have a number in mind, make an offer to purchase.

Never offer the seller the full asking price. While you want to go in with a good strong offer, you do not want to pay more for a property than you must. It is important to pay a visit to the courthouse before you buy to find out what the seller paid for the property, how much is owed on the property, and how much money the seller has poured into the property. Then you should be able to make a solid offer on the unit and feel good about it.

If you are going to ask the seller to take back a second mortgage, pay a portion of the closing costs, or even finance the purchase money mortgage, you cannot ask for a price reduction. However, over 30 years, at 6.5 percent interest, every $1,000 you finance will cost you something like $1,950 in interest. Therefore, you want to drive down the cost of the unit as much as possible.

When you begin writing out your offer to purchase, make sure you note the things you want to stay with the unit such as appliances, ceiling fans, and blinds. If the unit is supposed to be furnished, itemize the list and attach it to the offer to purchase so that you are sure you are getting everything with the unit that you understood came with the property. Closing usually occurs within 30 days of the offer to purchase but the best thing to do is to leave yourself a 60-day span to get your financing together and close on the property. "On or before" is a good way to stipulate your intentions in the offer to purchase.

SECURING THE FINANCING AND BUYING YOUR UNIT

After you find your unit and offer to purchase, you should know within a reasonable time whether the seller has accepted your offer. You will need to put down a good faith binder of $500-$1,000; the seller will ask good faith binder of 10 percent of the purchase price, steep for the buyer who wants to obtain a 97 percent loan.

A Little Tip

If you ask the seller to carry part or all of the note, you need to make sure you have the purchase price you are willing to offer along with an amortization schedule attached for the seller's review. Describe in detail the terms of the purchase money mortgage if you are going to have the seller carry the note. If you are interested in a lease option with the seller, describe the lease option terms as well.

Make sure you point out the terms to the seller when you present your offer to purchase. If the seller is in a financial position to carry the financing, pointing out the interest rate and the total money to the seller will help you present your offer in a positive light—a serious offer to purchase.

As soon as the seller accepts your offer, the retainer is deposited into an escrow account by either the agent or the seller. Either way, it will go toward the purchase of the home. After the seller accepts your offer, be prepared to spend time to secure your financing.

Before you commit to any loan package, you should shop for loans just as you shopped for your home. Visit several lenders.

Find the best terms and interest rates to meet your needs. When you have a specific loan in mind, it will be time to move ahead and begin to secure it. You may qualify for various loans so that selecting the best one to suit your shared ownership unit loan is crucial.

CLOSING THE DEAL

Before they set a closing date, your lender will require a plat (map) of the subdivision or development, a title search, a copy of the bylaws, an appraisal, and a termite inspection. You will want a home inspection for added peace of mind.

You will want to have title insurance and a final walkthrough before closing. Title insurance is good because errors do occur. It protects everyone. On closing day, take advantage of a final walkthrough. If you waive the walkthrough, do not be surprised if you find something amiss – too late.

Your walkthrough will examine only the interior unit. You will want to check all appliances to ensure they are in working order and check every inch of the unit to be sure there were no disasters during the previous owners' move. If you are buying a new unit, do not close until the builder does everything completely. If you notice something major left undone, do not close on the unit.

The builder does not have the right to leave the unit you are buying half finished even if he feels he is doing you a favor by financing or leasing to you. All appliances should be in place and in good working order before closing. Electrical wiring should be finished in your unit and covered properly. Heating, ventilation, and cooling should be in good working order, cabinetry and countertops finished, and all paint and trim work should be finished.

If you have good credit, you can obtain financing you need and if you go to the seller as a matter of convenience, you should never sacrifice quality for the financing option you chose to pursue.

THE BIG MOVING DAY

All the neighbors come out to say hello on moving day. They will not notice you are busy with a moving crew working for you on an hourly basis. Plan for interruptions and manage the stress. Try placing a note pad by the door and after someone stops in to say hello, jot down their name and what you remember about them. When you are busy, it is difficult to recall everything they want you to about them, but later on when you have a chance to look at your notes, you will remember them more clearly.

On moving day, you will have the opportunity to set those ground rules we talked about earlier. If you do not have children, and neighbors come over to introduce you to little Timmy, point out that you do not have children. Be aware that if you tell your neighbor you love children, Timmy may spend a great deal of time trying to get you to notice him whenever he sees you.

If you do have children, use moving day as a time to set ground rules. For instance, if the children come over to play and their parents are in tow, use the conversation they make to get in your rules. Let them know your children are inside and ready for bed before 9 p.m. and they mainly focus on school during the week and play on the weekends. If you do not set the rules in the beginning, you will regret it.

BEING A HAPPY HOMEOWNER

Being a happy homeowner in your complex will be up to you. If you want to be a social butterfly in the community, you will not have any trouble finding like people in a multi-family housing complex. However, even the most social individuals still like moments of privacy. If you see someone going into their unit with several friends, it is probably not a good time to send your four-year old over to play with their dog. Learning to be respectful of your neighbors is a big part in how well adjusted everyone is to the lifestyle of shared home ownership.

As a new homeowner in a shared housing environment, you should plan to attend the first homeowners association meeting after you move in. The other residents expect you to show up for the first meeting and you should use the opportunity to meet other residents.

The first association meetings can be intimidating, but you will learn more about your new home. At the first meeting, try to get to know your neighbors. Take the opportunity to meet everyone you can. Try not to approach the first meeting with your own agenda. You should be there to learn all you can about your new environment.

The first meeting is a great time to get some answers to your questions. If you have looked over the bylaws and have questions, take the time after the meeting to approach a board member and ask him or her to answer them for you.

As comical and trivial as it sounds, many board members protect their positions on the board. They feel that no one can represent the community as well as they can. Do not overstep their authority or act as if you have any interest in sitting on the board. You do not want to put your neighbors on guard.

15

THE PEOPLE YOU KNOW

———

"It is not what you know but who you know," works in real estate investing, particularly in the shared housing market. The more people you know, the easier your real estate transactions will be for you. There are people you will do business with daily. The more people you know and have in your corner, the easier it will be to conduct day-to-day business. Here are some of the players in your business world:

- Real estate agents

- Condominium boards and homeowners associations

- Attorneys

- Bankers and other lenders

- Sellers and buyers

When investing in townhouses, condos, and apartment buildings, you will need to master negotiations with the people above.

A real estate agent is crucial to your finding the perfect property. Sure, you can find a good property without using a real estate agent. However, you will probably make mistakes if you are not well informed on buying and selling real estate, particularly in the shared housing market.

Agents will confide what they know about the unit and the complex you are considering. If there are problems in the complex, an agent will pass that information along to you, saving you money. Here are some more advantages to working with agents:

- **They can help you with comparative market analysis.** When you are looking at condos, you want to look at several in the complex if there happens to be more than one unit for sale. See which unit meets your needs and ask your real estate agent to do a CMA report for you so you can see what other homes are selling for in the area. The report is the only way to determine the best market value for the home you want to buy.

- **They can help you with property management.** An agent who is working hard to help you buy and sell property might offer you a deal to represent your interests when it comes to rental managements.

- **They can represent your interests.** When investing in homes for rental or re-sale, you need to have a real estate agent whom you can trust working for you. One of the best agents in our area is stronger than ever because she is her client's agent before she is anything else. She does not care who gets mad or gets their feelings hurt; she is going to represent her client. She is straightforward in tough negotiations. If you are fortunate enough to find a real estate agent who will put your needs first, you could go far as an investor.

- **They can inform you on the market values.** You may think you are getting a good deal, but an informed agent can help you keep everything in perspective. If you have an educated real estate agent working for you, you can be assured each time you go to the closing table to purchase a new acquisition that things will go smoothly.

- **They can educate you about the particular complex you are considering.** The real estate community has inside knowledge that is not public information. If there are problems with an association's board that is so deeply rooted they are causing home values to depreciate, the agent will know.

- **They have the tools you need in real estate transactions.** Real estate agents have many tools they can use to help you save money. They can create a CMA that is effective and accurate. They have the contracts and documents you need and the knowledge to execute them.

- **They can pass along information to you.** If you need real estate information, an agent is someone who can provide you with good information and pass along information to you about what is coming up for sale on the market. (Agents do talk among themselves). They can pass along expired listings and help you secure good deals in your real estate transactions. Take care of your agents if they are not billing you for their time or taking commissions from sales.

- **They can help you maintain long-term perspective.** Investors and homeowners alike may have limited vision. Agents keep your focus where it needs to be—on the money.

- **They can help with buying, selling, and closing your transactions.** Real estate agents know how to get a deal to the closing table. They know about appraisals and surveys. They line up inspections and final walkthrough — in short, they can close your deals quickly and avoid problems.

- **They can save your time.** Time is a commodity. Save time and use an agent.

CASE STUDY: EUGENIA FOXWORTH

Investors have approached me to help them find investment properties. Harlem and Brooklyn were rather inexpensive seven years ago. A typical townhouse in Harlem was available for $250,000-$400,000 renovated. Within a year you could only purchase "shells" for $400,000. Now townhouses are the most sought after property in Harlem. Townhouses that need work are selling for $1.5 million, and a townhouse that is in good condition is selling for $1.9 million to $4 million.

There are so many investors in this market who are looking to purchase condos and buildings that have specific rent rolls. Europeans are investing because the Euro is so strong, and they are looking to purchase condos in prime locations to rent or to use as a pied-a-tier.

Russians are purchasing townhouses and homes that have particular zoning that will allow them to build mid-rise and high-rise condo buildings in all five boroughs in New York. I am presently working with a Russian investor, and we ran into a construction problem in Riverdale, which has hills and stone. The zoning was fine. The acreage was great. The problem was the stone. The investor owns a construction company, and he realized that it would be quite costly to rent special equipment to dig up the stone. He then realized that after doing so, he would have to shore up the land. We are back to the drawing board, but we will continue to work together.

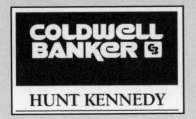
MORE INFORMATION CONCERNING THE CONDOMINIUM BOARD

The homeowner who buys into a complex without first researching the type of community he or she is joining is asking for problems. When you buy into a shared housing community, we have already determined that you are also buying into shared responsibilities. Bylaws of these communities describe the responsibilities of the homeowner's association and the homeowner.

However, the responsibilities of the association fall back upon the board. If you get to know them before buying into the complex, you can be sure of making an informed decision. If you think you are not investing in your community, think again. The dues you pay to the homeowners association are critical to the community and the complex where you buy.

By getting to know the people in charge of developing the complex, you will get the inside scoop on upcoming plans for the housing community. You can scope out management by talking to the president of the board. Asking questions will give you insight on how everything is managed, and meeting the people in key positions can help you make your buying decision.

CASE STUDY: BRUNO FRIIA

One attribute of a homeowner's association to look for is whether the association meets with and works with similar associations for other developments. Our property management division works directly with homeowners associations to guide them to work harmoniously with

each other so that they can become strong and productive. Strong associations work together for the good of the community; weak associations are typically dominated by one individual looking out for his own best interest, not the community as a whole.

Bruno Friia
Lambros Real Estate
Western Montana

ATTORNEYS ARE OUR FRIENDS — WELL, SOME OF THEM ARE

Do you have an attorney? Unless you are a business owner or rub shoulders with the judicial system frequently, chances are you do not. However, as an investor, you need a real estate attorney someone who can give you the ins and outs of a deal from a legal standpoint. Best of all, if you are moving many properties, an attorney may offer discount fees and move you quickly to the closing table when you need to close fast.

When considering engaging a lawyer, look for help in these areas:

- Assistance with the completion of your purchase.

- Advice on your rights, obligations and the programs which are available to help facilitate your purchase.

- Assistance with the closing transaction through Ontario's electronic registration system.

- Protection of your interests in the event of a dispute with your vendor.

APPRAISERS AND SURVEYORS

Knowing an appraiser and surveyor can be most beneficial, because they can answer questions for you and put your name at the top of their list to get things done in a rush. Your lender may have the final decision in appraiser and surveyor contacts, but in cash deals and seller financing, you choose. Try to stick with one appraiser and one surveyor as much as you can.

HOME INSPECTORS

Home inspectors do not have to work fast. In most areas, they are in such demand, they have steady work so they take names and addresses and move through them at their own pace. However, if you have a home inspector looking forward to doing business with you, your name may move to the top of the list.

BANKERS AND OTHER LENDERS

Bankers and lenders are my favorite people. It is all about their attitudes. You need to find lenders you can work with amicably. When in real estate, I had a few I loved dealing with and I let people know who they were. As an investor, you should have two bankers you like to go to for loans and a broker at a mortgage company. It is worth it to you to be kind to the people who can help you make money.

SELLERS AND BUYERS

If you cannot handle negotiations, find someone who can do it for you. I once had clients who were exceedingly likeable. It did not matter which side of the table they were on; they were well liked by both sides. I believe they were the only clients who could have a seller actually smile at the closing table after completely financing a real estate transaction, paying the closing costs, and the realtor's fees. Remarkable is the only word I can use to describe this couple. The lesson here: *become likeable.*

It is great to have friends and when you have the right connections, you can get things done. However, do not expect to have someone always on the move for you without anything in return. Learn to show appreciation and take care of those people who are looking out for you. Send them a gift certificate, drop them by a basket of muffins, or call them to tell them you appreciate them. It can make a difference.

NEW DEVELOPMENTS

O ne of the best times to buy a shared housing unit is when you have the opportunity to purchase directly from a builder or developer. There are numerous advantages if you are lucky enough to be one of the first to purchase your unit. Having the automatic built-in equity is the main reason to buy first.

CASE STUDY: BEN SMITH

My family and I vacation at the same spot in Hilton Head every year. We stay in a particular unit owned by a woman who bought her one bedroom unit during the building phase for less than a half a million dollars. Today, her oceanfront condo would sell for more than

$850,000 because of the location, the community, and the unit. The pre-developmental stage is when you want to buy. In some cases, the equity you realize is worth going through initial phases of development in the complex.

Ben Smith, Realtor
Johnson City, Tennessee
www.tricityareaproperties.com

BUYING YOUR NEW UNIT

When you are the first to buy in a new complex, you may be able to get a better deal than you would later because the builder wants to show his lender evidence of promise in the investment.

When you begin looking at a new complex, go beyond looking at the amenities or floor plans. The builder will have developed the bylaws of the homeowner's association. You want to be sure the community and the builder are sound financially. Will the builder be able to finish the project or if you buy, are you just a buyer who is helping his financial situation as he struggles to finish phase one of a five-phase project?

When developers take on the task of building a large complex, they may have big dreams without the financing to back them up. When they have not fully anticipated all costs, they are dependent on the lender who wants a return on the investment soon after the project is under roof. If units are not selling, lenders can bring construction to a standstill.

BEING THE FIRST

Being the first to buy may allow you to get a sweet deal. You may be able to buy your unit off the drawing board and it will likely be the best deal the developer will offer. In the pre-planning stages, anything can happen.

CASE STUDY: ANONYMOUS BUILDER & DEVELOPER, TN

As a developer, I know the first, second, and last units are the hardest units to sell. It may just be that way for me but it happened in more than 10 developments I initiated. I take a loss on all three of these units. I build it into the price of the other units because I know how

CHAPTER 16 - NEW DEVELOPMENTS

CASE STUDY: ANONYMOUS BUILDER & DEVELOPER, TN

much money I need to realize out of the entire project. I took a $20,000 loss on the first unit sold, but the profit on the complex had a couple of zeros added to it so it was worth it to get the first sale. By the last sale, I am ready for a change and may work a deal, but it is never as good for the buyer as the first one was. Never.

When you buy in the first stages of development, you can choose your colors, cabinets, countertops, and carpet. By buying during the pre-development stages, you can customize your unit in most situations. Some of the things you should expect to be able to choose during pre-construction phase are:

- Counter tops
- Carpet
- Hardwood floors / tile
- Appliance colors
- Cabinets within budget
- Cabinet hardware
- Ceiling fans / light fixtures within the set budget

If you are the first to buy in a development, make a ridiculously low offer. Expect to get the builder off his asking price 10 percent to 20 percent. The developer expects to haggle.

CASE STUDY: KIRK HANSEN

"Developers will come to us and offer commissions to help sell their new developments. About 30 percent of our business is from condo/townhouse sales."

Kirk Hansen, President
Century 21 Homes First
760-212-0062
Kirk.Hansen@Century21.com

KEEP YOUR BEST INTERESTS IN FOCUS

When you buy in a complex under construction, place a finish date in the offer to purchase with a penalty per day should the builder not finish on time. It may be countered with an offer, but you should be compensated if the builder or developer cannot finish on time. Often a developer will push back the date of completion so that he can finish a model unit first. Prevent delays by popping in on the job site repeatedly to let the builder know you are ready to move as quickly as possible. Become visible.

Sometimes, builders or developers get in too deeply, but if you are buying from reputable sellers with a good name in the community, you should not be concerned about this possibility. After all, the bank or lender has probably worked with them before and if they can sink their investing dollars into the project, your investment will be safe, too.

CASE STUDY: ANONYMOUS, MEMPHIS

"I would never buy from a new developer first. That is because the first home I bought was a two-bedroom condo in a new development. I was the first to buy and six months after I bought, there were still no takers in the complex, only me. It was because the builder had a horrible reputation for being a slacker.

"I, too, had trouble selling three years later because half of the units in the complex were still so new that no one had any reason to buy my unit. When you have run-off problems from drain issues, tile coming up in the bathroom because wafer board was not used, and countless other troubles, you have to wonder how the builder ever got his license and what you were thinking to take the plunge first. I would buy first again from an established builder but never from a new one again."

STAY FOCUSED ON WHAT IS IMPORTANT

Regardless of when you buy in a new housing complex, whether you are working with a real estate agent or alone, taking time to prepare a well thought out offer to purchase is crucial. In your offer to purchase, list everything your unit should include. Here are some suggestions:

- Express your choice. Are you choosing the carpet colors? The cabinets? Whatever you can choose, state it in the offer to purchase.

- Do not forget the blinds if you want blinds in your unit. You will have to ask to receive.

- Mention all appliances you plan to find in your unit.

- Mention switch plate covers and light fixtures. Indicate any ceiling fans promised to you and where each goes.

- If you are buying a unit with a deck or patio and it is important to you, spell it out so that if the builder changes his mind, you have redress.

- When do you expect to close and when do you want to occupy? Include both on your offer to purchase.

- If there are any special considerations for your pet and the bylaws are not in place yet, you need to amend the contract to allow your pet after the bylaws rule out pets.

Make sure you include everything that comes to mind because if you forget to mention something, you will regret it.

A Little Tip

I think you can get a great deal on buying first in new complexes, because I have seen it happen. However, I think if you give the builder your retainer and wait to close near the occupancy date, you will benefit more in the end. The builder has more of an incentive to finish your unit if you are not paying until you can move in.

ANOTHER OBSERVATION

I do not like to buy from an unknown person. If a builder or a developer is a serious businessman or woman in the community, he or she will be known by other builders or real estate professionals. Do not be too eager to jump on a good deal with an unknown builder. Even though people have to start somewhere, they should take the time to become active in the community if they are going to sell to the community. I hope that they will become members of the Chamber of Commerce and get involved with the area where they work.

CASE STUDY: ANONYMOUS, NC

"I know of three builders in my area who came from other parts of the United States after they developed a bad reputation for the quality of homes they built in their previous locations. They built homes and condos that were gorgeous on the outside, but on the inside, the stuff you cannot see, let the buyer beware."

You want to find a reputable developer who is able to build a quality home for you, and who has experience setting up a homeowners association so that you will make a good investment.

CONCLUSION

The Complete Guide to Purchasing a Condo, Townhouse, or Apartment: What Smart Investors Need to Know Explained Simply was written as a guide for investors and homeowners. The homeowner can see that investing in a shared housing unit can be wise. Peter Navarro wrote a book called *If It is Raining in Brazil, Buy Starbucks*. His book gives the investor reasons to buy contrary to trends. When I worked as a real estate agent, it was common to hear the myths of losing money in shared housing.

Tell them to Trump. Tell them to the men and women rebuilding Biloxi, Mississippi, who are investing in Bacaran Bay with up to 1,800 square feet of living space in an area recovering from a horrific devastation. Tell the real estate tycoons who have made their fortunes in large complexes housing hundreds of people. Investing in multi-family housing has made people wealthy.

The developers who are building these complexes are making money. The people who buy and sell the units in these complexes are making money, and the real estate agents who benefit from it all are making money in the shared housing market.

As an investor, you will find that shared housing units are easy to maintain—because you are not the person responsible for maintaining them. It is the smart way to invest because it is time-efficient when you are short on time. It encourages higher profits when that is the reason to own in the first place and enables the investor to keep rentals together making management easier.

While shared housing ownership is not for everyone, it is for every investor who wants to make the most money in multiple units. Tenants look at shared housing because of the amenities offered in these communities and as an investor, if you want to rent your units quickly, it is important to offer perquisites to your potential tenants, including tennis courts, swimming pools, hot tubs, boat docks, gazebos, and play grounds.

If you know you like the idea, it is a lifestyle you will enjoy because it allows you time to do things you enjoy, and it forces you to be social—often good for people who live alone or who wish to make new friends.

Outside of the social factor, the profitability is going to hold in the complexes where these units are housed. Decide on an apartment facing Central Park, a townhouse on the slopes, or a condo on the ocean and be assured you have invested, not bought, invested in a home. When you sell it someday, you will see you made the right decision.

Thank you for purchasing this book. I hope you enjoyed, it and I wish you wealth and happiness.

APPENDIX A

QUESTIONNAIRE FOR SUCCESS IN SHARED HOUSING

The following questionnaire will help you when you are searching for an apartment, condominium, or townhouse. Use this questionnaire to help you decide the shared housing complex you are considering is right for you.

SHARED HOUSING QUESTIONNAIRE	
Question	Answer
1. What time do you hear the most noise in the complex?	
2. What time do you hear the least noise in the complex?	
3. Are pets allowed in the complex and if so are they required to be leashed?	
4. Is security available on site and if not, should it be?	
5. Are junkers in driveways and on streets?	
6. Is there a noise ordinance? If not, should there be?	

SHARED HOUSING QUESTIONNAIRE	
Question	Answer
7. Have you met the neighbors? Do you feel comfortable around them?	
8. Are the neighbors happy with the area?	
9. What do you know about the homeowner's association?	
10. Does the association seem to have active participation from the owners in the complex?	
11. Who are the directors of the homeowners association?	
12. Are officers on the board chosen by a vote?	
13. Does the complex have adequate parking and if not, where does overflow parking go?	
14. Are parking permits and parking spaces assigned?	
15. Do you have to meet the approval of the board before you can move into the complex and if so, how?	
16. Are the units separated by firewalls?	
17. Why is the current owner selling?	
18. What seems to be the biggest complaint the other homeowners in the complex have? Is it something you will find bothersome?	
19. What is resale like in the area? Ask a real estate agent about the average days on market for the units there.	

SHARED HOUSING QUESTIONNAIRE	
Question	Answer
20. When was the last large assessment and how much was it?	
21. How much are the monthly homeowner's dues? In comparison to other homeowner's fees at other communities, are the fees reasonable or on the high side?	
22. Compare the unit you are buying to other units on the market in the same and in other complexes. Why does the unit you are buying cost more or less than the other units on the market?	
23. Are there more tenants than homeowners occupying the units?	
24. Does the complex offer adequate space for outside storage? Can you park a boat or an RV in a designated area? Is there storage in the interior space and outside around the deck or patio area?	
25. What restrictions exist if you choose to lease your unit? In vacation home rentals, will you need to let someone on the board know when you have someone arriving for a rental term? What is required of the tenants you rent to on a weekly or monthly basis if you choose to rent your unit?	
26. Will you be forbidden to place signs to advertise either an open house or that your unit is for sale?	

SUMMARY OF THE ABOVE QUESTIONNAIRE

If you are a working adult or a student who needs to have some down time and peace and quiet, check the noise level is in the complex. How many pets do you see on leashes and where are they going for their walks. Do the neighbors pass each other with a smile and do they chat? If it is a hub of activity, a working adult will never be happy there.

Parking can be a big issue. When you are considering a particular complex, ask about assigned parking areas. Talk to the current homeowner about where he or she parks. Is there anything in the deed to your property? It may be important to you later.

Find out why the current owner is selling. If it is a new complex and a new development, you know why the current owner is selling—for profit! However, if you are buying a unit that is occupied, ask why the owner is selling because it may become your reason for not buying. When there are many units on the market in one complex, there is a reason for it. Find out why and whether it is something that may prohibit your home from increasing or even holding its value.

GREAT AREAS TO BUY A GETAWAY

1. **St. George Island, Florida.** Still unscathed by the landscaping of industry and untouched by developers looking to commercialize it, St. George Island is an investment that can carry its weight. You will be able to afford ocean-side living and let your tenants in the vacation season help you pay for it all!

2. **The Outerbanks of North Carolina.** The Outerbanks

have always rented well. From Nags Head to Kitty Hawk, there are great investments just calling out the smart investor's name. While the area is known for the investment homes, there are some condos and townhouses for sale with an income you can rely on in the summer months.

3. **Myrtle Beach, South Carolina.** There is always a cheap buy in Myrtle Beach if you want to find one. So many times people are ready to dump a property or they have a fixer upper for sale and are willing to make a deal. If you want to make money in fixer-upper shared housing units, here is where your money needs to be.

4. **Hilton Head, South Carolina.** It is not cheap but property still holds its value in this area. Hilton Head Beach and Tennis Club is just one place you can go for evidence that property holds its value and is climbing. Best of all, these vacation units rent back to back in the vacation/sports season. If you want to ensure your vacation rental is always in demand, make it pet friendly, and you will be booked all the time.

5. **Fripp Island, South Carolina.** Two of South Carolina's best kept secrets are Harbour Island and Fripp Island. Not far from Hilton Head, this stretch of coastal beauty is an investor's dream. Limited space ensures fewer properties and higher value. The island is by far the most beautiful in South Carolina.

6. **Destin, Florida.** Imagine if you had bought something in Destin 10 years ago when baby boomers were swarming to the coastal playground on the Gulf of

Mexico. Evidence shows the homeowners who went to Destin intending to invest have made more money on their investment than they ever imagined. Watch for the fixer uppers for the most profit in this area.

7. **Fort Walton Beach, Florida.** Some of the more luxurious units are hidden in the heart of Fort Walton Beach. While neighboring Destin packs a powerful punch for vacationers, Fort Walton Beach has room for the investor. Some condominium complexes are sprouting up in the area. If you are going to invest in Fort Walton, check out the new and stay away from the old.

8. **Gatlinburg, Tennessee.** I have two friends who built cabins in Gatlinburg in the Great Smokey Mountains. They are making money because they built on mountainsides of undesirable land and named them Honeymoon Getaways and Family Weekend Adventures. They have added video libraries and pool tables to keep the family indoors at night while still only minutes from the hustle and bustle of the action in Gatlinburg and Pigeon Forge. It is worth checking into. They stay booked.

9. **Veil, Colorado.** Who loves to ski? If you like snow sports, a vacation home in Veil is a possibility. However, smart investors do not let go of their homes too cheaply. The only way to buy in Veil now is to hope for a cheap fixer upper (which is rare) or the opportunity to jump first on a foreclosure. However, if the opportunity presents itself, leap fast because Veil is renting, and the home values are holding.

10. **South Padre Island, Texas.** South Padre Island is coming back up. It is time to buy in Texas again, and South Padre Island prices are ripe for the picking. Choose the property you like best because the renters are repeaters—a good sign if you are looking for a vacation rental home.

11. **Biloxi, Mississippi.** The rebuilding stage has begun. Right now, you can go into Biloxi and make a fortune later. You can help a community in dire need rebuild while helping yourself to profits later on so it can be a win-win situation. I was in Biloxi about five months before Katrina hit. I know the potential in the area because I was also there in the beginning of the casino boom. This time the growth of bigger and better casinos to the area ensures an investor cannot go wrong in Biloxi or Gulfport.

ALL THE FURNISHINGS YOU NEED IN YOUR VACATION RENTAL HOME

When you are ready to buy an investment home in a shared housing environment where vacationing families expect to find comfortable surroundings on vacation, you may be surprised at how easy it is to furnish one of your vacation units. The more you provide, the more at home the vacationers will feel, but take a quick look the few items required to get you started in investing in a shared housing complex for vacation rentals.

VACATION RENTAL HOME FURNISHINGS NEEDED	
Patio Furniture	Two to four chairs and one or two end tables.

VACATION RENTAL HOME FURNISHINGS NEEDED	
Living Room Furniture	TV, video library of about 10 movies, bookshelf with several games such as ROOK cards, UNO Cards, and several board games, 10-15 books on crime or romance, sofa, two chairs, and a bean bag chair or two, VCR or DVD, end tables, and a coffee table.
Kitchen	Kitchen table with seating for four to six people. Stove, microwave, oven, refrigerator, and basic supplies such as bowls, plates, and silverware.
Bedroom Furniture	Bedrooms are simple. Each room is furnished with bed, dresser, and a chair or rocking chair and maybe a full length mirror. Fully furnished with mattresses, down comforters, and pillows.
Bathrooms	Towel rack, soap dish, waste bin, and hamper.

You can furnish a vacation unit for under $4,000 if you buy nice, inexpensive furniture. Throw a couple of cheap pictures on the wall and you are in business! As you rent the unit, you can make upgrades.

APPENDIX B

SAMPLE CONDOMINIUM BYLAWS OR RULES

Sample Copy of Rules and Regulations of On the Sea Condominiums. An attorney should prepare bylaws for a homeowner's association. The following is only a sample.

SAMPLE RULES AND REGULATIONS

Pursuant to the authority of the Board of On the Sea Condominium Association, Inc., ("Association"), the following rules and regulations of On the Sea Condominiums have been adopted by the Board of the Association ("Board") to govern the use of the Condominium Property.

1. Enforcement. All violations of these rules and regulations shall be reported to a member of the Board. Disagreements concerning the proper interpretation and effect of these rules shall be presented to and determined by the Board whose interpretation of these rules shall be held liable. In the event that any person, firm, or entity subject to these rules and regulations fails to abide by them, as interpreted by the Board, they shall be fined by the Association. (Most contracts will address enforcement for another paragraph or so.)

SAMPLE RULES AND REGULATIONS

2. Use of the Common Elements. The Common Elements of the Condominium ("Common Elements") are for the use of Unit Owners of the Condominium and their immediate families, lessees, and guests accompanied by a member, and no other person will be permitted to use the Common Elements unless accompanied by a Unit Owner or member of the owner's immediate family.

3. Noise. All noise, including, without limitation, talking, singing, television, radio, record player, tape recorder, or musical instrument should be kept at such volume level that the noise is not bothersome outside the unit where it originates. With respect to flooring, one-half inch cork or other soundproofing material will be installed under other hard surface flooring over living areas of other units to reduce noise. After 9 p.m. all noise, including running up and down the stairs in the breezeways, in any outdoor or indoor area on property will be kept at such volume level that the noise is not heard in any unit or bothersome to any of the tenants.

4. Children. Children under 13 will not play on or about the Condominium Property. The only exception is when they are under the care of a responsible adult. Property includes all pools, tennis courts, playgrounds, boats, and docks.

5. Pets.

a) Dogs must be kept on a leash and in control of the pet owner.

b) Pet feces deposited on common area must immediately be removed. The person in control of the pet should be responsible and clean up after the pet when taking the dog for a walk or exercise.

c) Each resident shall register pets with the association. Limit of one pet per unit. There are further restrictions on the number and weight of dogs as noted in parts 7 and 8 below. Pet restrictions are enforced by the Association.

d) Each condo owner is responsible for damages resulting from pet.

SAMPLE RULES AND REGULATIONS

e) No pet may be left unattended on any of the balconies at any time.

f) A resident may keep at most one dog per unit unless written permission is granted by the Association.

g) A pet dog may weigh at most 40 pounds.

6. Obstructions. There will be no cluttering of the Condominium Property, including sidewalks, driveways, automobile parking spaces, lawns, entrances, elevators, stairways, balconies, or any other areas marked as common area.

7. Destruction of Property. There shall be no marking, marring, damaging, destroying, or defacing of any part of the Condominium Property. Unit Owners will be held responsible for any defacing of the property even if the damage is done by one of the unit owner's tenants.

8. Hurricane Shutters. Upon issuance of hurricane warnings, standard hurricane shutters or panels, as approved by the Board, should be used but must be removed within 72 hours of the warning being lifted.

9. Patios, Screen Porches, Windows, and Doors. Nothing shall be dropped or thrown from any window. No plants, pots, receptacles, or other decorative articles can be kept, hung, or maintained on any rail or balcony ledge. All loose or movable objects should be removed from patios and screened porches upon notice of an approaching hurricane or other weather characterized by high wind. Patios, screened porches, windows, and doors cannot be altered as constructed. These items are expected to conform to the other units' patios, porches, windows, and doors.

10. Damage to Common Elements. All unit owners are responsible for and will bear expense of any damage to the Common Elements caused by moving to or removing from their unit household furnishings or other objects.

SAMPLE RULES AND REGULATIONS

11. Refuse. All waste, including bottles, cans, newspapers, magazines, and garbage shall be deposited in the covered trash bins. Any waste that does not fit in a waste bin shall be removed at the owner's expense.

12. Guests. Owners will notify the Association in writing in advance of the arrival and departure of guests who have permission to use a Unit in the Unit Owner's absence. No person under twenty one (21) years of age shall occupy a unit in this complex.

13. Signs. No sign will be inscribed or exposed on or at any window, door, balcony or terrace. This includes all real estate signs.

14. Keys. The Association shall maintain a key to each unit in the Condominium. In the event the homeowner changes the locks, the homeowners association should be presented with a new key within 24 hours or notified of the time the homeowner will be presenting the new key to the board.

15. Parking. Unauthorized parking shall include:

a) Vehicles parked so they block other parking spaces, drives, roads, or building entryways or parked in unauthorized spaces.

b) Trailers, campers, motor homes, trucks, or other oversized vehicles.

c) Parking of boats shall be in only those areas designated by the Association.

d) Parking in Covered Parking Spaces.

e) Parking of commercial vehicles, defined as those bearing commercial signs and/or commercial license plates, is prohibited.

f) Parking a vehicle without a valid parking permit is prohibited.

SAMPLE RULES AND REGULATIONS

16. Compliance with Documents. All Unit Owners and every guest of a Unit Owner shall comply with all the terms, conditions, covenants, restrictions, and limitations contained in the Declaration of Condominium and the Bylaws.

17. Rule Changes. The Board reserves the right to change or revoke existing rules and regulations and to make additional rules as necessary for the safety and protection of the buildings and their occupants, to promote cleanliness and good order of the Condominium Property, and to assure the comfort and convenience of Unit Owners.

18. Location for Posting Notices. All notices of owner meetings will be posted on the bulletin board located outside the clubhouse. The bulletin board is not a public forum to be used for anything other than notices that pertain to the homeowners specifically as a whole unity. Do not advertise cars for sale or yard sales. Fines of $300 each will be imposed for misuse of the community bulletin board.

19. Pool.

a) The use of the pool is restricted to residents and guests.

b) Children 13 and under must be accompanied by an adult either a parent or a legal guardian.

c) Pool Hours are Sunday -Thursday open 10 a.m. until 10 p.m. Friday and Saturday open 10 a.m. until 11 p.m.

d) Any type of glassware is prohibited in the pool area.

e) Please deposit all trash in trash bins before leaving the area.

f) Pets are not allowed in the pool or the pool area.

g) Earphones must be used with all radios and musical devices.

h) Appropriate swimwear must be worn in pool. Babies in diapers are not allowed in the pool unless protective covering is worn.

SAMPLE RULES AND REGULATIONS

i) No diving and no running in the pool area. Absolutely no horse playing in the pool area.

j) No lifeguard is on duty. Flotation devices are around the pool area for lifesaving measures only.

k) Swim at your own risk.

20. Air Conditioner. The length and width of the component outside your unit shall be no more than 36 inches.

21. Age. Restrictions and Use of Facilities.

a) A child must be at least 13 years old to use the pool unless accompanied by an adult.

b) A child must be at least 13 years of age to use the tennis and basketball courts.

c) A person must be at least 16 years old or accompanied by an adult to use the fitness facility.

d) To use the playground a child must be 13 years old or accompanied by a responsible adult.

APPENDIX C

SAMPLE ENGINEERING REPORT

D o not close the deal without a professional home inspection. A qualified, experienced inspector will find defects that were never considered by the property manager. Engineering reports are usually accompanied by a letter stating that the request for the inspection was fulfilled. This letter will include the property address, the date the request was fulfilled, and the results of the inspection. This report will include every aspect of the inspection including the exterior and interior as well as the grounds. It includes structural and architectural conditions, all mechanical/electrical systems, and everything else pertaining to the site.

The following is a sample of what you can expect to see in the engineering report for an apartment or other shared housing unit. This is not representative of a complete report but instead covers the basic report so the reader can understand it.

SAMPLE ENGINEERING REPORT

General Conditions

This property is an improved structure with a two-story stone and brick building with a crawl space considered grade. There is a total of eight individual home units.

All units share a common front and back, porches, steps, and breezeways. The common building consists of private storage spaces, electrical and gas meters, and all the water heaters in storage spaces outside each unit.

The building was constructed in (year). There are (number) units on each level. All units have two bedrooms and one bathroom.

There are 10 parking spaces on the north and south ends of the property.

The building has concrete foundation but is composed of brick and stone exterior walls. The floor and ceiling joists, rafters, stairs, and partition wall studs are all made of wood. The exterior walls are finished and covered with standard wallboard. The existing roof is in need of replacement. The windows are double-hung and insulated and each has appropriate insect screens.

Central heat and air are supplied using condensers (remote exterior) located on the north back roof.

It is my opinion that the building is architecturally sound but needs structural improvements.

All heating and plumbing systems seem to be new. The fixtures and devices are also new and seem to be in good working order.

Site and Building Exterior

The lot is (size). The paved area surrounding the building is used for parking and garbage disposal.

SAMPLE ENGINEERING REPORT

All the original vinyl windows appear to have been replaced recently. In all window openings, the lintels appear to be in good condition. The aluminum gutters are in excellent condition and the downspouts seem to be in good condition as well.

The main doors at the front and rear of the building are solid heavy steel. The concrete sidewalks and porches are in excellent condition.

Building Interior

It is my opinion that the common area appears to be in unsatisfactory condition.

I visited all eight units and found most of them in the remodeling stages. The remodeling work would include new kitchen appliances, new trim work, new flooring in the bathrooms, and new counter tops in the kitchen and bathroom.

Utility Operating System

(This section explains the heating and cooling systems and mention the standards they meet.)

I have been advised by the HVAC contractor that all furnaces are standard and meet the regulations implied.

The plumbing was recently updated by FGH Plumbing. It appears to be in working order. All fixtures are newly replaced or in the process of being replaced.

The water heaters for each individual unit are new and in excellent condition.

All piping, wiring, switches, and fixtures seem to be new or in like-new condition.

SUMMARY OF INSPECTION

In the summary of the inspection, the structure, mechanical systems, utilities, roofing, and environmental concerns will be addressed from the standpoint of the engineer. These are opinions only.

Most of the engineering reports are accompanied by a letter. Terminology is universal. Since I am not an engineer or one who is involved directly in inspections, this is only a sample. Most of the inspections are lengthy and describe every increment of the inspection in complete detailed order, but this sample gives the reader a summary of an inspection of a multi-family housing environment.

APPENDIX D

CALCULATING YOUR PAYMENT

The following examples show you how much you can afford to pay for a condo or townhouse. You need to add the homeowners association's dues onto your payment when calculating your total payment. For example, if your monthly payment is $300 and your homeowner's dues are $250 each month, you would need to be able to afford a $550 a month house payment.

THE FOLLOWING IS AN EXAMPLE OF A CONDOMINIUM WITH A SALES PRICE OF $50,000	
Cost of Home	$50,000
Down Payment at 10%	$5,000
Interest Rate *	7 percent
Authorization Period	20 years
Insurance Premium	$900
Mortgage	$45,000

Payment Frequency	Payment	Authorization	Balance
Monthly	$353.11	20 years	$39,531.35
Every Two Weeks	$176.56	16 years	$37,340.39
Weekly Payment	$88.28	16 years, 11 month(s)	$37,322.34

THE FOLLOWING IS AN EXAMPLE OF A CONDOMINIUM WITH A SALES PRICE OF $75,000

Cost of Home	$75,000
Down Payment	$7,500
Interest Rate *	7 percent
Amortization Period	20 years
Insurance Premium **	$1,350
Mortgage	$68,850

Payment Frequency	Payment	Authorization	Balance
Monthly	$529.67	20 years	$59,297.03
Every Two Weeks	$264.84	16 years	$56,010.59
Weekly Payment	$132.42	16 years, 11 month(s)	$55,983.51

THE FOLLOWING IS AN EXAMPLE OF A CONDOMINIUM WITH A SALES PRICE OF $100,000

Cost of Home	$100,000
Down Payment	$10,000
Interest Rate *	7 percent
Amortization Period	20 years
Insurance Premium **	$1,800
Mortgage	$91,800

Payment Frequency	Payment	Authorization	Balance
Monthly	$706.23	20 years	$79,062.70
Every Two Weeks	$353.11	16 years	$74,680.79
Weekly Payment	$176.56	16 years, 11 month(s)	$74,644.68

THE FOLLOWING IS AN EXAMPLE OF A CONDOMINIUM WITH A SALES PRICE OF $125,000

Cost of Home	$125,000
Down Payment	$12,500
Interest Rate *	7 percent

THE FOLLOWING IS AN EXAMPLE OF A CONDOMINIUM WITH A SALES PRICE OF $125,000	
Amortization Period	20 years
Insurance Premium **	$2,250
Mortgage	$114,750

Payment Frequency	Payment	Authorization	Balance
Monthly	$882.78	20 years	$98,828.38
Every Two Weeks	$441.39	16 years	$93,350.98
Weekly Payment	$220.70	16 years, 11 month(s)	$93,305.85

FULL AMORTIZATION TABLE BASED ON 30 YEARS

The following full table amortization chart is based on a townhouse with a sales price of $150,000 and an interest rate of 6.75 percent. The mortgage is amortized over 30 years.

The designated Prin/Pymt column shows what percentage of your regular payment is actually going toward the principal.

In this scenario, you will have a $972.90 payment. However, with homeowners association dues, your payment will be more than $1,000. Your monthly payment will be $972.90.

Year	Month	Principle	Prin/Pmt	Interest	Balance
2007	Jan.	129.15	13.274491	843.75	149870.85
2007	Feb.	129.87	13.349160	843.02	149740.98
2007	Mar.	130.60	13.424249	842.29	149610.38
2007	Apr.	131.34	13.499761	841.56	149479.04
2007	May	132.08	13.575697	840.82	149346.96
2007	Jun.	132.82	13.652060	840.08	149214.14
2007	TOTAL	1598.62	13.692969	10076.14	148401.38

2007	Jul.	133.57	13.728853	839.33	149080.57
2007	Aug.	134.32	13.806078	838.58	148946.25
2007	Sep.	135.07	13.883737	837.82	148811.18
2007	Oct.	135.83	13.961833	837.06	148675.34
2007	Nov.	136.60	14.040368	836.30	148538.74
2007	Dec.	137.37	14.119345	835.53	148401.38
2007	TOTAL	1598.62	13.692969	10076.14	148401.38

Year	Month	Principle	Prin/Pmt	Interest	Balance
2008	Jan.	138.14	14.198767	834.76	148263.24
2008	Feb.	138.92	14.278635	833.98	148124.32
2008	Mar.	139.70	14.358952	833.76	148263.24
2008	Apr.	140.48	14.439721	832.41	147844.14
2008	May	141.27	14.520944	831.62	147702.87
2008	Jun.	142.07	14.602625	830.03	147560.80
2008	Jul.	142.87	14.684765	830.03	147417.93
2008	Aug.	143.67	14.767366	829.23	147247.26
2008	Sep.	144.48	14.850433	828.42	147129.78
2008	Oct.	145.29	14.933966	827.61	146984.49
2008	Nov.	146.11	15.017970	826.79	146839.38
2008	Dec.	146.93	15.102446	825.97	146691.45
2008	TOTAL	1709.93	14.646382	9964.83	146691.45

Year	Month	Principle	Prin/Pmt	Interest	Balance
2009	Jan.	147.76	15.187397	825.14	146543.69
2009	Feb.	148.59	15.070826	824.31	146395.10
2009	Mar.	149.42	15.358736	823.47	146245.68
2009	Apr.	150.27	15.445129	822.63	146095.41
2009	May	151.11	15.532008	821.79	145944.30
2009	Jun.	151.96	15.619375	820.94	145792.34
2009	TOTAL	1828.99	15.666180	9845.75	144862.46

2009	Jul.	152.82	15.70734	820.08	145639.52
2009	Aug.	153.67	15.795588	819.22	145485.85
2009	Sep.	154.54	15.884438	818.36	145331.31
2009	Oct.	155.41	15.973788	817.49	145175.90
2009	Nov.	156.28	16.063640	816.61	145019.62
2009	Dec.	157.16	16.153998	815.74	144862.46
2009	TOTAL	1828.99	15.666180	9845.75	144862.46

Year	Month	Principle	Prin/Pmt	Interest	Balance
2010	Jan.	158.05	16.244864	814.85	144704.41
2010	Feb.	158.93	16.336242	813.96	144545.48
2010	Mar.	159.83	16.428133	813.07	144385.65
2010	Apr.	160.73	16.520541	812.17	144224.92
2010	May	161.63	16.613469	811.27	144063.29
2010	Jun.	162.54	16706920	810.36	143900.75
2010	Jul.	163.46	16.800897	809.44	143737.29
2010	Aug.	164.37	16.895402	808.52	143572.92
2010	Sep.	165.30	16.990438	807.60	143407.62
2010	Oct.	166.23	17.086010	806.67	143241.39
2010	Nov.	167.16	17.182118	805.73	143074.22
2010	Dec.	168.10	17.278768	804.79	142906.12
2010	TOTAL	1956.34	16.756984	9718.43	142906.12

Year	Month	Principle	Prin/Pmt	Interest	Balance
2011	Jan.	169.05	17.375961	803.85	142737.07
2011	Feb.	170.00	17.473701	802.85	142737.07
2011	Mar.	170.96	17.571990	801.94	142396.11
2011	Apr.	171.92	17.670833	800.98	142224.19
2011	May	172.89	17.770231	800.01	142051.30
2011	Jun.	173.86	17.870189	799.04	141877.45
2011	TOTAL	2092.55	17.923738	9582.21	140813.56

2011	Jul.	174.84	17.970708	798.06	141702.61
2011	Aug.	175.82	18.071794	797.08	141526.79
2011	Sep.	176.81	18.173448	796.09	141349.98
2011	Oct.	177.80	18.378474	794.09	140993.37
2011	Nov.	178.80	18.378474	794.09	140933.56
2011	Dec.	179.81	18.481853	797.09	140813.56
2011	TOTAL	2092.55	17.923738	9582.21	140813.56

Year	Month	Principle	Prin/Pmt	Interest	Balance
2012	Jan.	180.82	18.585813	792.08	140632.74
2012	Feb.	181.84	18.690358	791.06	140450.91
2012	Mar.	182.86	18.795492	790.04	140268.04
2012	Apr.	183.89	18.901216	789.01	140084.16
2012	May	184.92	19.007536	787.97	139899.23
2012	Jun.	185.96	19.114453	786.93	139713.27
2012	Jul.	187.01	19.221972	785.89	139526.26
2012	Aug.	188.06	19.330095	784.84	139338.20
2012	Sep.	189.12	19.438827	783.78	139149.08
2012	Oct.	190.18	19.548171	782.71	138958.89
2012	Nov.	191.25	19.658129	781.64	138767.64
2012	Dec.	192.33	19.768706	780.57	138575.31
2012	TOTAL	2238.25	19.171731	9436.51	138575.31

Year	Month	Principle	Prin/Pmt	Interest	Balance
2013	Jan.	193.41	19.879905	779.49	138381.90
2013	Feb.	194.50	19.991729	778.40	138187.40
2013	Mar.	195.59	20.104183	777.30	137991.81
2013	Apr.	196.69	20.217269	776.20	137795.11
2013	May	197.80	20.330991	775.10	137597.31
2013	Jun.	198.91	20.445353	773.98	137398.40
2013	TOTAL	2394.10	20.506619	9280.67	136181.21

2013	Jul.	200.03	20.560358	772.87	137198.37
2013	Aug.	201.16	20.676101	771.74	136997.21
2013	Sep.	202.29	20.792313	770.61	136794.93
2013	Oct.	203.43	20.909269	769.47	136591.50
2013	Nov.	204.57	21.026884	768.33	136386.93
2013	Dec.	205.72	21.145160	767.18	136181.21
2013	TOTAL	2394.10	20.506619	9280.67	136181.21

Year	Month	Principle	Prin/Pmt	Interest	Balance
2014	Jan.	206.88	21.264102	766.02	135974.33
2014	Feb.	208.04	21.383712	764.86	135766.29
2014	Mar.	209.21	21.503996	763.89	135557.08
2014	Apr.	210.39	21.624956	762.51	135346.69
2014	May	211.57	21.746596	762.51	135346.69
2014	Jun.	212.76	21.868921	760.14	134922.36
2014	Jul.	213.96	21.991933	758.94	134708.40
2014	Aug.	215.16	22.115638	756.52	134276.86
2014	Sep.	216.37	22.240038	756.52	134276.86
2014	Oct.	217.59	22.365139	755.31	134059.27
2014	Nov.	218.81	22.490943	754.08	133840.46
2014	Dec.	220.04	22.617454	752.85	133620.41
2014	TOTAL	2560.80	21.934452	9113.97	133620.41

Year	Month	Principle	Prin/Pmt	Interest	Balance
2015	Jan.	221.28	22.744677	751.61	133399.13
2015	Feb.	222.53	22.872616	750.37	133176.60
2015	Mar.	223.75	23.001275	749.12	132952.83
2015	Apr.	225.04	23.130657	747.86	132727.79
2015	May	226.30	23.260767	746.59	132501.49
2015	Jun.	227.58	23.391608	745.32	132273.91
2015	TOTAL	2739.10	23.461703	8935.67	130881.32

2015	Jul.	228.86	23.523186	744.04	132045.05
2015	Aug.	230.14	23.655504	742.75	131814.91
2015	Sep.	213.44	23.788566	741.46	131583.47
2015	Oct.	232.74	23.922377	740.16	131350.73
2015	Nov.	234.05	24.056940	738.85	131116.68
2015	Dec.	235.37	24.192261	737.53	130881.32
2015	TOTAL	2739.10	23.461703	8935.67	130881.32

Year	Month	Principle	Prin/Pmt	Interest	Balance
2016	Jan.	236.69	24.328342	736.21	130644.63
2016	Feb.	238.02	24.465189	734.88	130406.60
2016	Mar.	239.36	24.602806	733.54	130167.24
2016	Apr.	240.71	24.741197	732.19	129926.56
2016	May	242.06	24.880366	730.84	129684.48
2016	Jun.	243.42	25.020318	729.48	129441.06
2016	Jul.	244.79	25.161057	728.11	129196.26
2016	Aug.	246.19	25.302588	726.73	128950.10
2016	Sep.	247.55	25.444915	725.34	128702.54
2016	Oct.	248.95	25.588043	723.95	128453.60
2016	Nov.	250.35	25.731976	722.55	128203.25
2016	Dec.	251.75	25.876718	721.14	127951.50
2016	TOTAL	2929.82	25.09593	8744.95	127951.50

Year	Month	Principle	Prin/Pmt	Interest	Balance
2017	Jan.	253.17	26.022274	719.73	127698.33
2017	Feb.	254.59	26.168650	718.30	127443.73
2017	Mar.	256.03	26.315848	716.87	127187.71
2017	Apr.	257.47	26.463875	715.43	126930.24
2017	May	258.91	26.612734	713.98	126671.33
2017	Jun.	260.37	26.762431	712.53	126410.96
2017	TOTAL	3133.81	26.842626	8540.95	124817.68

2017	Jul.	261.84	26.912970	711.06	126149.12
2017	Aug.	263.31	27.064355	709.59	125885.81
2017	Sep.	264.79	27.216592	708.11	125621.02
2017	Oct.	266.28	27.369685	706.62	125354.74
2017	Nov.	267.78	27.523640	705.12	125086.97
2017	Dec.	269.28	27.678460	703.61	124817.68
2017	TOTAL	3133.81	26.842626	8540.95	124817.68

Year	Month	Principle	Prin/Pmt	Interest	Balance
2018	Jan.	280.07	28.786864	692.83	122889.81
2018	Feb.	272.32	27.990719	700.58	124274.57
2018	Mar.	273.85	28.148167	699.04	124000.71
2018	Apr.	275.39	28.306500	697.50	123725.32
2018	May	276.94	28.465724	695.95	123448.38
2018	Jun.	278.50	28.625844	694.40	123169.88
2018	Jul.	280.07	28.786864	692.83	122889.81
2018	Aug.	281.64	28.948790	691.26	122608.17
2018	Sep.	283.23	29.111627	689.67	122324.94
2018	Oct.	284.82	29.275380	688.08	122040.12
2018	Nov.	286.42	29.440054	686.48	121753.70
2018	Dec.	288.03	29.605655	684.86	121465.67
2018	TOTAL	3352.01	28.711623	8322.75	121465.67

Year	Month	Principle	Prin/Pmt	Interest	Balance
2019	Jan.	289.65	29.772186	683.24	121176.02
2019	Feb.	291.28	29.939655	681.62	120884.74
2019	Mar.	292.92	90.108065	679.98	120591.81
2019	Apr.	294.57	30.277421	678.33	120297.25
2019	May	296.23	30.447734	676.67	120001.02
2019	Jun.	297.89	30.619002	675.01	119703.13
2019	TOTAL	3585.41	30.710754	8089.36	117880.26

2019	Jul.	299.57	30.791234	673.33	119403.56
2019	Aug.	301.25	30.964435	671.65	119102.31
2019	Sep.	302.95	31.138610	669.95	118799.36
2019	Oct.	30465	31.313765	668.25	118494.71
2019	Nov.	306.36	31489904	66.53	118188.35
2019	Dec.	308.09	31.667035	664.81	117880.25
2019	TOTAL	3585.41	30.710754	8089.36	117880.26

Year	Month	Principle	Prin/Pmt	Interest	Balance
2020	Jan.	309.82	31.845162	663.08	117570.44
2020	Feb.	311.56	32.024291	661.33	117258.88
2020	Mar.	313.32	32.204428	659.58	116945.56
2020	Apr.	315.08	32.385578	657.82	116630.48
2020	May	316.85	32.567747	656.05	116313.63
2020	Jun.	318.63	32.850940	654.26	115995.00
2020	Jul.	320.43	32.935164	652.47	115674.57
2020	Aug.	322.23	33.120425	650.67	115352.35
2020	Sep.	324.04	33.306727	648.86	115028.31
2020	Oct.	325.86	33.494077	647.03	114702.44
2020	Nov.	327.70	33.682482	645.20	114374.75
2020	Dec.	329.54	33.871945	643.36	114045.21
2020	TOTAL	3835.05	32.849081	7838.71	114045.21

Year	Month	Principle	Prin/Pmt	Interest	Balance
2021	Jan.	331.39	34.06475	641.50	113713.82
2021	Feb.	333.26	34.254077	639.64	113380.56
2021	Mar.	335.13	34.446756	637.77	113045.43
2021	Apr.	337.02	34640519	635.88	112708.41
2021	May	338.91	94.835372	633.98	112369.50
2021	Jun.	340.82	35.031321	632.08	112028.68
2021	TOTAL	4102.08	35.136294	7572.69	109943.13

2021	Jul.	342.74	35.228372	630.16	111685.94
2021	Aug.	344.66	35.426531	628.23	111341.28
2021	Sep.	346.60	35.625806	626.29	110994.68
2021	Oct.	348.55	35826204	624.35	110646.13
2021	Nov.	350.51	36.027723	622.38	110295.61
2021	Dec.	352.48	36.230379	620.41	109943.13
2021	TOTAL	4102.08	35.136294	7572.69	109943.13

Year	Month	Principle	Prin/Pmt	Interest	Balance
2022	Jan.	354.47	36.434175	618.43	109588.66
2022	Feb.	356.46	36.639117	616.44	109232.20
2022	Mar.	358.47	36.845212	614.43	108873.73
2022	Apr.	360.48	37.052437	612.41	108873.73
2022	May	362.51	37.260887	610.39	108150.74
2022	Jun.	364.55	37.470479	608.35	107786.19
2022	Jul.	366.60	37.681251	606.30	107419.59
2022	Aug.	368.66	37.893208	604.24	107050.93
2022	Sep.	370.74	38.106357	602.16	106680.20
2022	Oct.	372.82	38.320705	600.08	106307.37
2022	Nov.	374.92	38.536259	597.98	105932.46
2022	Dec.	377.03	38.753026	595.87	105555.43
2022	TOTAL	4387.70	37.582762	7287.01	105555.43

Year	Month	Principle	Prin/Pmt	Interest	Balance
2023	Jan.	379.15	38.971011	593.75	105176.28
2023	Feb.	381.28	39.190223	591.62	104795.00
2023	Mar.	383.43	39.410668	589.62	104795.00
2023	Apr.	385.58	39.632353	587.32	104025.99
2023	May	387.75	39.855285	585.15	103638.24
2023	Jun.	389.93	40.079471	582.97	103248.31
2023	TOTAL	4693.21	40.199572	6981.56	100862.22

2023	Jul.	392.13	40.304918	580.77	102856.18
2023	Aug.	394.33	40.531634	578.57	102461.85
2023	Sep.	396.55	40.759624	576.35	102065.30
2023	Oct.	398.78	40.988897	576.35	101666.52
2023	Nov.	401.02	41.219459	571.87	101265.50
2023	Dec.	403.28	41.451319	569.62	100862.22
2023	TOTAL	4693.21	40.199572	6981.56	100862.22

Year	Month	Principle	Prin/Pmt	Interest	Balance
2024	Jan.	405.55	41.684483	567.35	100456.68
2024	Feb.	407.83	41.918958	565.07	100048.85
2024	Mar.	410.12	42.154752	562.77	99638.73
2024	Apr.	412.43	42.391872	560.47	99226.30
2024	May	414.75	42.630327	558.15	98811.55
2024	Jun.	417.08	42.870122	555.81	98394.46
2024	Jul.	419.43	43.111267	553.47	97975.04
2024	Aug.	421.79	43.597633	548.74	97553.25
2024	Sep.	424.16	43.597633	548.74	97129.09
2024	Oct.	426.55	43.842869	546.35	96702.54
2024	Nov.	428.95	44.089485	543.95	96273.60
2024	Dec.	431.36	44.337489	541.54	95842.24
2024	TOTAL	5019.98	42.998585	6654.78	95842.24

Year	Month	Principle	Prin/Pmt	Interest	Balance
2025	Jan.	433.78	44.586887	539.11	95408.45
2025	Feb.	436.22	44.837688	536.67	94972.23
2025	Mar.	438.68	45.089900	534.22	94533.55
2025	Apr.	441.15	45.343531	531.75	94092.41
2025	May	443.63	45.598588	529.27	93648.75
2025	Jun.	446.12	45.855080	526.77	93202.66
2025	TOTAL	5369.52	45.992488	6305.25	90472.72

Year	Month	Principle	Prin/Pmt	Interest	Balance
2025	Jul.	448.63	46.113015	524.26	92754.02
2025	Aug.	451.16	46.372401	521.74	92302.87
2025	Sep.	453.69	46.633246	519.20	91849.17
2025	Oct.	456.25	46.895558	516.65	91392.12
2025	Nov.	458.81	47.159345	514.09	90934.12
2025	Dec.	461.39	47.42617	511.50	90472.72
2025	TOTAL	5369.52	45.992488	6305.25	90472.72

Year	Month	Principle	Prin/Pmt	Interest	Balance
2026	Jan.	463.99	47.691380	508.91	90008.74
2026	Feb.	466.60	47.959644	506.30	89542.14
2026	Mar.	469.22	48.229417	503.67	89072.91
2026	Apr.	469.22	48.229417	501.04	88601.05
2026	May	474.52	48.773524	498.38	88126.54
2026	Jun.	477.19	49.047875	495.71	87649.35
2026	Jul.	479.87	49.323769	493.03	87169.48
2026	Aug.	482.57	49.601216	490.33	85585.91
2026	Sep.	485.82	49.880222	487.61	85201.63
2026	Oct.	488.01	50.160799	484.88	85713.62
2026	Nov.	490.76	50.442953	482.14	85222.86
2026	Dec.	493.52	50.726695	479.38	84729.34
2026	TOTAL	5743.38	49.194850	5931.38	84729.34

Year	Month	Principle	Prin/Pmt	Interest	Balance
2027	Jan.	496.29	51.012032	476.60	84233.05
2027	Feb.	499.09	51.298975	473.81	83733.96
2027	Mar.	501.89	51.587532	471.00	83282.07
2027	Apr.	504.72	51.877712	468.18	82727.35
2027	May	507.56	52.169524	465.34	82219.79
2027	Jun.	510.41	52.462977	462.49	81709.38
2027	TOTAL	6143.28	52.620186	5531.48	78586.06

2027	Jul.	513.28	52.758082	459.62	81196.10
2027	Aug.	516.17	53.054846	456.73	50679.93
2027	Sep.	519.07	53.353279	453.82	80160.86
2027	Oct.	521.99	53.653392	450.90	79638.87
2027	Nov.	524.93	53.955192	447.97	79113.94
2027	Dec.	527.88	54.258690	445.02	78586.06
2027	TOTAL	6143.28	52.620186	5531.48	78586.06

Year	Month	Principle	Prin/Pmt	Interest	Balance
2028	Jan.	530.85	54.563895	442.05	78055.21
2028	Feb.	533.84	54.870817	439.06	77521.37
2028	Mar.	536.84	55.179465	436.06	76984.53
2028	Apr.	539.86	55.489850	433.04	76444.67
2028	May	542.90	55.801980	430.00	75355.83
2028	Jun.	545.95	56.115866	426.95	75355.83
2028	Jul.	549.02	56.431518	423.88	74806.80
2028	Aug.	552.11	56.748945	420.79	74254.70
2028	Sep.	555.21	57.068158	417.68	73141.14
2028	Oct.	558.34	57.389166	414.56	73141.14
2028	Nov.	561.48	57.711981	411.42	72015.03
2028	Dec.	564.64	58.036610	408.26	72015.03
2028	TOTAL	6571.03	56.284021	5103.74	72015.03

Year	Month	Principle	Prin/Pmt	Interest	Balance
2029	Jan.	567.81	58.363066	405.08	71447.22
2029	Feb.	571.01	58.691359	401.89	70876.21
2029	Mar.	574.22	59.021498	398.68	70301.99
2029	Apr.	577.45	59.353493	395.45	69724.54
2029	May	580.70	59.687357	392.20	69143.85
2029	Jun.	583.96	60.023098	388.93	68559.88
2029	TOTAL	7028.55	60.202961	4646.21	64986.47

2029	Jul.	587.25	60.36728	385.65	67972.64
2029	Aug.	590.55	60.700257	382.35	67382.08
2029	Sep.	593.87	61.041696	379.02	66788.21
2029	Oct.	597.21	64.385056	375.68	66191.00
2029	Nov.	600.57	61.730347	372.32	65590.43
2029	Dec.	603.95	62077580	368.95	64986.47
2029	TOTAL	7028.55	60.202961	4646.21	64986.47

Year	Month	Principle	Prin/Pmt	Interest	Balance
2030	Jan.	607.35	62.426766	365.55	64379.13
2030	Feb.	610.76	62.777917	362.13	63768.36
2030	Mar.	614.20	63.131043	358.70	63154.16
2030	Apr.	617.65	63.486155	355.24	62536.51
2030	May	621.13	63.202383	351.77	61915.38
2030	Jun.	624.62	64.202383	348.27	61290.75
2030	Jul.	628.14	64.563521	344.76	60662.62
2030	Aug.	631.67	64.926691	341.23	60030.95
2030	Sep.	635.22	65.291904	337.67	59395.72
2030	Oct.	638.80	65.659170	334.10	58756.93
2030	Nov.	642.39	66.028503	330.51	58114.54
2030	Dec.	646.00	66.399914	326.89	57468.54
2030	TOTAL	7517.94	64.394769	4156.83	57468.57

Year	Month	Principle	Prin/Pmt	Interest	Balance
2031	Jan.	649.64	66.773413	323.26	56818.90
2031	Feb.	653.29	67.149014	319.61	56165.61
2031	Mar.	656.97	67.526727	315.93	55508.64
2031	Apr.	660.66	67.906565	312.24	54847.98
2031	May	664.38	68.288539	308.52	54183.60
2031	Jun.	668.11	68.672662	304.78	53515.49
2031	TOTAL	8041.40	68.878444	3633.37	49427.14

2031	Jul.	671.87	69.058946	301.02	52843.62
2031	Aug.	675.65	69.447402	297.25	52167.97
2031	Sep.	679.45	69.838044	293.44	51488.51
2031	Oct.	683.27	70.230883	289.62	50805.24
2031	Nov.	687.12	70.625932	285.78	50118.12
2031	Dec.	690.98	71.023203	281.91	49427.14
2031	TOTAL	8041.40	68.878444	3633.37	49427.14

Year	Month	Principle	Prin/Pmt	Interest	Balance
2032	Jan.	694.87	71.422708	278.03	48732.27
2032	Feb.	698.78	71.824661	274.12	48033.49
2032	Mar.	702.66	72.634759	266.24	46624.12
2032	Apr.	706.66	72.634759	266.24	46624.12
2032	May	710.64	73.043329	262.26	45913.48
2032	Jun.	714.63	73.454198	258.26	45198.85
2032	Jul.	718.65	73.867378	254.24	44480.20
2032	Aug.	722.70	74.282882	250.20	43757.50
2032	Sep.	726.76	74.700723	246.14	43030.74
2032	Oct.	730.85	75.120915	242.05	42299.89
2032	Nov.	734.96	75.543470	237.94	41564.93
2032	Dec.	739.09	75.968402	233.80	40825.84
2032	TOTAL	8601.30	73.674308	3079.46	40825.84

Year	Month	Principle	Prin/Pmt	Interest	Balance
2033	Jan.	743.26	76.395724	229.65	40082.58
2033	Feb.	747.43	76.825450	225.46	39336.15
2033	Mar.	751.64	77.257593	221.26	38583.51
2033	Apr.	755.86	77.692167	217.03	37827.65
2033	May	760.12	78.129185	212.75	37067.53
2033	Jun.	764.39	78.568662	208.50	36303.14
2033	TOTAL	9200.19	79.804098	2474.57	31625.64

2033	Jul.	768.69	79.010677	204.21	35534.45
2033	Aug.	773.02	79.010611	204.21	35534.45
2033	Sep.	777.36	79.901980	195.53	33984.07
2033	Oct.	781.74	80.351429	191.16	33202.33
2033	Nov.	786.13	80.801406	186.76	32416.20
2033	Dec.	790.56	81.257925	182.34	31625.64
2033	TOTAL	9200.19	79.804098	2474.57	31625.64

Year	Month	Principle	Prin/Pmt	Interest	Balance
2034	Jan.	795.00	81.715001	177.89	30830.64
2034	Feb.	799.47	82.174647	173.42	30031.16
2034	Mar.	803.97	82.636880	168.93	29227.19
2034	Apr.	808.49	83.101712	164.40	28418.70
2034	May	813.04	83.569159	159.83	27605.66
2034	Jun.	817.62	84.039236	155.28	26788.04
2034	Jul.	822.21	84.511957	150.62	25965.83
2034	Aug.	826.84	84.987336	146.06	25138.99
2034	Sep.	831.49	85.465390	141.41	24307.50
2034	Oct.	836.17	85.946133	136.73	23471.33
2034	Nov.	840.87	86.429580	132.03	22630.46
2034	Dec.	845.60	86.915746	127.30	21784.86
2034	TOTAL	9840.75	84.291065	1833.98	21784.86

Year	Month	Principle	Prin/Pmt	Interest	Balance
2035	Jan.	850.36	87.40467	122.54	20934.50
2035	Feb.	855.14	87.896299	117.16	20079.36
2035	Mar.	859.95	88.390715	112.95	19219.41
2035	Apr.	864.79	88.887913	108.11	18354.62
2035	May	869.65	89.387908	103.24	17484.97
2035	Jun.	874.54	89.890715	98.35	16610.42
2035	TOTAL	10525.98	90.160078	1148.79	11258.88

2035	Jul.	879.46	90.396350	93.43	15730.96
2035	Aug.	884.41	90.904829	88.49	14846.55
2035	Sep.	889.39	91.416169	83.51	13957.17
2035	Oct.	894.39	91.930385	78.51	13062.78
2035	Nov.	899.42	92.447493	71.48	12163.36
2035	Dec.	904.48	92.967510	68.42	11258.88
2035	TOTAL	10525.98	90.160078	1148.79	11258.88

Year	Month	Principle	Prin/Pmt	Interest	Balance
2036	Jan.	909.57	93.490453	63.33	10349.31
2036	Feb.	914.68	94.016336	58.21	9434.63
2036	Mar.	919.83	94.545178	53.01	8514.80
2036	Apr.	925.00	95.076995	47.90	7589.80
2036	May	930.20	95.611803	42.69	6659.60
2036	Jun.	935.44	96.149619	37.46	5724.16
2036	Jul.	940.70	96.690461	32.20	4783.46
2036	Aug.	945.99	97.234345	26.91	3837.47
2036	Sep.	951.31	97.791288	21.59	2886.16
2036	Oct.	956.66	98.331308	16.23	1929.50
2036	Nov.	962.04	98.884421	10.85	967.46
2036	Dec.	967.46	99.440646	5.44	0.00
2036	TOTAL	11258.88	96.437738	415.89	0.00

WHERE THE FINAL SUMMARY IS

- Monthly Payment: $ 972.90

- Total Interest: $ 200,242.97 (No pre-payment)

- Total Interest: $ 200,242.97

- Average Interest each Month: $ 556.23

Full Amortization Table Based on 15 Years

FOR THE GIVEN VALUES

- Principal : $ 150,000

- Interest Rate : 6.75 percent

- Amortization Period : 15 years

- Starting month : Jan

- Starting year : 2007

The Prin/Pymt column shows the percentage of your regular payment that your principal payment is. Your monthly payment will be $ 1,327.36

Year	Month	Principle	Prin/Pmt	Interest	Balance
2007	Jan.	483.61	36.434175	843.75	149516.39
2007	Feb.	486.33	36.639117	841.75	149516.39
2007	Mar.	489.07	36.845212	838.29	148540.98
2007	Apr.	491.82	37.052467	835.54	148049.16
2007	May	494.59	37.260887	832.78	147554.57
2007	Jun.	497.37	37.470473	829.99	147057.20
2007	Jul.	500.17	37.681251	827.20	146557.04
2007	Aug.	502.98	37.681251	827.20	146557.04
2007	Sep.	505.81	38.106357	821.55	145548.24
2007	Oct.	508.66	38.320705	818.71	145039.59
2007	Nov.	511.52	38.536259	815.85	144528.07
2007	Dec.	514.39	38.753026	812.97	144013.68
2007	TOTAL	5986.32	37.582762	9942.05	144013.68

Year	Month	Principle	Prin/Pmt	Interest	Balance
2008	Jan.	517.29	38.971011	810.08	143496.39
2008	Feb.	520.20	39.190223	807.17	142976.19
2008	Mar.	523.12	39.410668	804.24	142453.07
2008	Apr.	526.07	39.632353	801.30	141927.01
2008	May	529.02	39.855285	798.34	141397.98
2008	Jun.	532.00	40.079471	795.36	140865.98
2008	Jul.	534.99	40.304918	792.37	140330.99
2008	Aug.	538.00	40.531634	789.36	139792.98
2008	Sep.	541.03	40.759624	786.34	139251.96
2008	Oct.	544.07	40.988897	783.29	138707.88
2008	Nov.	547.13	41.219459	780.23	138160.75
2008	Dec.	550.21	41.451319	777.15	137610.54
2008	TOTAL	6403.14	40.199572	9525.23	137610.54

Year	Month	Principle	Prin/Pmt	Interest	Balance
2009	Jan.	553.30	41.684483	774.06	137057.24
2009	Feb.	556.42	41.918958	770.95	136500.82
2009	Mar.	559.55	42.154752	767.82	135941.27
2009	Apr.	562.69	42.391872	764.67	135378.58
2009	May	565.86	42.630327	761.50	134812.72
2009	Jun.	569.04	42.870122	758.32	134243.68
2009	Jul.	572.24	43.111267	755.12	133671.43
2009	Aug.	575.46	43.353768	751.90	133095.91
2009	Sep.	578.70	43.597633	748.66	132517.27
2009	Oct.	581.95	43.842869	745.41	131935.32
2009	Nov.	585.23	44.089485	742.14	131350.09
2009	Dec.	588.52	44.337489	738.84	130761.57
2009	TOTAL	6848.97	42.998585	9079.40	130761.57

Year	Month	Principle	Prin/Pmt	Interest	Balance
2010	Jan.	591.83	44.586887	735.53	130169.74
2010	Feb.	595.16	44.837688	732.20	129574.58
2010	Mar.	598.51	45.089900	728.86	128976.07
2010	Apr.	601.84	45.343531	725.49	128374.20
2010	May	605.26	45.598588	722.10	127768.94
2010	Jun.	608.66	45.855050	718.70	127160.27
2010	Jul.	612.09	46.113015	715.28	126548.19
2010	Aug.	615.53	46.372401	711.83	125935.66
2010	Sep.	618.99	46.633246	708.37	125313.66
2010	Oct.	622.47	46.895558	704.89	124691.19
2010	Nov.	625.98	48.159345	701.39	124065.21
2010	Dec.	629.50	47.424617	697.87	123435.71
2010	TOTAL	7325.85	45.992488	8602.52	123435.71

Year	Month	Principle	Prin/Pmt	Interest	Balance
2011	Jan.	633.04	47.691380	694.33	122802.68
2011	Feb.	636.60	47.959644	690.77	122166.08
2011	Mar.	640.18	48.229417	687.18	121525.90
2011	Apr.	643.78	48.500707	683.58	120882.12
2011	May	647.40	48.773524	679.96	120234.71
2011	Jun.	651.04	49.047875	676.32	119583.67
2011	Jul.	654.71	49.323769	682.66	118928.96
2011	Aug.	658.39	49.601216	668.98	118270.57
2011	Sep.	662.09	49.880222	665.27	117608.48
2011	Oct.	665.82	50.160799	661.55	116942.67
2011	Nov.	669.36	50.442953	657.80	116273.10
2011	Dec.	673.33	50.726695	654.04	115599.78
2011	TOTAL	7835.94	49.194850	8092.43	115599.78

Year	Month	Principle	Prin/Pmt	Interest	Balance
2012	Jan.	677.12	51.012032	650.25	114922.66
2012	Feb.	680.92	51.298975	646.44	114241.74
2012	Mar.	684.75	51.587532	642.61	113556.98
2012	Apr.	688.61	51.877712	638.76	112868.38
2012	May	692.48	52.169524	634.88	112175.90
2012	Jun.	696.37	52.462977	630.99	111479.52
2012	Jul.	700.29	52.758082	627.07	110075.00
2012	Aug.	704.23	53.054846	623.13	110075.00
2012	Sep.	708.19	53.353279	619.17	109366.81
2012	Oct.	712.18	53.653392	615.19	108654.63
2012	Nov.	716.18	53955192	611.18	107938.45
2012	Dec.	720..21	54.258690	607.15	107218.24
2012	TOTAL	881.34	52.620186	7546.83	107218.24

Year	Month	Principle	Prin/Pmt	Interest	Balance
2013	Jan.	724.26	54.563895	603.10	106493.98
2013	Feb.	728.34	54.870817	599.03	105765.64
2013	Mar.	732.43	55.179465	594.93	105033.21
2013	Apr.	736.55	55.489850	590.81	104296.66
2013	May	740.70	55.801980	586.67	103555.96
2013	Jun.	744.86	56.115866	582.50	102811.10
2013	Jul.	749.05	56.431518	578.31	102062.05
2013	Aug.	753.27	56.748945	574.10	101308.78
2013	Sep.	757.27	56.748945	574.10	100551.28
2013	Oct.	761.76	57.389166	565.60	99789.52
2013	Nov.	766.05	57.711981	561.32	99023.47
2013	Dec.	770.36	58.036610	557.01	98253.11
2013	TOTAL	8965.13	56.284021	6963.24	98253.11

Year	Month	Principle	Prin/Pmt	Interest	Balance
2014	Jan.	774.69	58.363066	552.67	97478.42
2014	Feb.	779.05	58.691359	548.32	96699.97
2014	Mar.	783.43	59.021498	543.93	95915.94
2014	Apr.	787.84	59.353493	539.53	95128.11
2014	May	792.27	59.687357	535.10	94335.84
2014	Jun.	796.73	60.023098	530.64	93539.11
2014	Jul.	801.21	60.360728	526.16	92737.90
2014	Aug.	805.71	60.700257	521.65	91932.19
2014	Sep.	810.25	61.041696	517.12	91121.95
2014	Oct.	814.80	61.385056	512.56	90307.14
2014	Nov.	819.39	61.730347	507.98	89487.76
2014	Dec.	824.00	62.077580	503.37	88663.76
2014	TOTAL	9589.35	60.202961	6339.02	88663.76

Year	Month	Principle	Prin/Pmt	Interest	Balance
2015	Jan.	828.63	62.426766	498.73	87835.13
2015	Feb.	833.29	62.777917	494.07	87001.84
2015	Mar.	837.98	63.131043	489.39	86163.86
2015	Apr.	842.69	63.486155	484.67	85321.17
2015	May	847.43	63.843264	479.93	84473.73
2015	Jun.	852.20	64.202383	475.16	83621.53
2015	Jul.	856.99	64.563521	470.37	82764.54
2015	Aug.	861.81	64.926691	465.55	81902.73
2015	Sep.	866.66	65.291904	460.70	81036.07
2015	Oct.	871.56	65.659170	455.83	80164.53
2015	Nov.	876.44	66.028503	450.93	79288.09
2015	Dec.	881.37	66.399914	446.00	78406.72
2015	TOTAL	10257.04	64.394769	5671.33	78406.72

Year	Month	Principle	Prin/Pmt	Interest	Balance
2016	Jan.	886.33	66.773413	441.04	77520.40
2016	Feb.	890.31	67.149014	436.05	76629.08
2016	Mar.	896.33	67.526727	431.04	75732.76
2016	Apr.	901.37	67.906565	426.00	74831.39
2016	May	906.44	68.288539	420.93	73924.95
2016	Jun.	911.54	68.288539	420.93	73924.95
2016	Jul.	916.66	69.058946	410.70	72096.75
2016	Aug.	921.82	69.447402	405.54	71174.93
2016	Sep.	927.01	69.838044	400.36	70247.93
2016	Oct.	932.22	70.625932	389.90	68378.25
2016	Nov.	937.46	70.625932	389.90	68378.25
2016	Dec.	942.74	71.023203	384.63	67435.51
2016	TOTAL	10971.21	68.878444	4957.16	67435.51

Year	Month	Principle	Prin/Pmt	Interest	Balance
2017	Jan.	948.04	71.422708	379.32	66487.47
2017	Feb.	953.37	71.824461	373.99	65534.10
2017	Mar.	958.73	72.228473	368.63	64575.36
2017	Apr.	964.13	72.634759	363.24	63611.23
2017	May	969.55	73.043329	357.81	62641.68
2017	Jun.	975.00	73.454198	352.36	61666.68
2017	Jul.	980.49	73.867378	346.88	60686.19
2017	Aug.	986.00	74.282882	341.36	59700.19
2017	Sep.	991.55	74.700723	335.81	58708.64
2017	Oct.	997.13	75.120915	330.24	57711.51
2017	Nov.	1002.74	75.543470	324.63	56708.77
2017	Dec.	1008.38	75.968402	318.99	55700.39
2017	TOTAL	11735.12	73.674308	4193.25	55700.39

Year	Month	Principle	Prin/Pmt	Interest	Balance
2018	Jan.	1014.05	76.395724	313.31	54686.34
2018	Feb.	1019.75	76.825450	307.61	53666.59
2018	Mar.	1025.49	77.257593	301.87	52641.10
2018	Apr.	1031.06	77.692167	296.11	51609.84
2018	May	1037.06	78.129185	290.31	50572.78
2018	Jun.	1042.89	78.568662	284.47	49529.89
2018	Jul.	1048.76	79.010611	287.61	48481.13
2018	Aug.	1054.66	79.455046	272.71	46365.88
2018	Sep.	1060.59	79.901980	266.77	46365.88
2018	Oct.	1066.56	80.351429	260.81	45299.33
2018	Nov.	1072.56	80.803406	254.81	44226.77
2018	Dec.	1078.59	81.257925	248.78	43148.18
2018	TOTAL	12552.21	78.804098	3376.16	43148.18

Year	Month	Principle	Prin/Pmt	Interest	Balance
2019	Jan.	1084.66	81.715001	242.71	42063.53
2019	Feb.	1090.76	82174647	236.61	40972.77
2019	Mar.	1096.89	82.636880	230.47	39875.88
2019	Apr.	1103.06	83.101712	224.30	38772.82
2019	May	1109.27	83.569159	218.10	37663.55
2019	Jun.	1115.51	84.039236	211.86	36548.04
2019	Jul.	1121.78	84.511957	205.58	35426.26
2019	Aug.	1128.09	84.987336	199.27	34298.17
2019	Sep.	1134.44	85.465390	192.93	33163.73
2019	Oct.	1140.82	85.946133	186.55	32022.91
2019	Nov.	1147.24	86.429580	180.13	30875.68
2019	Dec.	1153.69	86.915746	173.68	29721.99
2019	TOTAL	13426.19	84.291065	2502.18	29721.99

Year	Month	Principle	Prin/Pmt	Interest	Balance
2020	Jan.	1160.18	87.404647	167.19	28561.81
2020	Feb.	1166.70	87.896299	160.66	27395.11
2020	Mar.	1179.27	88.390715	154.10	26221.84
2020	Apr.	1179.87	88.887913	147.50	25041.98
2020	May	1186.50	89.387908	140.86	23855.47
2020	Jun.	1193.18	89.890715	134.19	22662.30
2020	Jul.	1199.89	90.396350	127.48	21462.41
2020	Aug.	1206.64	90.904829	120.73	20255.77
2020	Sep.	1213.43	91.416169	113.94	19042.34
2020	Oct.	1220.25	91.930385	107.11	17822.09
2020	Nov.	1227.11	92.447493	100.25	16594.98
2020	Dec.	1234.02	92.967510	93.35	15360.96
2020	TOTAL	14361.03	90.160075	1567.34	15360.96

Year	Month	Principle	Prin/Pmt	Interest	Balance
2021	Jan.	1240.96	93.490453	86.41	14120.00
2021	Feb.	1247.94	94.016336	79.43	12872.06
2021	Mar.	1254.96	94.545178	72.41	11617.10
2021	Apr.	1262.02	95.076995	65.35	10355.09
2021	May	1269.12	95.611803	58.25	9085.97
2021	Jun.	1276.26	96.149619	51.11	7809.71
2021	Jul.	1283.43	96.690461	43.93	6526.28
2021	Aug.	1290.65	97.234345	36.71	5235.62
2021	Sep.	1297.91	97.781288	29.45	3937.71
2021	Oct.	1305.21	98.331308	22.15	2632.50
2021	Nov.	1312.56	98.884421	14.81	1319.94
2021	Dec.	1319.94	99.440646	7.42	0.00
2021	TOTAL	15360.96	96.437738	567.41	0.00

WHERE THE FINAL SUMMARY IS

- Monthly Payment: $ 1,327.36

- Total Interest: $ 88,925.55

- Average Interest each Month: $ 494.03

Comparing 15, 20, 30-year charts

When working out the details of your mortgage, you should compare what you can afford with terms of the loan. Below are three tables to consider. The loan amount is $375,000. It shows the difference in payments based on a 15, 20, and 30 year mortgage.

Based on 15 years at 7 percent interest, the payments would be $4354.07.

Month	Loan Balance	Interest	Principal	Total Interest
Sep 2006	373,816.89	2,187.50	1,183.11	2,187.50
Oct 2006	372,626.89	2,180.60	1,190.01	4,368.10
Nov 2006	371,429.94	2,173.66	1,196.95	6,541.76
Dec 2006	370,226.01	2,166.67	1,203.93	8,708.43
Month	Loan Balance	Interest	Principal	Total Interest
Jan 2007	369,015.05	2,159.65	1,210.95	10,868.08
Feb 2007	367,797.03	2,152.59	1,218.02	13,020.67
Mar 2007	366,571.91	2,145.48	1,225.12	15,166.15
Apr 2007	365,339.64	2,138.34	1,232.27	17,304.49
May 2007	364,100.18	2,131.15	1,239.46	19,435.64
Jun 2007	362,853.49	2,123.92	1,246.69	21,559.55
Jul 2007	361,599.53	2,116.65	1,253.96	23,676.20
Aug 2007	360,338.26	2,109.33	1,261.28	25,785.53
Sep 2007	359,069.62	2,101.97	1,268.63	27,887.50
Oct 2007	357,793.59	2,094.57	1,276.03	29,982.08

Nov 2007	356,510.12	2,087.13	1,283.48	32,069.21
Dec 2007	355,219.15	2,079.64	1,290.96	34,148.85
Month	Loan Balance	Interest	Principal	Total Interest
Jan 2008	353,920.66	2,072.11	1,298.49	36,220.96
Feb 2008	352,614.59	2,064.54	1,306.07	38,285.50
Mar 2008	351,300.90	2,056.92	1,313.69	40,342.42
Apr 2008	349,979.55	2,049.26	1,321.35	42,391.67
May 2008	348,650.49	2,041.55	1,329.06	44,433.22
Jun 2008	347,313.68	2,033.79	1,336.81	46,467.01
Jul 2008	345,969.07	2,026.00	1,344.61	48,493.01
Aug 2008	344,616.62	2,018.15	1,352.45	50,511.16
Sep 2008	343,256.27	2,010.26	1,360.34	52,521.43
Oct 2008	341,888.00	2,002.33	1,368.28	54,523.75
Nov 2008	340,511.74	1,994.35	1,376.26	56,518.10
Dec 2008	339,127.45	1,986.32	1,384.29	58,504.42
Month	Loan Balance	Interest	Principal	Total Interest
Jan 2009	337,735.09	1,978.24	1,392.36	60,482.66
Feb 2009	336,334.60	1,970.12	1,400.48	62,452.78
Mar 2009	334,925.95	1,961.95	1,408.65	64,414.74
Apr 2009	333,509.08	1,953.73	1,416.87	66,368.47
May 2009	332,083.94	1,945.47	1,425.14	68,313.94
Jun 2009	330,650.49	1,937.16	1,433.45	70,251.10
Jul 2009	329,208.68	1,928.79	1,441.81	72,179.89
Aug 2009	327,758.46	1,920.38	1,450.22	74,100.27
Sep 2009	326,299.78	1,911.92	1,458.68	76,012.20
Oct 2009	324,832.59	1,903.42	1,467.19	77,915.61
Nov 2009	323,356.84	1,894.86	1,475.75	79,810.47
Dec 2009	321,872.48	1,886.25	1,484.36	81,696.72
Month	Loan Balance	Interest	Principal	Total Interest
Jan 2010	320,379.46	1,877.59	1,493.02	83,574.31
Feb 2010	318,877.74	1,868.88	1,501.73	85,443.19
Mar 2010	317,367.25	1,860.12	1,510.49	87,303.31

Month	Loan Balance	Interest	Principal	Total Interest
Apr 2010	315,847.95	1,851.31	1,519.30	89,154.62
May 2010	314,319.79	1,842.45	1,528.16	90,997.06
Jun 2010	312,782.72	1,833.53	1,537.07	92,830.60
Jul 2010	311,236.68	1,824.57	1,546.04	94,655.16
Aug 2010	309,681.62	1,815.55	1,555.06	96,470.71
Sep 2010	308,117.49	1,806.48	1,564.13	98,277.19
Oct 2010	306,544.24	1,797.35	1,573.25	100,074.54
Nov 2010	304,961.81	1,788.17	1,582.43	101,862.71
Dec 2010	303,370.14	1,778.94	1,591.66	103,641.66
Month	Loan Balance	Interest	Principal	Total Interest
Jan 2011	301,769.20	1,769.66	1,600.95	105,411.32
Feb 2011	300,158.91	1,760.32	1,610.29	107,171.64
Mar 2011	298,539.23	1,750.93	1,619.68	108,922.56
Apr 2011	296,910.10	1,741.48	1,629.13	110,664.04
May 2011	295,271.47	1,731.98	1,638.63	112,396.02
Jun 2011	293,623.29	1,722.42	1,648.19	114,118.43
Jul 2011	291,965.48	1,712.80	1,657.80	115,831.24
Aug 2011	290,298.01	1,703.13	1,667.47	117,534.37
Sep 2011	288,620.81	1,693.41	1,677.20	119,227.77
Oct 2011	286,933.82	1,683.62	1,686.98	120,911.40
Nov 2011	285,237.00	1,673.78	1,696.83	122,585.18
Dec 2011	283,530.27	1,663.88	1,706.72	124,249.06
Month	Loan Balance	Interest	Principal	Total Interest
Jan 2012	281,813.59	1,653.93	1,716.68	125,902.99
Feb 2012	280,086.90	1,643.91	1,726.69	127,546.90
Mar 2012	278,350.13	1,633.84	1,736.77	129,180.74
Apr 2012	276,603.24	1,623.71	1,746.90	130,804.45
May 2012	274,846.15	1,613.52	1,757.09	132,417.97
Jun 2012	273,078.81	1,603.27	1,767.34	134,021.24
Jul 2012	271,301.17	1,592.96	1,777.65	135,614.19
Aug 2012	269,513.15	1,582.59	1,788.02	137,196.79
Sep 2012	267,714.71	1,572.16	1,798.45	138,768.95

Oct 2012	265,905.77	1,561.67	1,808.94	140,330.61
Nov 2012	264,086.28	1,551.12	1,819.49	141,881.73
Dec 2012	262,256.18	1,540.50	1,830.10	143,422.23
Month	Loan Balance	Interest	Principal	Total Interest
Jan 2013	260,415.40	1,529.83	1,840.78	144,952.06
Feb 2013	258,563.88	1,519.09	1,851.52	146,471.15
Mar 2013	256,701.57	1,508.29	1,862.32	147,979.44
Apr 2013	254,828.39	1,497.43	1,873.18	149,476.87
May 2013	252,944.28	1,486.50	1,884.11	150,963.37
Jun 2013	251,049.18	1,475.51	1,895.10	152,438.87
Jul 2013	249,143.03	1,464.45	1,906.15	153,903.33
Aug 2013	247,225.76	1,453.33	1,917.27	155,356.66
Sep 2013	245,297.30	1,442.15	1,928.46	156,798.81
Oct 2013	243,357.60	1,430.90	1,939.71	158,229.71
Nov 2013	241,406.58	1,419.59	1,951.02	159,649.30
Dec 2013	239,444.17	1,408.21	1,962.40	161,057.50
Month	Loan Balance	Interest	Principal	Total Interest
Jan 2014	237,470.33	1,396.76	1,973.85	162,454.26
Feb 2014	235,484.96	1,385.24	1,985.36	163,839.51
Mar 2014	233,488.02	1,373.66	1,996.94	165,213.17
Apr 2014	231,479.43	1,362.01	2,008.59	166,575.18
May 2014	229,459.12	1,350.30	2,020.31	167,925.48
Jun 2014	227,427.02	1,338.51	2,032.09	169,263.99
Jul 2014	225,383.08	1,326.66	2,043.95	170,590.65
Aug 2014	223,327.20	1,314.73	2,055.87	171,905.38
Sep 2014	221,259.34	1,302.74	2,067.86	173,208.12
Oct 2014	219,179.41	1,290.68	2,079.93	174,498.80
Nov 2014	217,087.35	1,278.55	2,092.06	175,777.35
Dec 2014	214,983.09	1,266.34	2,104.26	177,043.69
Month	Loan Balance	Interest	Principal	Total Interest
Jan 2015	212,866.55	1,254.07	2,116.54	178,297.76
Feb 2015	210,737.67	1,241.72	2,128.88	179,539.48

Month	Loan Balance	Interest	Principal	Total Interest
Mar 2015	208,596.37	1,229.30	2,141.30	180,768.79
Apr 2015	206,442.57	1,216.81	2,153.79	181,985.60
May 2015	204,276.21	1,204.25	2,166.36	183,189.85
Jun 2015	202,097.22	1,191.61	2,178.99	184,381.46
Jul 2015	199,905.51	1,178.90	2,191.71	185,560.36
Aug 2015	197,701.02	1,166.12	2,204.49	186,726.47
Sep 2015	195,483.67	1,153.26	2,217.35	187,879.73
Oct 2015	193,253.39	1,140.32	2,230.28	189,020.05
Nov 2015	191,010.09	1,127.31	2,243.29	190,147.36
Dec 2015	188,753.71	1,114.23	2,256.38	191,261.59
Month	Loan Balance	Interest	Principal	Total Interest
Jan 2016	186,484.17	1,101.06	2,269.54	192,362.65
Feb 2016	184,201.39	1,087.82	2,282.78	193,450.48
Mar 2016	181,905.29	1,074.51	2,296.10	194,524.98
Apr 2016	179,595.80	1,061.11	2,309.49	195,586.10
May 2016	177,272.84	1,047.64	2,322.96	196,633.74
Jun 2016	174,936.32	1,034.09	2,336.51	197,667.83
Jul 2016	172,586.18	1,020.46	2,350.14	198,688.29
Aug 2016	170,222.32	1,006.75	2,363.85	199,695.05
Sep 2016	167,844.68	992.96	2,377.64	200,688.01
Oct 2016	165,453.17	979.09	2,391.51	201,667.10
Nov 2016	163,047.71	965.14	2,405.46	202,632.25
Dec 2016	160,628.21	951.11	2,419.49	203,583.36
Month	Loan Balance	Interest	Principal	Total Interest
Jan 2017	158,194.60	937.00	2,433.61	204,520.36
Feb 2017	155,746.80	922.80	2,447.80	205,443.16
Mar 2017	153,284.72	908.52	2,462.08	206,351.68
Apr 2017	150,808.27	894.16	2,476.45	207,245.84
May 2017	148,317.38	879.71	2,490.89	208,125.56
Jun 2017	145,811.96	865.18	2,505.42	208,990.74
Jul 2017	143,291.92	850.57	2,520.04	209,841.31
Aug 2017	140,757.19	835.87	2,534.74	210,677.18

Month	Loan Balance	Interest	Principal	Total Interest
Sep 2017	138,207.66	821.08	2,549.52	211,498.26
Oct 2017	135,643.27	806.21	2,564.39	212,304.48
Nov 2017	133,063.92	791.25	2,579.35	213,095.73
Dec 2017	130,469.52	776.21	2,594.40	213,871.93
Month	Loan Balance	Interest	Principal	Total Interest
Jan 2018	127,859.98	761.07	2,609.53	214,633.01
Feb 2018	125,235.23	745.85	2,624.76	215,378.86
Mar 2018	122,595.16	730.54	2,640.07	216,109.40
Apr 2018	119,939.69	715.14	2,655.47	216,824.53
May 2018	117,268.73	699.65	2,670.96	217,524.18
Jun 2018	114,582.19	684.07	2,686.54	218,208.25
Jul 2018	111,879.98	668.40	2,702.21	218,876.65
Aug 2018	109,162.01	652.63	2,717.97	219,529.28
Sep 2018	106,428.18	636.78	2,733.83	220,166.06
Oct 2018	103,678.41	620.83	2,749.77	220,786.89
Nov 2018	100,912.59	604.79	2,765.82	221,391.68
Dec 2018	98,130.64	588.66	2,781.95	221,980.34
Month	Loan Balance	Interest	Principal	Total Interest
Jan 2019	95,332.47	572.43	2,798.18	222,552.76
Feb 2019	92,517.97	556.11	2,814.50	223,108.87
Mar 2019	89,687.05	539.69	2,830.92	223,648.56
Apr 2019	86,839.62	523.17	2,847.43	224,171.73
May 2019	83,975.58	506.56	2,864.04	224,678.30
Jun 2019	81,094.83	489.86	2,880.75	225,168.16
Jul 2019	78,197.28	473.05	2,897.55	225,641.21
Aug 2019	75,282.82	456.15	2,914.46	226,097.36
Sep 2019	72,351.36	439.15	2,931.46	226,536.51
Oct 2019	69,402.81	422.05	2,948.56	226,958.56
Nov 2019	66,437.05	404.85	2,965.76	227,363.41
Dec 2019	63,453.99	387.55	2,983.06	227,750.96
Month	Loan Balance	Interest	Principal	Total Interest
Jan 2020	60,453.54	370.15	3,000.46	228,121.11

Feb 2020	57,435.58	352.65	3,017.96	228,473.75
Mar 2020	54,400.01	335.04	3,035.57	228,808.79
Apr 2020	51,346.74	317.33	3,053.27	229,126.13
May 2020	48,275.66	299.52	3,071.08	229,425.65
Jun 2020	45,186.66	281.61	3,089.00	229,707.26
Jul 2020	42,079.64	263.59	3,107.02	229,970.85
Aug 2020	38,954.50	245.46	3,125.14	230,216.31
Sep 2020	35,811.13	227.23	3,143.37	230,443.54
Oct 2020	32,649.42	208.90	3,161.71	230,652.44
Nov 2020	29,469.27	190.45	3,180.15	230,842.90
Dec 2020	26,270.57	171.90	3,198.70	231,014.80
Month	Loan Balance	Interest	Principal	Total Interest
Jan 2021	23,053.21	153.24	3,217.36	231,168.05
Feb 2021	19,817.08	134.48	3,236.13	231,302.52
Mar 2021	16,562.07	115.60	3,255.01	231,418.12
Apr 2021	13,288.08	96.61	3,273.99	231,514.74
May 2021	9,994.98	77.51	3,293.09	231,592.25
Jun 2021	6,682.68	58.30	3,312.30	231,650.55
Jul 2021	3,351.06	38.98	3,331.62	231,689.54
Aug 2021	0.00	19.55	3,351.06	231,709.08

Based on 20 years at 7 percent interest, the payments would be $2907.37.

Month	Loan Balance	Interest	Principal	Total Interest
Sep 2006	374,280.13	2,187.50	719.87	2,187.50
Oct 2006	373,556.06	2,183.30	724.07	4,370.80
Nov 2006	372,827.76	2,179.08	728.29	6,549.88
Dec 2006	372,095.22	2,174.83	732.54	8,724.71
Month	Loan Balance	Interest	Principal	Total Interest
Jan 2007	371,358.41	2,170.56	736.82	10,895.26
Feb 2007	370,617.29	2,166.26	741.11	13,061.52
Mar 2007	369,871.86	2,161.93	745.44	15,223.45

Apr 2007	369,122.07	2,157.59	749.79	17,381.04
May 2007	368,367.91	2,153.21	754.16	19,534.25
Jun 2007	367,609.35	2,148.81	758.56	21,683.06
Jul 2007	366,846.37	2,144.39	762.98	23,827.45
Aug 2007	366,078.94	2,139.94	767.43	25,967.39
Sep 2007	365,307.03	2,135.46	771.91	28,102.85
Oct 2007	364,530.61	2,130.96	776.41	30,233.81
Nov 2007	363,749.67	2,126.43	780.94	32,360.24
Dec 2007	362,964.17	2,121.87	785.50	34,482.11
Month	Loan Balance	Interest	Principal	Total Interest
Jan 2008	362,174.09	2,117.29	790.08	36,599.40
Feb 2008	361,379.40	2,112.68	794.69	38,712.08
Mar 2008	360,580.08	2,108.05	799.32	40,820.13
Apr 2008	359,776.09	2,103.38	803.99	42,923.51
May 2008	358,967.42	2,098.69	808.68	45,022.21
Jun 2008	358,154.02	2,093.98	813.39	47,116.18
Jul 2008	357,335.88	2,089.23	818.14	49,205.42
Aug 2008	356,512.97	2,084.46	822.91	51,289.87
Sep 2008	355,685.26	2,079.66	827.71	53,369.53
Oct 2008	354,852.72	2,074.83	832.54	55,444.36
Nov 2008	354,015.32	2,069.97	837.40	57,514.34
Dec 2008	353,173.04	2,065.09	842.28	59,579.43
Month	Loan Balance	Interest	Principal	Total Interest
Jan 2009	352,325.84	2,060.18	847.19	61,639.60
Feb 2009	351,473.71	2,055.23	852.14	63,694.84
Mar 2009	350,616.60	2,050.26	857.11	65,745.10
Apr 2009	349,754.49	2,045.26	862.11	67,790.36
May 2009	348,887.36	2,040.23	867.14	69,830.60
Jun 2009	348,015.16	2,035.18	872.19	71,865.78
Jul 2009	347,137.88	2,030.09	877.28	73,895.86
Aug 2009	346,255.48	2,024.97	882.40	75,920.83
Sep 2009	345,367.93	2,019.82	887.55	77,940.66

Oct 2009	344,475.21	2,014.65	892.72	79,955.30
Nov 2009	343,577.27	2,009.44	897.93	81,964.74
Dec 2009	342,674.10	2,004.20	903.17	83,968.94
Month	Loan Balance	Interest	Principal	Total Interest
Jan 2010	341,765.66	1,998.93	908.44	85,967.88
Feb 2010	340,851.93	1,993.63	913.74	87,961.51
Mar 2010	339,932.86	1,988.30	919.07	89,949.81
Apr 2010	339,008.43	1,982.94	924.43	91,932.75
May 2010	338,078.61	1,977.55	929.82	93,910.30
Jun 2010	337,143.36	1,972.13	935.25	95,882.43
Jul 2010	336,202.66	1,966.67	940.70	97,849.10
Aug 2010	335,256.47	1,961.18	946.19	99,810.28
Sep 2010	334,304.76	1,955.66	951.71	101,765.94
Oct 2010	333,347.50	1,950.11	957.26	103,716.05
Nov 2010	332,384.66	1,944.53	962.84	105,660.58
Dec 2010	331,416.20	1,938.91	968.46	107,599.49
Month	Loan Balance	Interest	Principal	Total Interest
Jan 2011	330,442.09	1,933.26	974.11	109,532.75
Feb 2011	329,462.30	1,927.58	979.79	111,460.33
Mar 2011	328,476.79	1,921.86	985.51	113,382.20
Apr 2011	327,485.53	1,916.11	991.26	115,298.31
May 2011	326,488.49	1,910.33	997.04	117,208.64
Jun 2011	325,485.64	1,904.52	1,002.85	119,113.16
Jul 2011	324,476.93	1,898.67	1,008.70	121,011.82
Aug 2011	323,462.35	1,892.78	1,014.59	122,904.61
Sep 2011	322,441.84	1,886.86	1,020.51	124,791.47
Oct 2011	321,415.38	1,880.91	1,026.46	126,672.38
Nov 2011	320,382.93	1,874.92	1,032.45	128,547.30
Dec 2011	319,344.46	1,868.90	1,038.47	130,416.20
Month	Loan Balance	Interest	Principal	Total Interest
Jan 2012	318,299.93	1,862.84	1,044.53	132,279.05
Feb 2012	317,249.31	1,856.75	1,050.62	134,135.80

Month	Loan Balance	Interest	Principal	Total Interest
Mar 2012	316,192.56	1,850.62	1,056.75	135,986.42
Apr 2012	315,129.65	1,844.46	1,062.91	137,830.87
May 2012	314,060.53	1,838.26	1,069.11	139,669.13
Jun 2012	312,985.18	1,832.02	1,075.35	141,501.15
Jul 2012	311,903.56	1,825.75	1,081.62	143,326.90
Aug 2012	310,815.62	1,819.44	1,087.93	145,146.33
Sep 2012	309,721.34	1,813.09	1,094.28	146,959.43
Oct 2012	308,620.68	1,806.71	1,100.66	148,766.13
Nov 2012	307,513.60	1,800.29	1,107.08	150,566.42
Dec 2012	306,400.05	1,793.83	1,113.54	152,360.25
Month	Loan Balance	Interest	Principal	Total Interest
Jan 2013	305,280.02	1,787.33	1,120.04	154,147.58
Feb 2013	304,153.45	1,780.80	1,126.57	155,928.38
Mar 2013	303,020.30	1,774.23	1,133.14	157,702.61
Apr 2013	301,880.55	1,767.62	1,139.75	159,470.23
May 2013	300,734.15	1,760.97	1,146.40	161,231.20
Jun 2013	299,581.06	1,754.28	1,153.09	162,985.48
Jul 2013	298,421.25	1,747.56	1,159.81	164,733.04
Aug 2013	297,254.67	1,740.79	1,166.58	166,473.83
Sep 2013	296,081.28	1,733.99	1,173.39	168,207.82
Oct 2013	294,901.05	1,727.14	1,180.23	169,934.96
Nov 2013	293,713.93	1,720.26	1,187.11	171,655.21
Dec 2013	292,519.89	1,713.33	1,194.04	173,368.54
Month	Loan Balance	Interest	Principal	Total Interest
Jan 2014	291,318.89	1,706.37	1,201.00	175,074.91
Feb 2014	290,110.88	1,699.36	1,208.01	176,774.27
Mar 2014	288,895.82	1,692.31	1,215.06	178,466.58
Apr 2014	287,673.68	1,685.23	1,222.15	180,151.81
May 2014	286,444.40	1,678.10	1,229.27	181,829.91
Jun 2014	285,207.96	1,670.93	1,236.45	183,500.83
Jul 2014	283,964.30	1,663.71	1,243.66	185,164.54
Aug 2014	282,713.39	1,656.46	1,250.91	186,821.00

Sep 2014	281,455.18	1,649.16	1,258.21	188,470.16
Oct 2014	280,189.63	1,641.82	1,265.55	190,111.99
Nov 2014	278,916.70	1,634.44	1,272.93	191,746.43
Dec 2014	277,636.34	1,627.01	1,280.36	193,373.44
Month	Loan Balance	Interest	Principal	Total Interest
Jan 2015	276,348.51	1,619.55	1,287.83	194,992.99
Feb 2015	275,053.17	1,612.03	1,295.34	196,605.02
Mar 2015	273,750.28	1,604.48	1,302.89	198,209.50
Apr 2015	272,439.79	1,596.88	1,310.49	199,806.37
May 2015	271,121.65	1,589.23	1,318.14	201,395.60
Jun 2015	269,795.82	1,581.54	1,325.83	202,977.15
Jul 2015	268,462.26	1,573.81	1,333.56	204,550.96
Aug 2015	267,120.92	1,566.03	1,341.34	206,116.99
Sep 2015	265,771.75	1,558.21	1,349.17	207,675.19
Oct 2015	264,414.71	1,550.34	1,357.04	209,225.53
Nov 2015	263,049.76	1,542.42	1,364.95	210,767.95
Dec 2015	261,676.85	1,534.46	1,372.91	212,302.40
Month	Loan Balance	Interest	Principal	Total Interest
Jan 2016	260,295.93	1,526.45	1,380.92	213,828.85
Feb 2016	258,906.95	1,518.39	1,388.98	215,347.24
Mar 2016	257,509.87	1,510.29	1,397.08	216,857.53
Apr 2016	256,104.64	1,502.14	1,405.23	218,359.67
May 2016	254,691.21	1,493.94	1,413.43	219,853.62
Jun 2016	253,269.54	1,485.70	1,421.67	221,339.32
Jul 2016	251,839.57	1,477.41	1,429.97	222,816.72
Aug 2016	250,401.27	1,469.06	1,438.31	224,285.79
Sep 2016	248,954.57	1,460.67	1,446.70	225,746.46
Oct 2016	247,499.43	1,452.23	1,455.14	227,198.70
Nov 2016	246,035.81	1,443.75	1,463.62	228,642.44
Dec 2016	244,563.65	1,435.21	1,472.16	230,077.65
Month	Loan Balance	Interest	Principal	Total Interest
Jan 2017	243,082.90	1,426.62	1,480.75	231,504.27

Month	Loan Balance	Interest	Principal	Total Interest
Feb 2017	241,593.51	1,417.98	1,489.39	232,922.26
Mar 2017	240,095.43	1,409.30	1,498.08	234,331.55
Apr 2017	238,588.62	1,400.56	1,506.81	235,732.11
May 2017	237,073.01	1,391.77	1,515.60	237,123.88
Jun 2017	235,548.57	1,382.93	1,524.45	238,506.80
Jul 2017	234,015.23	1,374.03	1,533.34	239,880.84
Aug 2017	232,472.95	1,365.09	1,542.28	241,245.92
Sep 2017	230,921.67	1,356.09	1,551.28	242,602.02
Oct 2017	229,361.34	1,347.04	1,560.33	243,949.06
Nov 2017	227,791.91	1,337.94	1,569.43	245,287.00
Dec 2017	226,213.33	1,328.79	1,578.58	246,615.79
Month	Loan Balance	Interest	Principal	Total Interest
Jan 2018	224,625.54	1,319.58	1,587.79	247,935.36
Feb 2018	223,028.48	1,310.32	1,597.06	249,245.68
Mar 2018	221,422.11	1,301.00	1,606.37	250,546.68
Apr 2018	219,806.37	1,291.63	1,615.74	251,838.31
May 2018	218,181.20	1,282.20	1,625.17	253,120.51
Jun 2018	216,546.55	1,272.72	1,634.65	254,393.24
Jul 2018	214,902.37	1,263.19	1,644.18	255,656.42
Aug 2018	213,248.60	1,253.60	1,653.77	256,910.02
Sep 2018	211,585.17	1,243.95	1,663.42	258,153.97
Oct 2018	209,912.05	1,234.25	1,673.12	259,388.22
Nov 2018	208,229.17	1,224.49	1,682.88	260,612.71
Dec 2018	206,536.47	1,214.67	1,692.70	261,827.38
Month	Loan Balance	Interest	Principal	Total Interest
Jan 2019	204,833.89	1,204.80	1,702.57	263,032.17
Feb 2019	203,121.38	1,194.86	1,712.51	264,227.04
Mar 2019	201,398.89	1,184.87	1,722.50	265,411.91
Apr 2019	199,666.34	1,174.83	1,732.54	266,586.74
May 2019	197,923.69	1,164.72	1,742.65	267,751.46
Jun 2019	196,170.88	1,154.55	1,752.82	268,906.01
Jul 2019	194,407.84	1,144.33	1,763.04	270,050.34

Month	Loan Balance	Interest	Principal	Total Interest
Aug 2019	192,634.51	1,134.05	1,773.33	271,184.39
Sep 2019	190,850.84	1,123.70	1,783.67	272,308.09
Oct 2019	189,056.77	1,113.30	1,794.07	273,421.39
Nov 2019	187,252.23	1,102.83	1,804.54	274,524.22
Dec 2019	185,437.16	1,092.30	1,815.07	275,616.52
Month	Loan Balance	Interest	Principal	Total Interest
Jan 2020	183,611.51	1,081.72	1,825.65	276,698.24
Feb 2020	181,775.20	1,071.07	1,836.30	277,769.31
Mar 2020	179,928.19	1,060.36	1,847.02	278,829.66
Apr 2020	178,070.40	1,049.58	1,857.79	279,879.24
May 2020	176,201.77	1,038.74	1,868.63	280,917.99
Jun 2020	174,322.24	1,027.84	1,879.53	281,945.83
Jul 2020	172,431.75	1,016.88	1,890.49	282,962.71
Aug 2020	170,530.23	1,005.85	1,901.52	283,968.56
Sep 2020	168,617.62	994.76	1,912.61	284,963.32
Oct 2020	166,693.85	983.60	1,923.77	285,946.92
Nov 2020	164,758.86	972.38	1,934.99	286,919.30
Dec 2020	162,812.58	961.09	1,946.28	287,880.40
Month	Loan Balance	Interest	Principal	Total Interest
Jan 2021	160,854.95	949.74	1,957.63	288,830.14
Feb 2021	158,885.90	938.32	1,969.05	289,768.46
Mar 2021	156,905.37	926.83	1,980.54	290,695.29
Apr 2021	154,913.28	915.28	1,992.09	291,610.57
May 2021	152,909.57	903.66	2,003.71	292,514.24
Jun 2021	150,894.17	891.97	2,015.40	293,406.21
Jul 2021	148,867.01	880.22	2,027.16	294,286.42
Aug 2021	146,828.03	868.39	2,038.98	295,154.81
Sep 2021	144,777.16	856.50	2,050.87	296,011.31
Oct 2021	142,714.32	844.53	2,062.84	296,855.85
Nov 2021	140,639.45	832.50	2,074.87	297,688.35
Dec 2021	138,552.48	820.40	2,086.97	298,508.74
Month	Loan Balance	Interest	Principal	Total Interest

Month	Loan Balance	Interest	Principal	Total Interest
Jan 2022	136,453.33	808.22	2,099.15	299,316.96
Feb 2022	134,341.93	795.98	2,111.39	300,112.94
Mar 2022	132,218.22	783.66	2,123.71	300,896.60
Apr 2022	130,082.13	771.27	2,136.10	301,667.88
May 2022	127,933.57	758.81	2,148.56	302,426.69
Jun 2022	125,772.48	746.28	2,161.09	303,172.97
Jul 2022	123,598.78	733.67	2,173.70	303,906.64
Aug 2022	121,412.40	720.99	2,186.38	304,627.63
Sep 2022	119,213.27	708.24	2,199.13	305,335.87
Oct 2022	117,001.31	695.41	2,211.96	306,031.28
Nov 2022	114,776.44	682.51	2,224.86	306,713.79
Dec 2022	112,538.60	669.53	2,237.84	307,383.32
Month	Loan Balance	Interest	Principal	Total Interest
Jan 2023	110,287.71	656.48	2,250.90	308,039.80
Feb 2023	108,023.68	643.34	2,264.03	308,683.14
Mar 2023	105,746.45	630.14	2,277.23	309,313.28
Apr 2023	103,455.93	616.85	2,290.52	309,930.13
May 2023	101,152.05	603.49	2,303.88	310,533.63
Jun 2023	98,834.73	590.05	2,317.32	311,123.68
Jul 2023	96,503.90	576.54	2,330.84	311,700.22
Aug 2023	94,159.47	562.94	2,344.43	312,263.16
Sep 2023	91,801.36	549.26	2,358.11	312,812.42
Oct 2023	89,429.50	535.51	2,371.86	313,347.93
Nov 2023	87,043.80	521.67	2,385.70	313,869.60
Dec 2023	84,644.18	507.76	2,399.62	314,377.35
Month	Loan Balance	Interest	Principal	Total Interest
Jan 2024	82,230.57	493.76	2,413.61	314,871.11
Feb 2024	79,802.88	479.68	2,427.69	315,350.79
Mar 2024	77,361.02	465.52	2,441.85	315,816.31
Apr 2024	74,904.92	451.27	2,456.10	316,267.58
May 2024	72,434.50	436.95	2,470.43	316,704.53
Jun 2024	69,949.66	422.53	2,484.84	317,127.06

Jul 2024	67,450.33	408.04	2,499.33	317,535.10
Aug 2024	64,936.42	393.46	2,513.91	317,928.56
Sep 2024	62,407.85	378.80	2,528.58	318,307.36
Oct 2024	59,864.52	364.05	2,543.33	318,671.40
Nov 2024	57,306.36	349.21	2,558.16	319,020.61
Dec 2024	54,733.27	334.29	2,573.08	319,354.90
Month	Loan Balance	Interest	Principal	Total Interest
Jan 2025	52,145.18	319.28	2,588.09	319,674.18
Feb 2025	49,541.99	304.18	2,603.19	319,978.36
Mar 2025	46,923.61	288.99	2,618.38	320,267.35
Apr 2025	44,289.96	273.72	2,633.65	320,541.07
May 2025	41,640.95	258.36	2,649.01	320,799.43
Jun 2025	38,976.49	242.91	2,664.47	321,042.34
Jul 2025	36,296.48	227.36	2,680.01	321,269.70
Aug 2025	33,600.84	211.73	2,695.64	321,481.43
Sep 2025	30,889.47	196.00	2,711.37	321,677.43
Oct 2025	28,162.29	180.19	2,727.18	321,857.62
Nov 2025	25,419.20	164.28	2,743.09	322,021.90
Dec 2025	22,660.10	148.28	2,759.09	322,170.18
Month	Loan Balance	Interest	Principal	Total Interest
Jan 2026	19,884.92	132.18	2,775.19	322,302.36
Feb 2026	17,093.54	116.00	2,791.38	322,418.36
Mar 2026	14,285.88	99.71	2,807.66	322,518.07
Apr 2026	11,461.85	83.33	2,824.04	322,601.41
May 2026	8,621.34	66.86	2,840.51	322,668.27
Jun 2026	5,764.26	50.29	2,857.08	322,718.56
Jul 2026	2,890.51	33.62	2,873.75	322,752.18
Aug 2026	0.00	16.86	2,890.51	322,769.04

Finally, financing for 30 years at 7 percent interest, the following chart shows cheaper payments but not that much of a difference for an additional 10 years with the payments set at $2,494.88:

Month	Loan Balance	Interest	Principal	Total Interest
Sep 2006	374,692.62	2,187.50	307.38	2,187.50
Oct 2006	374,383.44	2,185.71	309.18	4,373.21
Nov 2006	374,072.46	2,183.90	310.98	6,557.11
Dec 2006	373,759.66	2,182.09	312.80	8,739.20
Month	Loan Balance	Interest	Principal	Total Interest
Jan 2007	373,445.04	2,180.26	314.62	10,919.46
Feb 2007	373,128.59	2,178.43	316.45	13,097.89
Mar 2007	372,810.29	2,176.58	318.30	15,274.48
Apr 2007	372,490.13	2,174.73	320.16	17,449.20
May 2007	372,168.10	2,172.86	322.03	19,622.06
Jun 2007	371,844.20	2,170.98	323.90	21,793.04
Jul 2007	371,518.41	2,169.09	325.79	23,962.13
Aug 2007	371,190.71	2,167.19	327.69	26,129.33
Sep 2007	370,861.11	2,165.28	329.61	28,294.60
Oct 2007	370,529.58	2,163.36	331.53	30,457.96
Nov 2007	370,196.12	2,161.42	333.46	32,619.38
Dec 2007	369,860.71	2,159.48	335.41	34,778.86
Month	Loan Balance	Interest	Principal	Total Interest
Jan 2008	369,523.35	2,157.52	337.36	36,936.38
Feb 2008	369,184.02	2,155.55	339.33	39,091.93
Mar 2008	368,842.71	2,153.57	341.31	41,245.51
Apr 2008	368,499.40	2,151.58	343.30	43,397.09
May 2008	368,154.10	2,149.58	345.30	45,546.67
Jun 2008	367,806.78	2,147.57	347.32	47,694.24
Jul 2008	367,457.44	2,145.54	349.34	49,839.78
Aug 2008	367,106.05	2,143.50	351.38	51,983.28
Sep 2008	366,752.62	2,141.45	353.43	54,124.73
Oct 2008	366,397.13	2,139.39	355.49	56,264.12
Nov 2008	366,039.56	2,137.32	357.57	58,401.44
Dec 2008	365,679.90	2,135.23	359.65	60,536.67
Month	Loan Balance	Interest	Principal	Total Interest

Month	Loan Balance	Interest	Principal	Total Interest
Jan 2009	365,318.15	2,133.13	361.75	62,669.80
Feb 2009	364,954.29	2,131.02	363.86	64,800.82
Mar 2009	364,588.31	2,128.90	365.98	66,929.72
Apr 2009	364,220.19	2,126.77	368.12	69,056.49
May 2009	363,849.92	2,124.62	370.27	71,181.11
Jun 2009	363,477.49	2,122.46	372.43	73,303.56
Jul 2009	363,102.90	2,120.29	374.60	75,423.85
Aug 2009	362,726.11	2,118.10	376.78	77,541.95
Sep 2009	362,347.13	2,115.90	378.98	79,657.85
Oct 2009	361,965.94	2,113.69	381.19	81,771.54
Nov 2009	361,582.52	2,111.47	383.42	83,883.01
Dec 2009	361,196.87	2,109.23	385.65	85,992.24
Month	Loan Balance	Interest	Principal	Total Interest
Jan 2010	360,808.96	2,106.98	387.90	88,099.22
Feb 2010	360,418.80	2,104.72	390.17	90,203.94
Mar 2010	360,026.36	2,102.44	392.44	92,306.39
Apr 2010	359,631.63	2,100.15	394.73	94,406.54
May 2010	359,234.59	2,097.85	397.03	96,504.39
Jun 2010	358,835.25	2,095.54	399.35	98,599.93
Jul 2010	358,433.57	2,093.21	401.68	100,693.13
Aug 2010	358,029.54	2,090.86	404.02	102,783.99
Sep 2010	357,623.17	2,088.51	406.38	104,872.50
Oct 2010	357,214.42	2,086.14	408.75	106,958.63
Nov 2010	356,803.28	2,083.75	411.13	109,042.39
Dec 2010	356,389.75	2,081.35	413.53	111,123.74
Month	Loan Balance	Interest	Principal	Total Interest
Jan 2011	355,973.81	2,078.94	415.94	113,202.68
Feb 2011	355,555.44	2,076.51	418.37	115,279.19
Mar 2011	355,134.63	2,074.07	420.81	117,353.27
Apr 2011	354,711.36	2,071.62	423.27	119,424.88
May 2011	354,285.63	2,069.15	425.73	121,494.03
Jun 2011	353,857.41	2,066.67	428.22	123,560.70

Month	Loan Balance	Interest	Principal	Total Interest
Jul 2011	353,426.69	2,064.17	430.72	125,624.87
Aug 2011	352,993.46	2,061.66	433.23	127,686.52
Sep 2011	352,557.71	2,059.13	435.76	129,745.65
Oct 2011	352,119.41	2,056.59	438.30	131,802.24
Nov 2011	351,678.55	2,054.03	440.85	133,856.27
Dec 2011	351,235.13	2,051.46	443.43	135,907.73
Month	Loan Balance	Interest	Principal	Total Interest
Jan 2012	350,789.12	2,048.87	446.01	137,956.60
Feb 2012	350,340.50	2,046.27	448.61	140,002.87
Mar 2012	349,889.27	2,043.65	451.23	142,046.52
Apr 2012	349,435.41	2,041.02	453.86	144,087.54
May 2012	348,978.89	2,038.37	456.51	146,125.92
Jun 2012	348,519.72	2,035.71	459.17	148,161.63
Jul 2012	348,057.87	2,033.03	461.85	150,194.66
Aug 2012	347,593.32	2,030.34	464.55	152,225.00
Sep 2012	347,126.06	2,027.63	467.26	154,252.62
Oct 2012	346,656.08	2,024.90	469.98	156,277.52
Nov 2012	346,183.36	2,022.16	472.72	158,299.69
Dec 2012	345,707.88	2,019.40	475.48	160,319.09
Month	Loan Balance	Interest	Principal	Total Interest
Jan 2013	345,229.62	2,016.63	478.26	162,335.72
Feb 2013	344,748.58	2,013.84	481.04	164,349.56
Mar 2013	344,264.73	2,011.03	483.85	166,360.59
Apr 2013	343,778.05	2,008.21	486.67	168,368.80
May 2013	343,288.54	2,005.37	489.51	170,374.17
Jun 2013	342,796.17	2,002.52	492.37	172,376.69
Jul 2013	342,300.93	1,999.64	495.24	174,376.33
Aug 2013	341,802.80	1,996.76	498.13	176,373.09
Sep 2013	341,301.77	1,993.85	501.03	178,366.94
Oct 2013	340,797.81	1,990.93	503.96	180,357.87
Nov 2013	340,290.91	1,987.99	506.90	182,345.85
Dec 2013	339,781.06	1,985.03	509.85	184,330.88

Month	Loan Balance	Interest	Principal	Total Interest
Jan 2014	339,268.23	1,982.06	512.83	186,312.94
Feb 2014	338,752.41	1,979.06	515.82	188,292.00
Mar 2014	338,233.58	1,976.06	518.83	190,268.06
Apr 2014	337,711.73	1,973.03	521.86	192,241.09
May 2014	337,186.83	1,969.99	524.90	194,211.07
Jun 2014	336,658.87	1,966.92	527.96	196,178.00
Jul 2014	336,127.83	1,963.84	531.04	198,141.84
Aug 2014	335,593.69	1,960.75	534.14	200,102.59
Sep 2014	335,056.43	1,957.63	537.25	202,060.22
Oct 2014	334,516.05	1,954.50	540.39	204,014.71
Nov 2014	333,972.50	1,951.34	543.54	205,966.06
Dec 2014	333,425.79	1,948.17	546.71	207,914.23
Month	Loan Balance	Interest	Principal	Total Interest
Jan 2015	332,875.89	1,944.98	549.90	209,859.21
Feb 2015	332,322.78	1,941.78	553.11	211,800.99
Mar 2015	331,766.45	1,938.55	556.33	213,739.54
Apr 2015	331,206.87	1,935.30	559.58	215,674.84
May 2015	330,644.02	1,932.04	562.84	217,606.88
Jun 2015	330,077.90	1,928.76	566.13	219,535.64
Jul 2015	329,508.47	1,925.45	569.43	221,461.09
Aug 2015	328,935.72	1,922.13	572.75	223,383.23
Sep 2015	328,359.62	1,918.79	576.09	225,302.02
Oct 2015	327,780.17	1,915.43	579.45	227,217.45
Nov 2015	327,197.34	1,912.05	582.83	229,129.50
Dec 2015	326,611.10	1,908.65	586.23	231,038.15
Month	Loan Balance	Interest	Principal	Total Interest
Jan 2016	326,021.45	1,905.23	589.65	232,943.38
Feb 2016	325,428.36	1,901.79	593.09	234,845.18
Mar 2016	324,831.81	1,898.33	596.55	236,743.51
Apr 2016	324,231.77	1,894.85	600.03	238,638.36
May 2016	323,628.24	1,891.35	603.53	240,529.71

Month	Loan Balance	Interest	Principal	Total Interest
Jun 2016	323,021.19	1,887.83	607.05	242,417.54
Jul 2016	322,410.59	1,884.29	610.59	244,301.83
Aug 2016	321,796.44	1,880.73	614.16	246,182.56
Sep 2016	321,178.70	1,877.15	617.74	248,059.71
Oct 2016	320,557.36	1,873.54	621.34	249,933.25
Nov 2016	319,932.39	1,869.92	624.97	251,803.17
Dec 2016	319,303.78	1,866.27	628.61	253,669.44
Month	Loan Balance	Interest	Principal	Total Interest
Jan 2017	318,671.50	1,862.61	632.28	255,532.05
Feb 2017	318,035.53	1,858.92	635.97	257,390.96
Mar 2017	317,395.86	1,855.21	639.68	259,246.17
Apr 2017	316,752.45	1,851.48	643.41	261,097.65
May 2017	316,105.29	1,847.72	647.16	262,945.37
Jun 2017	315,454.35	1,843.95	650.94	264,789.32
Jul 2017	314,799.61	1,840.15	654.73	266,629.47
Aug 2017	314,141.06	1,836.33	658.55	268,465.80
Sep 2017	313,478.67	1,832.49	662.39	270,298.29
Oct 2017	312,812.41	1,828.63	666.26	272,126.91
Nov 2017	312,142.26	1,824.74	670.15	273,951.65
Dec 2017	311,468.21	1,820.83	674.05	275,772.48
Month	Loan Balance	Interest	Principal	Total Interest
Jan 2018	310,790.22	1,816.90	677.99	277,589.38
Feb 2018	310,108.28	1,812.94	681.94	279,402.32
Mar 2018	309,422.36	1,808.96	685.92	281,211.29
Apr 2018	308,732.44	1,804.96	689.92	283,016.25
May 2018	308,038.49	1,800.94	693.95	284,817.19
Jun 2018	307,340.50	1,796.89	697.99	286,614.08
Jul 2018	306,638.44	1,792.82	702.06	288,406.90
Aug 2018	305,932.28	1,788.72	706.16	290,195.63
Sep 2018	305,222.00	1,784.60	710.28	291,980.23
Oct 2018	304,507.57	1,780.46	714.42	293,760.69
Nov 2018	303,788.98	1,776.29	718.59	295,536.99

Dec 2018	303,066.20	1,772.10	722.78	297,309.09
Month	Loan Balance	Interest	Principal	Total Interest
Jan 2019	302,339.20	1,767.89	727.00	299,076.97
Feb 2019	301,607.97	1,763.65	731.24	300,840.62
Mar 2019	300,872.46	1,759.38	735.50	302,600.00
Apr 2019	300,132.67	1,755.09	739.80	304,355.09
May 2019	299,388.56	1,750.77	744.11	306,105.86
Jun 2019	298,640.10	1,746.43	748.45	307,852.30
Jul 2019	297,887.29	1,742.07	752.82	309,594.36
Aug 2019	297,130.08	1,737.68	757.21	311,332.04
Sep 2019	296,368.45	1,733.26	761.63	313,065.30
Oct 2019	295,602.38	1,728.82	766.07	314,794.11
Nov 2019	294,831.85	1,724.35	770.54	316,518.46
Dec 2019	294,056.82	1,719.85	775.03	318,238.31
Month	Loan Balance	Interest	Principal	Total Interest
Jan 2020	293,277.26	1,715.33	779.55	319,953.65
Feb 2020	292,493.16	1,710.78	784.10	321,664.43
Mar 2020	291,704.49	1,706.21	788.67	323,370.64
Apr 2020	290,911.21	1,701.61	793.27	325,072.25
May 2020	290,113.31	1,696.98	797.90	326,769.23
Jun 2020	289,310.75	1,692.33	802.56	328,461.56
Jul 2020	288,503.52	1,687.65	807.24	330,149.21
Aug 2020	287,691.57	1,682.94	811.95	331,832.14
Sep 2020	286,874.89	1,678.20	816.68	333,510.34
Oct 2020	286,053.44	1,673.44	821.45	335,183.78
Nov 2020	285,227.20	1,668.65	826.24	336,852.42
Dec 2020	284,396.14	1,663.83	831.06	338,516.25
Month	Loan Balance	Interest	Principal	Total Interest
Jan 2021	283,560.23	1,658.98	835.91	340,175.23
Feb 2021	282,719.45	1,654.10	840.78	341,829.33
Mar 2021	281,873.76	1,649.20	845.69	343,478.53
Apr 2021	281,023.14	1,644.26	850.62	345,122.79

Month	Loan Balance	Interest	Principal	Total Interest
May 2021	280,167.56	1,639.30	855.58	346,762.09
Jun 2021	279,306.99	1,634.31	860.57	348,396.40
Jul 2021	278,441.39	1,629.29	865.59	350,025.69
Aug 2021	277,570.75	1,624.24	870.64	351,649.93
Sep 2021	276,695.03	1,619.16	875.72	353,269.10
Oct 2021	275,814.20	1,614.05	880.83	354,883.15
Nov 2021	274,928.23	1,608.92	885.97	356,492.07
Dec 2021	274,037.09	1,603.75	891.14	358,095.82
Month	Loan Balance	Interest	Principal	Total Interest
Jan 2022	273,140.76	1,598.55	896.33	359,694.37
Feb 2022	272,239.19	1,593.32	901.56	361,287.69
Mar 2022	271,332.37	1,588.06	906.82	362,875.75
Apr 2022	270,420.26	1,582.77	912.11	364,458.52
May 2022	269,502.83	1,577.45	917.43	366,035.97
Jun 2022	268,580.04	1,572.10	922.78	367,608.07
Jul 2022	267,651.87	1,566.72	928.17	369,174.79
Aug 2022	266,718.29	1,561.30	933.58	370,736.09
Sep 2022	265,779.27	1,555.86	939.03	372,291.95
Oct 2022	264,834.76	1,550.38	944.51	373,842.33
Nov 2022	263,884.75	1,544.87	950.01	375,387.20
Dec 2022	262,929.19	1,539.33	955.56	376,926.52
Month	Loan Balance	Interest	Principal	Total Interest
Jan 2023	261,968.06	1,533.75	961.13	378,460.28
Feb 2023	261,001.32	1,528.15	966.74	379,988.42
Mar 2023	260,028.94	1,522.51	972.38	381,510.93
Apr 2023	259,050.90	1,516.84	978.05	383,027.77
May 2023	258,067.14	1,511.13	983.75	384,538.90
Jun 2023	257,077.65	1,505.39	989.49	386,044.29
Jul 2023	256,082.38	1,499.62	995.26	387,543.91
Aug 2023	255,081.31	1,493.81	1,001.07	389,037.72
Sep 2023	254,074.40	1,487.97	1,006.91	390,525.70
Oct 2023	253,061.62	1,482.10	1,012.78	392,007.80

Month	Loan Balance	Interest	Principal	Total Interest
Nov 2023	252,042.93	1,476.19	1,018.69	393,483.99
Dec 2023	251,018.29	1,470.25	1,024.63	394,954.24
Month	Loan Balance	Interest	Principal	Total Interest
Jan 2024	249,987.68	1,464.27	1,030.61	396,418.51
Feb 2024	248,951.06	1,458.26	1,036.62	397,876.78
Mar 2024	247,908.39	1,452.21	1,042.67	399,328.99
Apr 2024	246,859.64	1,446.13	1,048.75	400,775.12
May 2024	245,804.77	1,440.01	1,054.87	402,215.14
Jun 2024	244,743.75	1,433.86	1,061.02	403,649.00
Jul 2024	243,676.53	1,427.67	1,067.21	405,076.67
Aug 2024	242,603.09	1,421.45	1,073.44	406,498.12
Sep 2024	241,523.39	1,415.18	1,079.70	407,913.30
Oct 2024	240,437.40	1,408.89	1,086.00	409,322.19
Nov 2024	239,345.06	1,402.55	1,092.33	410,724.74
Dec 2024	238,246.36	1,396.18	1,098.70	412,120.92
Month	Loan Balance	Interest	Principal	Total Interest
Jan 2025	237,141.25	1,389.77	1,105.11	413,510.69
Feb 2025	236,029.69	1,383.32	1,111.56	414,894.01
Mar 2025	234,911.64	1,376.84	1,118.04	416,270.85
Apr 2025	233,787.07	1,370.32	1,124.57	417,641.17
May 2025	232,655.95	1,363.76	1,131.13	419,004.93
Jun 2025	231,518.22	1,357.16	1,137.72	420,362.09
Jul 2025	230,373.86	1,350.52	1,144.36	421,712.61
Aug 2025	229,222.82	1,343.85	1,151.04	423,056.46
Sep 2025	228,065.07	1,337.13	1,157.75	424,393.59
Oct 2025	226,900.57	1,330.38	1,164.50	425,723.97
Nov 2025	225,729.27	1,323.59	1,171.30	427,047.56
Dec 2025	224,551.14	1,316.75	1,178.13	428,364.31
Month	Loan Balance	Interest	Principal	Total Interest
Jan 2026	223,366.14	1,309.88	1,185.00	429,674.19
Feb 2026	222,174.22	1,302.97	1,191.92	430,977.16
Mar 2026	220,975.35	1,296.02	1,198.87	432,273.18

Month	Loan Balance	Interest	Principal	Total Interest
Apr 2026	219,769.49	1,289.02	1,205.86	433,562.20
May 2026	218,556.60	1,281.99	1,212.90	434,844.19
Jun 2026	217,336.63	1,274.91	1,219.97	436,119.11
Jul 2026	216,109.54	1,267.80	1,227.09	437,386.90
Aug 2026	214,875.29	1,260.64	1,234.25	438,647.54
Sep 2026	213,633.85	1,253.44	1,241.45	439,900.98
Oct 2026	212,385.16	1,246.20	1,248.69	441,147.18
Nov 2026	211,129.19	1,238.91	1,255.97	442,386.09
Dec 2026	209,865.89	1,231.59	1,263.30	443,617.68
Month	Loan Balance	Interest	Principal	Total Interest
Jan 2027	208,595.23	1,224.22	1,270.67	444,841.90
Feb 2027	207,317.15	1,216.81	1,278.08	446,058.70
Mar 2027	206,031.61	1,209.35	1,285.53	447,268.05
Apr 2027	204,738.58	1,201.85	1,293.03	448,469.90
May 2027	203,438.00	1,194.31	1,300.58	449,664.21
Jun 2027	202,129.84	1,186.72	1,308.16	450,850.93
Jul 2027	200,814.05	1,179.09	1,315.79	452,030.02
Aug 2027	199,490.58	1,171.42	1,323.47	453,201.44
Sep 2027	198,159.39	1,163.70	1,331.19	454,365.13
Oct 2027	196,820.44	1,155.93	1,338.95	455,521.06
Nov 2027	195,473.67	1,148.12	1,346.77	456,669.18
Dec 2027	194,119.05	1,140.26	1,354.62	457,809.45
Month	Loan Balance	Interest	Principal	Total Interest
Jan 2028	192,756.53	1,132.36	1,362.52	458,941.81
Feb 2028	191,386.05	1,124.41	1,370.47	460,066.22
Mar 2028	190,007.59	1,116.42	1,378.47	461,182.64
Apr 2028	188,621.08	1,108.38	1,386.51	462,291.02
May 2028	187,226.49	1,100.29	1,394.59	463,391.31
Jun 2028	185,823.76	1,092.15	1,402.73	464,483.46
Jul 2028	184,412.84	1,083.97	1,410.91	465,567.43
Aug 2028	182,993.70	1,075.74	1,419.14	466,643.17
Sep 2028	181,566.28	1,067.46	1,427.42	467,710.64

Month	Loan Balance	Interest	Principal	Total Interest
Oct 2028	180,130.53	1,059.14	1,435.75	468,769.77
Nov 2028	178,686.41	1,050.76	1,444.12	469,820.54
Dec 2028	177,233.86	1,042.34	1,452.55	470,862.87
Month	Loan Balance	Interest	Principal	Total Interest
Jan 2029	175,772.84	1,033.86	1,461.02	471,896.74
Feb 2029	174,303.30	1,025.34	1,469.54	472,922.08
Mar 2029	172,825.19	1,016.77	1,478.12	473,938.85
Apr 2029	171,338.45	1,008.15	1,486.74	474,947.00
May 2029	169,843.04	999.47	1,495.41	475,946.47
Jun 2029	168,338.90	990.75	1,504.13	476,937.22
Jul 2029	166,826.00	981.98	1,512.91	477,919.20
Aug 2029	165,304.26	973.15	1,521.73	478,892.35
Sep 2029	163,773.65	964.27	1,530.61	479,856.62
Oct 2029	162,234.12	955.35	1,539.54	480,811.97
Nov 2029	160,685.60	946.37	1,548.52	481,758.34
Dec 2029	159,128.05	937.33	1,557.55	482,695.67
Month	Loan Balance	Interest	Principal	Total Interest
Jan 2030	157,561.41	928.25	1,566.64	483,623.92
Feb 2030	155,985.63	919.11	1,575.78	484,543.02
Mar 2030	154,400.66	909.92	1,584.97	485,452.94
Apr 2030	152,806.45	900.67	1,594.21	486,353.61
May 2030	151,202.94	891.37	1,603.51	487,244.98
Jun 2030	149,590.07	882.02	1,612.87	488,127.00
Jul 2030	147,967.79	872.61	1,622.28	488,999.61
Aug 2030	146,336.06	863.15	1,631.74	489,862.75
Sep 2030	144,694.80	853.63	1,641.26	490,716.38
Oct 2030	143,043.97	844.05	1,650.83	491,560.43
Nov 2030	141,383.51	834.42	1,660.46	492,394.86
Dec 2030	139,713.36	824.74	1,670.15	493,219.59
Month	Loan Balance	Interest	Principal	Total Interest
Jan 2031	138,033.47	814.99	1,679.89	494,034.59
Feb 2031	136,343.78	805.20	1,689.69	494,839.78

Month	Loan Balance	Interest	Principal	Total Interest
Mar 2031	134,644.23	795.34	1,699.55	495,635.12
Apr 2031	132,934.77	785.42	1,709.46	496,420.55
May 2031	131,215.34	775.45	1,719.43	497,196.00
Jun 2031	129,485.88	765.42	1,729.46	497,961.42
Jul 2031	127,746.33	755.33	1,739.55	498,716.76
Aug 2031	125,996.63	745.19	1,749.70	499,461.94
Sep 2031	124,236.73	734.98	1,759.90	500,196.92
Oct 2031	122,466.56	724.71	1,770.17	500,921.64
Nov 2031	120,686.06	714.39	1,780.50	501,636.03
Dec 2031	118,895.18	704.00	1,790.88	502,340.03
Month	Loan Balance	Interest	Principal	Total Interest
Jan 2032	117,093.85	693.56	1,801.33	503,033.58
Feb 2032	115,282.02	683.05	1,811.84	503,716.63
Mar 2032	113,459.61	672.48	1,822.41	504,389.11
Apr 2032	111,626.57	661.85	1,833.04	505,050.96
May 2032	109,782.84	651.16	1,843.73	505,702.11
Jun 2032	107,928.36	640.40	1,854.48	506,342.51
Jul 2032	106,063.06	629.58	1,865.30	506,972.09
Aug 2032	104,186.87	618.70	1,876.18	507,590.80
Sep 2032	102,299.75	607.76	1,887.13	508,198.55
Oct 2032	100,401.61	596.75	1,898.14	508,795.30
Nov 2032	98,492.40	585.68	1,909.21	509,380.98
Dec 2032	96,572.06	574.54	1,920.35	509,955.52
Month	Loan Balance	Interest	Principal	Total Interest
Jan 2033	94,640.51	563.34	1,931.55	510,518.85
Feb 2033	92,697.69	552.07	1,942.81	511,070.92
Mar 2033	90,743.55	540.74	1,954.15	511,611.66
Apr 2033	88,778.00	529.34	1,965.55	512,141.00
May 2033	86,800.99	517.87	1,977.01	512,658.87
Jun 2033	84,812.44	506.34	1,988.55	513,165.21
Jul 2033	82,812.30	494.74	2,000.15	513,659.95
Aug 2033	80,800.48	483.07	2,011.81	514,143.02

Month	Loan Balance	Interest	Principal	Total Interest
Sep 2033	78,776.94	471.34	2,023.55	514,614.35
Oct 2033	76,741.58	459.53	2,035.35	515,073.89
Nov 2033	74,694.36	447.66	2,047.23	515,521.55
Dec 2033	72,635.19	435.72	2,059.17	515,957.26
Month	Loan Balance	Interest	Principal	Total Interest
Jan 2034	70,564.01	423.71	2,071.18	516,380.97
Feb 2034	68,480.75	411.62	2,083.26	516,792.59
Mar 2034	66,385.34	399.47	2,095.41	517,192.06
Apr 2034	64,277.70	387.25	2,107.64	517,579.31
May 2034	62,157.77	374.95	2,119.93	517,954.26
Jun 2034	60,025.47	362.59	2,132.30	518,316.85
Jul 2034	57,880.74	350.15	2,144.74	518,667.00
Aug 2034	55,723.49	337.64	2,157.25	519,004.64
Sep 2034	53,553.66	325.05	2,169.83	519,329.69
Oct 2034	51,371.17	312.40	2,182.49	519,642.09
Nov 2034	49,175.95	299.67	2,195.22	519,941.75
Dec 2034	46,967.93	286.86	2,208.02	520,228.61
Month	Loan Balance	Interest	Principal	Total Interest
Jan 2035	44,747.02	273.98	2,220.90	520,502.59
Feb 2035	42,513.16	261.02	2,233.86	520,763.62
Mar 2035	40,266.27	247.99	2,246.89	521,011.61
Apr 2035	38,006.27	234.89	2,260.00	521,246.50
May 2035	35,733.09	221.70	2,273.18	521,468.20
Jun 2035	33,446.65	208.44	2,286.44	521,676.64
Jul 2035	31,146.87	195.11	2,299.78	521,871.75
Aug 2035	28,833.68	181.69	2,313.19	522,053.44
Sep 2035	26,506.99	168.20	2,326.69	522,221.63
Oct 2035	24,166.73	154.62	2,340.26	522,376.26
Nov 2035	21,812.82	140.97	2,353.91	522,517.23
Dec 2035	19,445.18	127.24	2,367.64	522,644.47
Month	Loan Balance	Interest	Principal	Total Interest
Jan 2036	17,063.72	113.43	2,381.45	522,757.90

Feb 2036	14,668.38	99.54	2,395.35	522,857.44
Mar 2036	12,259.06	85.57	2,409.32	522,943.01
Apr 2036	9,835.68	71.51	2,423.37	523,014.52
May 2036	7,398.17	57.37	2,437.51	523,071.89
Jun 2036	4,946.45	43.16	2,451.73	523,115.05
Jul 2036	2,480.42	28.85	2,466.03	523,143.90
Aug 2036	0.00	14.47	2,480.42	523,158.37

As you can see from the charts above, there is not that much difference in amortizing over 20 or 30 years because you are initially only paying the interest anyway. Most people can afford the payments on a 20 year mortgage as easily as they can a 30 year mortgage, and they will have their home paid for sooner than they imagined.

Before you finance anything, look at the sample amortization charts and tables throughout this book and weigh the pros and cons of amortizing a loan over 10, 15, 20 or 30 years. Decide how much you can afford, knowing that the fewer years you finance your home, the quicker you will own it!

REFERENCES

1. Eldred, Gary, (PHD) *The Beginner's Guide to Real Estate Investing*, John Wiley and Sons, 2004, ISBN 0-471-64711-X.

2. Eldred, Gary, (PHD), *Make Money with Condominiums and Townhouses*, John Wiley and Sons, 2003, ISBN 0-471-43344-6.

3. Navarro, Peter, *If It Is Raining in Brazil Buy Starbucks*, McGraw-Hill, 2002, ISBN 0-07-141611-0.

4. Cummings, Jack, *Real Estate Finance and Investment Manual*, Prentice Hall, 1997, ISBN 0-13-493388-5.

5. Friedman, Jack P. and Harris, Jack C. PhDs, Keys to Purchasing a Condo or Co-Op, Barron's, 2000, ISBN 0-7641-1305-4.

6. Weiss, Mark B. Condos, Co-Ops, and Townhouses, Dearborn Trade Publishing, 2003, ISBN 0-7931-7840-1.

7. Berges, Steve, The Complete Guide to Buying and Selling Apartment Buildings Second Edition, 2005, ISBN 0-471-68405-8.

8. **www.mortgage-x.com**

ABOUT THE AUTHOR

———

Susan Alvis has her Tennessee real estate license in retirement. She is the author of *How to Creatively Finance Your Real Estate Investments and Build Your Personal Fortune: What Smart Investors Need to Know*; *How to Buy Real Estate Without a Down Payment in any Market: Insider Secrets From the Experts Who do it Everyday*, and *How to Become a Million Dollar Real Estate Agent in Your First Year*. Currently, she is working on several non-fiction books on gambling related material as a ghost writer and under her own name. She has started writing romance novelettes under a pen name and is realizing success in fiction writing as well. Susan also speaks to teens and young adults in a gripping message every teenager in America should hear. She lives in Northeast Tennessee with her husband, Brent, and their two children, Matthew and Amber. You can visit her on her Web site at **www.SusanAlvis.com**.

GLOSSARY

401(k)/403(b) An investment plan sponsored by an employer that enables individuals to set aside pre-tax income for retirement or emergency purposes. 401(k) plans are provided by private corporations. 403(b) plans are provided by non-profit organizations.

401(k)/403(b) Loan Type of financing using a loan against the money accumulated in a 401(k)/403(b) plan.

Abatement May be referred to as free rent or early occupancy. A condition that could happen in addition to the primary term of the lease.

Above Building Standard Finishes and specialized designs that have been upgraded in order to accommodate a tenant's requirements.

Absorption Rate The speed and amount of time at which rentable space, in square feet, is filled.

Abstract or Title Search The process of reviewing all transactions that have been recorded publicly in order to determine whether any defects in the title exist that could interfere with a clear property ownership transfer.

Accelerated Cost Recovery System A calculation for taxes to provide more depreciation for the first few years of ownership.

Accelerated Depreciation A method of depreciation where the value of a property depreciates faster in the first few years after purchasing it.

Acceleration Clause A clause in a contract that gives the lender the right to demand immediate payment of the balance of the loan if the borrower defaults on the loan.

Acceptance The seller's written approval of a buyer's offer.

Ad Valorem A Latin phrase that translates as "according to value". Refers to a tax imposed on a property's value typically based on the local government's evaluation of the property.

Addendum An addition or update for an existing contract between parties.

Additional Principal Payment Additional money paid to the lender, apart from the scheduled loan payments, to pay more of the principal balance, shortening the length of the loan.

Adjustable-Rate Mortgage (ARM) A home loan with an interest rate that is adjusted periodically in order to reflect changes in a specific financial resource.

Adjusted Funds From Operations (AFFO) The rate of REIT performance or ability to pay dividends that is used by many analysts who have concerns about the quality of earnings as measured by Funds From Operations (FFO).

Adjustment Date The date at which the interest rate is adjusted for an adjustable-rate mortgage (ARM).

Adjustment Period The amount of time between adjustments for an interest rate in an ARM.

Administrative Fee A percentage of the value of the assets under management, or a fixed annual dollar amount charged to manage an account.

Advances The payments the servicer makes when the borrower fails to send a payment.

Adviser A broker or investment banker who represents an owner in a transaction and is paid a retainer and/or a performance fee once a financing or sales transaction has closed.

Agency Closing A type of closing in which a lender uses a title company or other firm as an agent to finish a loan.

Agency Disclosure A requirement in most states that agents who act for both buyers or sellers must disclose who they are working for in the transaction.

Aggregation Risk The risk that is associated with warehousing mortgages during the process of pooling them for future security.

Agreement of Sale A legal document the buyer and seller must approve and sign that details the price and terms in the transaction.

Alienation Clause The provision in a loan that requires the borrower to pay the total balance of the loan at once if the property is sold or the ownership transferred.

Alternative Mortgage A home loan that does not match the standard terms of a fixed-rate mortgage.

Alternative or Specialty Investments Types of property that are not considered to be conventional real estate investments, such as self-storage facilities, mobile homes, timber, agriculture, or parking lots.

Amortization The usual process of paying a loan's interest and principal via scheduled monthly payments.

Amortization Schedule Chart or table that shows the percentage of each payment that will be applied toward principal and interest over the life of the mortgage and how the loan balance decreases until it reaches zero.

Amortization Tables Mathematical tables that are used to calculate what a borrower's monthly payment will be.

Amortization Term The number of months it will take to amortize the loan.

Anchor The business or individual who is serving as the primary draw to a commercial property.

Annual Mortgagor Statement A yearly statement to borrowers which details the remaining principal balance and amounts paid throughout the year for taxes and interest.

Annual Percentage Rate (APR) The interest rate that states the actual cost of borrowing money over the course of a year.

Annuity The regular payments of a fixed sum.

Application The form a borrower must complete in order to apply for a mortgage loan, including information such as income, savings, assets, and debts.

Application Fee A fee some lenders charge that may include charges for items such as property appraisal or a credit report unless those fees are included elsewhere.

Appraisal The estimate of the value of a property on a particular date given by a professional appraiser, usually presented in a written document.

Appraisal Fee The fee charged by a professional appraiser for his estimate of the market value of a property.

Appraisal Report The written report presented by an appraiser regarding the value of a property.

Appraised Value The dollar amount a professional appraiser assigned to the value of a property in his report.

Appraiser A certified individual who is qualified by education, training, and experience to estimate the value of real and personal property.

Appreciation An increase in the home's or property's value.

Appreciation Return The amount gained when the value of the real estate assets increases during the current quarter.

Arbitrage The act of buying securities in one market and selling them immediately in another market in order to profit from the difference in price.

ARM Index A number that is publicly published and used as the basis for interest rate adjustments on an ARM.

As-Is Condition Phrase in a purchase or lease contract in which the new tenant accepts the existing condition of the premises and any physical defects.

Assessed Value The value placed on a home that is determined by a tax assessor in order to calculate a tax base.

Assessment (1) The approximate value of a property. (2) A fee charged in addition to taxes in order to help pay for items such as water, sewer, street improvements, etc.

Assessor A public officer who estimates the value of a property for the purpose of taxation.

Asset A property or item of value owned by an individual or company.

Asset Management Fee A fee that is charged to investors based on the amount of money they have invested into real estate assets for the particular fund or account.

Asset Management The various tasks and areas around managing real estate assets from the initial investment until the time it is sold.

Asset Turnover The rate of total revenues for the previous 12 months divided by the average total assets.

Assets Under Management The amount of the current market value of real estate assets that a manager is responsible to manage and invest.

Assignee Name The individual or business to whom the lease, mortgage, or other contract has been re-assigned.

Assignment The transfer of rights and responsibilities from one party to another for paying a debt. The original party remains liable for the debt should the second party default.

Assignor The person who transfers the rights and interests of a property to another.

Assumable Mortgage A mortgage that is capable of being transferred to a different borrower.

Assumption The act of assuming the mortgage of the seller.

Assumption Clause A contractual provision that enables the buyer to take responsibility for the mortgage loan from the seller.

Assumption Fee A fee charged to the buyer for processing new records when they are assuming an existing loan.

Attorn To agree to recognize a new owner of a property and to pay rent to the new landlord.

Average Common Equity The sum of the common equity for the last five quarters divided by five.

Average Downtime The number of months that are expected between a lease's expiration and the beginning of a replacement lease under the current market conditions.

Average Free Rent The number of months the rent abatement concession is expected to be granted to a tenant as part of an incentive to lease under current market conditions.

Average Occupancy The average rate of each of the previous 12 months that a property was occupied.

Average Total Assets The sum of the total assets of a company for the previous five quarters divided by five.

Back Title Letter A letter that an attorney receives from a title insurance company before examining the title for insurance purposes.

Back-End Ratio The calculation lenders use to compare a borrower's gross monthly income to their total debt.

Balance Sheet A statement that lists an individual's assets, liabilities, and net worth.

Balloon Loan A type of mortgage in which the monthly payments are not large enough to repay the loan by the end of the term, and the final payment is one large payment of the remaining balance.

Balloon Payment The final huge payment due at the end of a balloon mortgage.

Balloon Risk The risk that a borrower may not be able to come up with the funds for the balloon payment at maturity.

Bankrupt The state an individual or business is in if they are unable to repay their debt when it is due.

Bankruptcy A legal proceeding where a debtor can obtain relief from payment of certain obligations through restructuring their finances.

Base Loan Amount The amount that forms the basis for the loan payments.

Base Principal Balance The original loan amount once adjustments for subsequent fundings and principal payments have been made without including accrued interest or other unpaid debts.

Base Rent A certain amount that is used as a minimum rent, providing for rent increases over the term of the lease agreement.

Base Year The sum of actual taxes and operating expenses during a given year, often that in which a lease begins.

Basis Point A term for 1/100 of one percentage point.

Before-Tax Income An individual's income before taxes have been deducted.

Below-Grade Any structure or part of a structure that is below the surface of the ground that surrounds it.

Beneficiary An employee who is covered by the benefit plan his or her company provides.

Beta The measurement of common stock price volatility for a company in comparison to the market.

Bid The price or range an investor is willing to spend on whole loans or securities.

Bill of Sale A written legal document that transfers the ownership of personal property to another party.

Binder (1) A report describing the conditions of a property's title. (2) An early agreement between seller and buyer.

Biweekly Mortgage A mortgage repayment plan that requires payments every two weeks to help repay the loan over a shorter amount of time.

Blanket Mortgage A rare type of mortgage that covers more than one of the borrower's properties.

Blind Pool A mixed fund that accepts capital from investors without specifying property assets.

Bond Market The daily buying and selling of thirty-year treasury bonds that also affects fixed rate mortgages.

Book Value The value of a property based on its purchase amount plus upgrades or other additions with depreciation subtracted.

Break-Even Point The point at which a landlord's income from rent matches expenses and debt.

Bridge Loan A short-term loan for individuals or companies that are still seeking more permanent financing.

Broker A person who serves as a go-between for a buyer and seller.

Brokerage The process of bringing two or more parties together in exchange for a fee, commission, or other compensation.

Buildable Acres The portion of land that can be built on after allowances for roads, setbacks, anticipated open spaces, and unsuitable areas have been made.

Building Code The laws set forth by the local government regarding end use of a given piece of property. These law codes may dictate the design, materials used, and/or types of improvements that will be allowed.

Building Standard Plus Allowance A detailed list provided by the landlord stating the standard building materials and costs necessary to make the premises inhabitable.

Build-Out Improvements to a property's space that have been implemented according to the tenant's specifications.

Build-to-Suit A way of leasing property, usually for commercial purposes, in which the developer or landlord builds to a tenant's specifications.

Buydown A term that usually refers to a fixed-rate mortgage for which additional payments can be applied to the interest rate for a temporary period, lowering payments for a period of one to three years.

Buydown Mortgage A style of home loan in which the lender receives a higher payment in order to convince them to reduce the interest rate during the initial years of the mortgage.

Buyer's Remorse A nervousness that first-time home buyers tend to feel after signing a sales contract or closing the purchase of a house.

Call Date The periodic or continuous right a lender has to call for payment of the total remaining balance prior to the date of maturity.

Call Option A clause in a loan agreement that allows a lender to demand repayment of the entire principal balance at any time.

Cap A limit on how much the monthly payment or interest rate is allowed to increase in an adjustable-rate mortgage.

Capital Appreciation The change in a property's or portfolio's market value after it has been adjusted for capital improvements and partial sales.

Capital Expenditures The purchase of long-term assets, or the expansion of existing ones, that prolongs the life or efficiency of those assets.

Capital Gain The amount of excess when the net proceeds from the sale of an asset are higher than its book value.

Capital Improvements Expenses that prolong the life of a property or add new improvements to it.

Capital Markets Public and private markets where individuals or businesses can raise or borrow capital.

Capitalization The mathematical process that investors use to derive the value of a property using the rate of return on investments.

Capitalization Rate The percentage of return as it is estimated from the net income of a property.

Carryback Financing A type of

funding in which a seller agrees to hold back a note for a specified portion of the sales price.

Carrying Charges Costs incurred to the landlord when initially leasing out a property and then during the periods of vacancy.

Cash Flow The amount of income an investor receives on a rental property after operating expenses and loan payments have been deducted.

Cashier's Check A check the bank draws on its own resources instead of a depositor's account.

Cash-on-Cash Yield The percentage of a property's net cash flow and the average amount of invested capital during the specified operating year.

Cash-Out Refinance The act of refinancing a mortgage for an amount that is higher than the original amount for the purpose of using the leftover cash for personal use.

Certificate of Deposit A type of deposit that is held in a bank for a limited time and pays a certain amount of interest to the depositor.

Certificate of Deposit Index (CODI) A rate that is based on interest rates of six-month CDs and is often used to determine interest rates for some ARMs.

Certificate of Eligibility A type of

document that the Department of Veterans Affairs issues to verify the eligibility of a veteran for a VA loan.

Certificate of Occupancy (CO) A written document issued by a local government or building agency that states that a home or other building is inhabitable after meeting all building codes.

Certificate of Reasonable Value (CRV) An appraisal presented by the Department of Veterans Affairs that shows the current market value of a property.

Certificate of Veteran Status A document veterans or reservists receive if they have served 90 days of continuous active duty (including training time).

Chain of Title The official record of all transfers of ownership over the history of a piece of property.

Chapter 11 The part of the federal bankruptcy code that deals with reorganizations of businesses.

Chapter 7 The part of the federal bankruptcy code that deals with liquidations of businesses.

Circulation Factor The interior space that is required for internal office circulation and is not included in the net square footage.

Class A A property rating that is

usually assigned to those that will generate the maximum rent per square foot, due to superior quality and/or location.

Class B A good property that most potential tenants would find desirable but lacks certain attributes that would bring in the top dollar.

Class C A building that is physically acceptable but offers few amenities, thereby becoming cost-effective space for tenants who are seeking a particular image.

Clear Title A property title that is free of liens, defects, or other legal encumbrances.

Clear-Span Facility A type of building, usually a warehouse or parking garage, consisting of vertical columns on the outer edges of the structure and clear spaces between the columns.

Closed-End Fund A mixed fund with a planned range of investor capital and a limited life.

Closing The final act of procuring a loan and title in which documents are signed between the buyer and seller and/or their respective representation and all money concerned in the contract changes hands.

Closing Costs The expenses that are related to the sale of real estate including loan, title, and appraisal fees and are beyond the price of the property itself.

Closing Statement See: Settlement Statement.

Cloud on Title Certain conditions uncovered in a title search that present a negative impact to the title for the property.

Commercial Mortgage-Backed Securities (CMBS) A type of securities that is backed by loans on commercial real estate.

Collateralized Mortgage Obligation (CMO) Debt that is fully based on a pool of mortgages.

Co-Borrower Another individual who is jointly responsible for the loan and is on the title to the property.

Cost of Funds Index (COFI) An index used to determine changes in the interest rates for certain ARMs.

Co-Investment Program A separate account for an insurance company or investment partnership in which two or more pension funds may co-invest their capital in an individual property or a portfolio of properties.

Co-Investment The condition that occurs when two or more pension funds or groups of funds are sharing ownership of a real estate investment.

Collateral The property for which a

borrower has obtained a loan, thereby assuming the risk of losing the property if the loan is not repaid according to the terms of the loan agreement.

Collection The effort on the part of a lender, due to a borrower defaulting on a loan, which involves mailing and recording certain documents in the event that the foreclosure procedure must be implemented.

Commercial Mortgage A loan used to purchase a piece of commercial property or building.

Commercial Mortgage Broker A broker specialized in commercial mortgage applications.

Commercial Mortgage Lender A lender specialized in funding commercial mortgage loans.

Commingled Fund A pooled fund that enables qualified employee benefit plans to mix their capital in order to achieve professional management, greater diversification, or investment positions in larger properties.

Commission A compensation to salespeople that is paid out of the total amount of the purchase transaction.

Commitment The agreement of a lender to make a loan with given terms for a specific period.

Commitment Fee The fee a lender charges for the guarantee of specified

loan terms, to be honored at some point in the future.

Common Area Assessments Sometimes called Homeowners' Association Fees. Charges paid to the homeowners' association by the individual unit owners, in a condominium or planned unit development (PUD), that are usually used to maintain the property and common areas.

Common Area Maintenance The additional charges the tenant must pay in addition to the base rent to pay for the maintenance of common areas.

Common Areas The portions of a building, land, and amenities, owned or managed by a planned unit development (PUD) or condominium's homeowners' association, that are used by all of the unit owners who share in the common expense of operation and maintenance.

Common Law A set of unofficial laws that were originally based on English customs and used to some extent in several states.

Community Property Property that is acquired by a married couple during the course of their marriage and is considered in many states to be owned jointly, unless certain circumstances are in play.

Comparable Sales Also called Comps or Comparables. The recent selling prices of similar properties in the area that are used to help determine the market value of a property.

Compound Interest The amount of interest paid on the principal balance of a mortgage in addition to accrued interest.

Concessions Cash, or the equivalent, that the landlord pays or allows in the form of rental abatement, additional tenant finish allowance, moving expenses, or other costs expended in order to persuade a tenant to sign a lease.

Condemnation A government agency's act of taking private property, without the owner's consent, for public use through the power of eminent domain.

Conditional Commitment A lender's agreement to make a loan providing the borrower meets certain conditions.

Conditional Sale A contract to sell a property that states that the seller will retain the title until all contractual conditions have been fulfilled.

Condominium A type of ownership in which all of the unit owners own the property, common areas, and buildings jointly, and have sole ownership in the unit to which they hold the title.

Condominium Conversion Changing an existing rental property's ownership to the condominium form of ownership.

Condominium Hotel A condominium project that involves registration desks, short-term occupancy, food and telephone services, and daily cleaning services, and is generally operated as a commercial hotel even though the units are individually owned.

Conduit A strategic alliance between lenders and unaffiliated organizations that acts as a source of funding by regularly purchasing loans, usually with a goal of pooling and securitizing them.

Conforming Loan A type of mortgage that meets the conditions to be purchased by Fannie Mae or Freddie Mac.

Construction Documents The drawings and specifications an architect and/or engineer provides to describe construction requirements for a project.

Construction Loan A short-term loan to finance the cost of construction, usually dispensed in stages throughout the construction project.

Construction Management The process of ensuring that the stages of the construction project are completed in a timely and seamless manner.

Construction-to-Permanent Loan A construction loan that can be converted to a longer-term traditional mortgage after construction is complete.

Consultant Any individual or company that provides the services to institutional investors, such as defining real estate investment policies, making recommendations to advisers or managers, monitoring and reporting on portfolio performance, and/or reviewing specified investment opportunities.

Consumer Price Index (CPI) A measurement of inflation, relating to the change in the prices of goods and services that are regularly purchased by a specific population during a certain period of time.

Contiguous Space Refers to several suites or spaces on a floor (or connected floors) in a given building that can be combined and rented to a single tenant.

Contingency A specific condition that must be met before either party in a contract can be legally bound.

Contract An agreement, either verbal or written, to perform or not to perform a certain thing.

Contract Documents See: Construction Documents.

Contract Rent Also known as Face Rent. The dollar amount of the rental obligation specified in a lease.

Conventional Loan A long-term loan from a non-governmental lender that a borrower obtains for the purchase of a home.

Convertible Adjustable-Rate Mortgage Type of mortgage that begins as a traditional ARM but contains a provision to enable the borrower to change to a fixed-rate mortgage during a certain time period.

Convertible Debt The point in a mortgage at which the lender has the option to convert to a partially or fully owned property within a certain period of time.

Convertible Preferred Stock Preferred stock that can be converted to common stock under certain conditions that have been specified by the issuer.

Conveyance The act of transferring a property title between parties by deed.

Cooperative Also called a Co-op. A type of ownership by multiple residents of a multi-unit housing complex in which they all own shares in the cooperative corporation that owns the property, thereby having the right to occupy a particular apartment or unit.

Cooperative Mortgage Any loan that is related to a cooperative residential project.

Core Properties The main types of property, specifically office, retail, industrial, and multi-family.

Co-Signer A second individual or party who also signs a promissory note or loan agreement, thereby taking responsibility for the debt in the event that the primary borrower cannot pay.

Cost-Approach Improvement Value The current expenses for constructing a copy or replacement for an existing structure, but subtracting an estimate of the accrued depreciation.

Cost-Approach Land Value The estimated value of the basic interest in the land, as if it were available for development to its highest and best use.

Cost-of-Sale Percentage An estimate of the expenses of selling an investment that represents brokerage commissions, closing costs, fees, and other necessary sales costs.

Coupon The token or expected interest rate the borrower is charged on a promissory note or mortgage.

Courier Fee The fee that is charged at closing for the delivery of documents between all parties concerned in a real estate transaction.

Covenant Written agreement, included in deeds or other legal documents, that defines the requirements for certain acts or use of a property.

Credit An agreement in which a borrower promises to repay the lender at a later date and receives something of value in exchange.

Credit Enhancement The necessary credit support, in addition to mortgage collateral, in order to achieve the desired credit rating on mortgage-backed securities.

Credit History An individual's record which details his current and past financial obligations and performance.

Credit Life Insurance A type of insurance that pays the balance of a mortgage if the borrower dies.

Credit Rating The degree of creditworthiness a person is assigned based on his credit history and current financial status.

Credit Report A record detailing an individual's credit, employment, and residence history used to determine the individual's creditworthiness.

Credit Repository A company that records and updates credit applicants' financial and credit information from various sources.

Credit Score Sometimes called a Credit Risk Score. The number contained in a consumer's credit report that represents a statistical summary of the information.

Creditor A party to whom other parties owe money.

Cross-Collateralization A group of mortgages or properties that jointly secures one debt obligation.

Cross-Defaulting A provision that allows a trustee or lender to require full payment on all loans in a group, if any single loan in the group is in default.

Cumulative Discount Rate A percentage of the current value of base rent with all landlord lease concessions taken into account.

Current Occupancy The current percentage of units in a building or property that is leased.

Current Yield The annual rate of return on an investment, expressed as a percentage.

Deal Structure The type of agreement in financing an acquisition. The deal can be un-leveraged, leveraged, traditional debt, participating debt, participating/ convertible debt, or joint ventures.

Debt Any amount one party owes to another party.

Debt Service Coverage Ratio (DSCR) A property's yearly net operating income divided by the yearly cost of debt service.

Debt Service The amount of money that is necessary to meet all interest and principal payments during a specific period.

Debt-to-Income Ratio The percentage of a borrower's monthly payment on long-term debts divided by his gross monthly income.

Dedicate To change a private property to public ownership for a particular public use.

Deed A legal document that conveys property ownership to the buyer.

Deed in Lieu of Foreclosure A situation in which a deed is given to a lender in order to satisfy a mortgage debt and to avoid the foreclosure process.

Deed of Trust A provision that allows a lender to foreclose on a property in the event that the borrower defaults on the loan.

Default The state that occurs when a borrow fails to fulfill a duty or take care of an obligation, such as making monthly mortgage payments.

Deferred Maintenance Account A type of account that a borrower must fund to provide for maintenance of a property.

Deficiency Judgment The legal assignment of personal liability to a borrower for the unpaid balance of a mortgage, after foreclosing on the property has failed to yield the full amount of the debt.

Defined-Benefit Plan A type of benefit provided by an employer that defines an employee's benefits either as a fixed amount or a percentage of the beneficiary's salary when he retires.

Defined-Contribution Plan A type of benefit plan provided by an employer in which an employee's retirement benefits are determined by the amount that has been contributed by the employer and/or employee during the time of employment, and by the actual investment earnings on those contributions over the life of the fund.

Delinquency A state that occurs when the borrower fails to make mortgage payments on time, eventually resulting in foreclosure, if severe enough.

Delinquent Mortgage A mortgage in which the borrower is behind on payments.

Demising Wall The physical partition between the spaces of two tenants or from the building's common areas.

Deposit Also referred to as Earnest Money. The funds that the buyer provides when offering to purchase property.

Depreciation A decline in the value of property or an asset, often used as a tax-deductible item.

Derivative Securities A type of securities that has been created from other financial instruments.

Design/Build An approach in which a single individual or business is responsible for both the design and construction.

Disclosure A written statement, presented to a potential buyer, that lists information relevant to a piece of property, whether positive or negative.

Discount Points Fees that a lender charges in order to provide a lower interest rate.

Discount Rate A figure used to translate present value from future payments or receipts.

Discretion The amount of authority an adviser or manager is granted for investing and managing a client's capital.

Distraint The act of seizing a tenant's personal property when the tenant is in default, based on the right the landlord has in satisfying the debt.

Diversification The act of spreading individual investments out to insulate a portfolio against the risk of reduced yield or capital loss.

Dividend Yield The percentage of a security's market price that represents the annual dividend rate.

Dividend Distributions of cash or stock that stockholders receive.

Dividend-Ex Date The initial date on which a person purchasing the stock can no longer receive the most recently announced dividend.

Document Needs List The list of

documents a lender requires from a potential borrower who is submitting a loan application.

Documentation Preparation Fee A fee that lenders, brokers, and/or settlement agents charge for the preparation of the necessary closing documents.

Dollar Stop An agreed amount of taxes and operating expenses each tenant must pay out on a prorated basis.

Down Payment The variance between the purchase price and the portion that the mortgage lender financed.

DOWNREIT A structure of organization that makes it possible for REITs to purchase properties using partnership units.

Draw A payment from the construction loan proceeds made to contractors, subcontractors, home builders, or suppliers.

Due Diligence The activities of a prospective purchaser or mortgager of real property for the purpose of confirming that the property is as represented by the seller and is not subject to environmental or other problems.

Due on Sale Clause The standard mortgage language that states the loan must still be repaid if the property is resold.

Earnest Money See: Deposit.

Earthquake Insurance A type of insurance policy that provides coverage against earthquake damage to a home.

Easement The right given to a non-ownership party to use a certain part of the property for specified purposes, such as servicing power lines or cable lines.

Economic Feasibility The viability of a building or project in terms of costs and revenue where the degree of viability is established by extra revenue.

Economic Rent The market rental value of a property at a particular point in time.

Effective Age An estimate of the physical condition of a building presented by an appraiser.

Effective Date The date on which the sale of securities can commence once a registration statement becomes effective.

Effective Gross Income (EGI) The total property income that rents and other sources generate after subtracting a vacancy factor estimated to be appropriate for the property.

Effective Gross Rent (EGR) The net rent that is generated after adjusting for tenant improvements and other capital costs, lease commissions, and other sales expenses.

Effective Rent The actual rental rate that the landlord achieves after deducting the concession value from the base rental rate a tenant pays.

Electronic Authentication A way of providing proof that a particular electronic document is genuine, has arrived unaltered, and came from the indicated source.

Eminent Domain The power of the government to pay the fair market value for a property, appropriating it for public use.

Encroachment Any improvement or upgrade that illegally intrudes onto another party's property.

Encumbrance Any right or interest in a property that interferes with using it or transferring ownership.

End Loan Result of converting to permanent financing from a construction loan.

Entitlement A benefit of a VA home loan. Often referred to as Eligibility.

Environmental Impact Statement Legally required documents that must accompany major project proposals where there will likely be an impact on the surrounding environment.

Equal Credit Opportunity Act (ECOA) A federal law that requires a lender or other creditor to make credit available for applicants regardless of sex, marital status, race, religion, or age.

Equifax One of the three primary credit-reporting bureaus.

Equity The value of a property after existing liabilities have been deducted.

Employee Retirement Income Security Act (ERISA) A legislation that controls the investment activities, mainly of corporate and union pension plans.

Errors and Omissions Insurance A type of policy that insures against the mistakes of a builder or architect.

Escalation Clause The clause in a lease that provides for the rent to be increased to account for increases in the expenses the landlord must pay.

Escrow A valuable item, money, or documents deposited with a third party for delivery upon the fulfillment of a condition.

Escrow Account Also referred to as an Impound Account. An account established by a mortgage lender or servicing company for the purpose of holding funds for the payment of items, such as homeowner's insurance and property taxes.

Escrow Agent A neutral third party who makes sure that all conditions of a real estate transaction have been met before any funds are transferred or property is recorded.

Escrow Agreement A written agreement between an escrow agent and the contractual parties that defines the basic obligations of each party, the money (or other valuables) to be deposited in escrow, and how the escrow agent is to dispose of the money on deposit.

Escrow Analysis An annual investigation a lender performs to make sure they are collecting the appropriate amount of money for anticipated expenditures.

Escrow Closing The event in which all conditions of a real estate transaction have been met, and the property title is transferred to the buyer.

Escrow Company A neutral company that serves as a third party to ensure that all conditions of a real estate transaction are met.

Escrow Disbursements The dispensing of escrow funds for the payment of real estate taxes, hazard insurance, mortgage insurance, and other property expenses as they are due.

Escrow Payment The funds that are withdrawn by a mortgage servicer from a borrower's escrow account to pay property taxes and insurance.

Estate The total assets, including property, of an individual after he has died.

Estimated Closing Costs An estimation of the expenses relating to the sale of real estate.

Estimated Hazard Insurance An estimation of hazard insurance, or homeowner's insurance, that will cover physical risks.

Estimated Property Taxes An estimation of the property taxes that must be paid on the property, according to state and county tax rates.

Estoppel Certificate A signed statement that certifies that certain factual statements are correct as of the date of the statement and can be relied upon by a third party, such as a prospective lender or purchaser.

Eviction The legal removal of an occupant from a piece of property.

Examination of Title A title company's inspection and report of public records and other documents for the purpose of determining the chain of ownership of a property.

Exclusive Agency Listing A written agreement between a property owner and a real estate broker in which the owner promises to pay the broker a commission if certain property is leased during the listing period.

Exclusive Listing A contract that allows a licensed real estate agent to be the only agent who can sell a property for a given time.

Executed Contract An agreement in which all parties involved have fulfilled their duties.

Executor The individual who is named in a will to administer an estate. Executrix is the feminine form.

Exit Strategy An approach investors may use when they wish to liquidate all or part of their investment.

Experian One of the three primary credit-reporting bureaus.

Face Rental Rate The rental rate that the landlord publishes.

Facility Space The floor area in a hospitality property that is dedicated to activities, such as restaurants, health clubs, and gift shops, that interactively service multiple people and is not directly related to room occupancy.

Funds Available for Distribution (FAD) The income from operations, with cash expenditures subtracted, that may be used for leasing commissions and tenant improvement costs.

FAD Multiple The price per share of a REIT divided by its funds available for distribution.

Fair Credit Reporting Act (FCRA) The federal legislation that governs the processes credit reporting agencies must follow.

Fair Housing Act The federal legislation that prohibits the refusal to rent or sell to anyone based on race, color, religion, sex, family status, or disability.

Fair Market Value The highest price that a buyer would be willing to pay, and the lowest a seller would be willing to accept.

Fannie Mae See: Federal National Mortgage Association.

Fannie Mae's Community Home Buyer's Program A community lending model based on borrower income in which mortgage insurers and Fannie Mae offer flexible underwriting guidelines in order to increase the buying power for a low- or moderate-income family and to decrease the total amount of cash needed to purchase a home.

Farmer's Home Administration (FMHA) An agency within the U.S. Department of Agriculture that provides credit to farmers and other rural residents.

Federal Home Loan Mortgage Corporation (FHLMC) Also known as Freddie Mac. The company that buys mortgages from lending institutions, combines them with other loans, and sells shares to investors.

Federal Housing Administration (FHA) A government agency that provides low-rate mortgages to buyers who are able to make a down payment as low as 3 percent.

Federal National Mortgage Association (FNMA) Also known as Fannie Mae. A congressionally chartered, shareholder-owned company that is the nation's largest supplier of home mortgage funds. The company buys mortgages from lenders and resells them as securities on the secondary mortgage market.

Fee Simple The highest possible interest a person can have in a piece of real estate.

Fee Simple Estate An unconditional, unlimited inheritance estate in which the owner may dispose of or use the property as desired.

Fee Simple Interest The state of owning all the rights in a real estate parcel.

Funds From Operations (FFO) A ratio that is meant to highlight the amount of cash a company's real estate portfolio generates relative to its total operating cash flow.

FFO Multiple The price of a REIT share divided by its funds from operations.

FHA Loans Mortgages that the Federal Housing Administration (FHA) insures.

FHA Mortgage Insurance A type of insurance that requires a fee to

be paid at closing in order to insure the loan with the Federal Housing Administration (FHA).

Fiduciary Any individual who holds authority over a plan's asset management, administration or disposition, or renders paid investment advice regarding a plan's assets.

Finance Charge The amount of interest to be paid on a loan or credit card balance.

Firm Commitment A written agreement a lender makes to loan money for the purchase of property.

First Mortgage The main mortgage on a property.

First Refusal Right/ Right of First Refusal A lease clause that gives a tenant the first opportunity to buy a property or to lease additional space in a property at the same price and terms as those contained in an offer from a third party that the owner has expressed a willingness to accept.

First-Generation Space A new space that has never before been occupied by a tenant and is currently available for lease.

First-Loss Position A security's position that will suffer the first economic loss if the assets below it lose value or are foreclosed on.

Fixed Costs Expenses that remain

the same despite the level of sales or production.

Fixed Rate An interest rate that does not change over the life of the loan.

Fixed Time The particular weeks of a year that the owner of a timeshare arrangement can access his or her accommodations.

Fixed-Rate Mortgage A loan with an unchanging interest rate over the life of the loan.

Fixture Items that become a part of the property when they are permanently attached to the property.

Flat Fee An amount of money that an adviser or manager receives for managing a portfolio of real estate assets.

Flex Space A building that provides a flexible configuration of office or showroom space combined with manufacturing, laboratory, warehouse, distribution, etc.

Float The number of freely traded shares owned by the public.

Flood Certification The process of analyzing whether a property is located in a known flood zone.

Flood Insurance A policy that is required in designated flood zones to protect against loss due to flood damage.

Floor Area Ratio (FAR) A measurement of a building's gross square footage compared to the square footage of the land on which it is located.

For Sale By Owner (FSBO) A method of selling property in which the property owner serves as the selling agent and directly handles the sales process with the buyer or buyer's agent.

Force Majeure An external force that is not controlled by the contractual parties and prevents them from complying with the provisions of the contract.

Foreclosure The legal process in which a lender takes over ownership of a property once the borrower is in default in a mortgage arrangement.

Forward Commitments Contractual agreements to perform certain financing duties according to any stated conditions.

Four Quadrants of the Real Estate Capital Markets The four market types that consist of Private Equity, Public Equity, Private Debt, and Public Debt.

Freddie Mac See: Federal Home Loan Mortgage Corporation.

Front-End Ratio The measurement a lender uses to compare a borrower's monthly housing expense to gross monthly income.

Full Recourse A loan on which the responsibility of a loan is transferred to an endorser or guarantor in the event of default by the borrower.

Full-Service Rent A rental rate that includes all operating expenses and real estate taxes for the first year.

Fully Amortized ARM An ARM with a monthly payment that is sufficient to amortize the remaining balance at the current interest accrual rate over the amortization term.

Fully Diluted Shares The number of outstanding common stock shares if all convertible securities were converted to common shares.

Future Proposed Space The space in a commercial development that has been proposed but is not yet under construction, or the future phases of a multi-phase project that has not yet been built.

General Contractor The main person or business that contracts for the construction of an entire building or project, rather than individual duties.

General Partner The member in a partnership who holds the authority to bind the partnership and shares in its profits and losses.

Gift Money a buyer has received from a relative or other source that will not have to be repaid.

Ginnie Mae See: Government National Mortgage Association.

Going-In Capitalization Rate The rate that is computed by dividing the expected net operating income for the first year by the value of the property.

Good Faith Estimate A lender's or broker's estimate that shows all costs associated with obtaining a home loan including loan processing, title, and inspection fees.

Government Loan A mortgage that is insured or guaranteed by the FHA, the Department of Veterans Affairs (VA), or the Rural Housing Service (RHS).

Government National Mortgage Association (GNMA) Also known as Ginnie Mae. A government-owned corporation under the U.S. Department of Housing and Urban Development (HUD) that performs the same role as Fannie Mae and Freddie Mac in providing funds to lenders for making home loans, but only purchases loans that are backed by the federal government.

Grace Period A defined time period in which a borrower may make a loan payment after its due date without incurring a penalty.

Graduated Lease A lease, usually long-term, in which rent payments vary in accordance with future contingencies.

Graduated Payment Mortgage A

mortgage that requires low payments during the first years of the loan, but eventually requires larger monthly payments over the term of the loan that become fixed later in the term.

Grant To give or transfer an interest in a property by deed or other documented method.

Grantee The party to whom an interest in a property is given.

Grantor The party who is transferring an interest in a property.

Gross Building Area The sum of areas at all floor levels, including the basement, mezzanine, and penthouses included in the principal outside faces of the exterior walls without allowing for architectural setbacks or projections.

Gross Income The total income of a household before taxes or expenses have been subtracted.

Gross Investment in Real Estate (Historic Cost) The total amount of equity and debt that is invested in a piece of real estate minus proceeds from sales or partial sales.

Gross Leasable Area The amount of floor space that is designed for tenants' occupancy and exclusive use.

Gross Lease A rental arrangement in which the tenant pays a flat sum for rent, and the landlord must pay all building expenses out of that amount.

Gross Real Estate Asset Value The total market value of the real estate investments under management in a fund or individual accounts, usually including the total value of all equity positions, debt positions, and joint venture ownership positions.

Gross Real Estate Investment Value The market value of real estate investments that are held in a portfolio without including debt.

Gross Returns The investment returns generated from operating a property without adjusting for adviser or manager fees.

Ground Lease Land being leased to an individual that has absolutely no residential dwelling on the property; or if it does, the ground (or land) is the only portion of the property being leased.

Ground Rent A long-term lease in which rent is paid to the land owner, normally to build something on that land.

Growing-Equity Mortgage A fixed-rate mortgage in which payments increase over a specified amount of time with the extra funds being applied to the principal.

Guarantor The part who makes a guaranty.

Guaranty An agreement in which the guarantor promises to satisfy the debt or obligations of another, if and when the debtor fails to do so.

Hard Cost The expenses attributed to actually constructing property improvements.

Hazard Insurance Also known as Homeowner's Insurance or Fire Insurance. A policy that provides coverage for damage from forces such as fire and wind.

Highest and Best Use The most reasonable, expected, legal use of a piece of vacant land or improved property that is physically possible, supported appropriately, financially feasible, and that results in the highest value.

High-Rise In a suburban district, any building taller than six stories. In a business district, any building taller than 25 stories.

Holdbacks A portion of a loan funding that is not dispersed until an additional condition is met, such as the completion of construction.

Holding Period The expected length of time, from purchase to sale, that an investor will own a property.

Hold-Over Tenant A tenant who retains possession of the leased premises after the lease has expired.

Home Equity Conversion Mortgage (HECM) Also referred to as a Reverse Annuity Mortgage. A type of mortgage

in which the lender makes payments to the owner, thereby enabling older homeowners to convert equity in their homes into cash in the form of monthly payments.

Home Equity Line An open-ended amount of credit based on the equity a homeowner has accumulated.

Home Equity Loan A type of loan that allows owners to borrow against the equity in their homes up to a limited amount.

Home Inspection A pre-purchase examination of the condition a home is in by a certified inspector.

Home Inspector A certified professional who determines the structural soundness and operating systems of a property.

Home Price The price that a buyer and seller agree upon, generally based on the home's appraised market value.

Homeowners' Association (HOA) A group that governs a community, condominium building, or neighborhood and enforces the covenants, conditions, and restrictions set by the developer.

Homeowners' Association Dues The monthly payments that are paid to the homeowners' association for maintenance and communal expenses.

Homeowner's Insurance A policy

that includes coverage for all damages that may affect the value of a house as defined in the terms of the insurance policy.

Homeowner's Warranty A type of policy home buyers often purchase to cover repairs, such as heating or air-conditioning, should they stop working within the coverage period.

Homestead The property an owner uses as his primary residence.

Housing Expense Ratio The percentage of gross income that is devoted to housing costs each month.

HUD (Housing and Urban Development) A federal agency that oversees a variety of housing and community development programs, including the FHA.

HUD Median Income The average income for families in a particular area, which is estimated by HUD.

HUD-1 Settlement Statement Also known as the Closing Statement or Settlement Sheet. An itemized listing of the funds paid at closing.

HUD-1 Uniform Settlement Statement A closing statement for the buyer and seller that describes all closing costs for a real estate transaction or refinancing.

HVAC Heating, ventilating, and air-conditioning.

Hybrid Debt A position in a mortgage that has equity-like features of participation in both cash flow and the appreciation of the property at the point of sale or refinance.

Implied Cap Rate The net operating income divided by the sum of a REIT's equity market capitalization and its total outstanding debt.

Impounds The part of the monthly mortgage payment that is reserved in an account in order to pay for hazard insurance, property taxes, and private mortgage insurance.

Improvements The upgrades or changes made to a building to improve its value or usefulness.

Incentive Fee A structure in which the fee amount charged is based on the performance of the real estate assets under management.

Income Capitalization Value The figure derived for an income-producing property by converting its expected benefits into property value.

Income Property A particular property that is used to generate income but is not occupied by the owner.

Income Return Percentage of the total return generated by the income from property, fund, or account operations.

Index Financial table that lenders use for calculating interest rates on ARMs.

Indexed Rate The sum of the published index with a margin added.

Indirect Costs Expenses of development other than the costs of direct material and labor that are related directly to the construction of improvements.

Individual Account Management The process of maintaining accounts that have been established for individual plan sponsors or other investors for investment in real estate, where a firm acts as an adviser in obtaining and/or managing a real estate portfolio.

Inflation Hedge An investment whose value tends to increase at a greater rate than inflation, contributing to the preservation of the purchasing power of a portfolio.

Inflation The rate at which consumer prices increase each year.

Initial Interest Rate The original interest rate on an ARM which is sometimes subject to a variety of adjustments throughout the mortgage.

Initial Public Offering (IPO) The first time a previously private company offers securities for public sale.

Initial Rate Cap The limit specified by some ARMs as the maximum amount the interest rate may increase when the initial interest rate expires.

Initial Rate Duration The date specified by most ARMs at which the initial rate expires.

Inspection Fee The fee that a licensed property inspector charges for determining the current physical condition of the property.

Inspection Report A written report of the property's condition presented by a licensed inspection professional.

Institutional-Grade Property A variety of types of real estate properties usually owned or financed by tax-exempt institutional investors.

Insurance Binder A temporary insurance policy implemented while a permanent policy is drawn up or obtained.

Insurance Company Separate Account A real estate investment vehicle only offered by life insurance companies, which enables an ERISA-governed fund to avoid creating unrelated taxable income for certain types of property investments and investment structures.

Insured Mortgage A mortgage that is guaranteed by the FHA or by private mortgage insurance (PMI).

Interest Accrual Rate The rate at which a mortgage accrues interest.

Interest-Only Loan Mortgage where the borrower pays only the interest that accrues on the balance each month.

Interest Paid over Life of Loan The total amount that has been paid to the lender during the time the money was borrowed.

Interest Rate The percentage that is charged for a loan.

Interest Rate Buy-Down Plans A plan in which a seller uses funds from the sale of the home to buy down the interest rate and reduce the buyer's monthly payments.

Interest Rate Cap The highest interest rate charge allowed on the monthly payment of an ARM during an adjustment period.

Interest Rate Ceiling The maximum interest rate a lender can charge for an ARM.

Interest Rate Floor The minimum possible interest rate a lender can charge for an ARM.

Interest Price paid for use of capital.

Interest-Only Strip A derivative security that consists of all or part of the portion of interest in the underlying loan or security.

Interim Financing Also known as Bridge or Swing Loans. Short-term financing a seller uses to bridge the gap between the sale of one house and the purchase of another.

Internal Rate of Return (IRR) The calculation of a discounted cash flow analysis that is used to determine the potential total return of a real estate asset during a particular holding period.

Inventory The entire space of a certain proscribed market without concern for its availability or condition.

Investment Committee The governing body that is charged with overseeing corporate pension investments and developing investment policies for board approval.

Investment Manager An individual or company that assumes authority over a specified amount of real estate capital, invests that capital in assets using a separate account, and provides asset management.

Investment Policy A document that formalizes an institution's goals, objectives, and guidelines for asset management, investment advisory contracting, fees, and utilization of consultants and other outside professionals.

Investment Property A piece of real estate that generates some form of income.

Investment Strategy The methods used by a manager in structuring a portfolio and selecting the real estate assets for a fund or an account.

Investment Structures Approaches to investing that include un-leveraged acquisitions, leveraged acquisitions, traditional debt, participating debt, convertible debt, triple-net leases, and joint ventures.

Investment-Grade CMBS Commercial mortgage-backed securities that have ratings of AAA, AA, A, or BBB.

Investor Status The position an investor is in, either taxable or tax-exempt.

Joint Liability The condition in which responsibility rests with two or more people for fulfilling the terms of a home loan or other financial debt.

Joint Tenancy A form of ownership in which two or more people have equal shares in a piece of property, and rights pass to the surviving owner(s) in the event of death.

Joint Venture An investment business formed by more than one party for the purpose of acquiring or developing and managing property and/or other assets.

Judgment The decision a court of law makes.

Judicial Foreclosure The usual foreclosure proceeding some states use, which is handled in a civil lawsuit.

Jumbo Loan A type of mortgage that exceeds the required limits set by Fannie Mae and Freddie Mac each year.

Junior Mortgage A loan that is a lower priority behind the primary loan.

Just Compensation The amount that is fair to both the owner and the government when property is appropriated for public use through eminent domain.

Landlord's Warrant The warrant a landlord obtains to take a tenant's personal property to sell at a public sale to compel payment of the rent or other stipulation in the lease.

Late Charge Fee that is imposed by a lender when the borrower has not made a payment when it was due.

Late Payment Payment made to the lender after the due date has passed.

Lead Manager The investment banking firm that has primary responsibility for coordinating the new issuance of securities.

Lease A contract between a property owner and tenant that defines payments and conditions under which the tenant may occupy the real estate for a given period of time.

Lease Commencement Date Date the terms of the lease are implemented.

Lease Expiration Exposure Schedule A chart of the total square footage of all current leases that expire in each of the next five years, without taking renewal options into account.

Lease Option A financing option that provides for home buyers to lease a home with an option to buy, with part of the rental payments being applied toward the down payment.

Leasehold Limited right to inhabit a piece of real estate held by a tenant.

Leasehold State A way of holding a property title in which the mortgagor does not actually own the property but has a long-term lease on it.

Leasehold Interest The right to hold or use property for a specific period of time at a given price without transferring ownership.

Lease-Purchase A contract that defines the closing date and solutions for the seller in the event that the buyer defaults.

Legal Blemish A negative count against a piece of property such as a zoning violation or fraudulent title claim.

Legal Description A way of describing and locating a piece of real estate that is recognized by law.

Legal Owner The party who holds the title to the property, although the title may carry no actual rights to the property other than as a lien.

Lender A bank or other financial institution that offers home loans.

Letter of Credit Promise from a bank or other party that the issuer will honor drafts or requests for payment upon complying with the requirements specified in the letter of credit.

Letter of Intent An initial agreement defining the proposed terms for the end contract.

Leverage Process of increasing the return on an investment by borrowing some of the funds at an interest rate less than the return on the project.

Liabilities Borrower's debts and financial obligations, whether long- or short-term.

Liability Insurance A type of policy that protects owners against negligence, personal injury, or property damage claims.

London InterBank Offered Rate (LIBOR) The interest rate offered on Eurodollar deposits traded between banks and used to determine changes in interest rate for ARMs.

Lien A claim put by one party on the property of another as collateral for money owed.

Lien Waiver A waiver of a mechanic's lien rights that is sometimes required before the general contractor can receive money under the payment provisions of a construction loan and contract.

Life Cap A limit on the amount an ARM's interest rate can increase during the mortgage term.

Lifecycle The stages of development for a property: pre-development, development, leasing, operating, and rehabilitation.

Lifetime Payment Cap A limit on the amount that payments can increase or decrease over the life of an ARM.

Lifetime Rate Cap The highest possible interest rate that may be charged, under any circumstances, over the entire life of an ARM.

Like-Kind Property A term that refers to real estate that is held for productive use in a trade or business or for investment.

Limited Partnership A type of partnership in which some partners manage the business and are personally liable for partnership debts, but some partners contribute capital and share in profits without the responsibility of management.

Line of Credit An amount of credit granted by a financial institution up to a specified amount for a certain period of time to a borrower.

Liquid Asset A type of asset that can be easily converted into cash.

Liquidity The ease with which an individual's or company's assets can be converted to cash without losing their value.

Listing Agreement An agreement between a property owner and a real estate broker that authorizes the broker to attempt to sell or lease the property at a specified price and terms in return for a commission or other compensation.

Loan An amount of money that is borrowed and usually repaid with interest.

Loan Application A document that presents a borrower's income, debt, and other obligations to determine credit worthiness, as well as some basic information on the target property.

Loan Application Fee A fee lenders charge to cover expenses relating to reviewing a loan application.

Loan Commitment An agreement by a lender or other financial institution to make or ensure a loan for the specified amount and terms.

Loan Officer An official representative of a lending institution who is authorized to act on behalf of the lender within specified limits.

Loan Origination The process of obtaining and arranging new loans.

Loan Origination Fee A fee lenders charge to cover the costs related to arranging the loan.

Loan Servicing Process a lending institution goes through for all loans it manages. This involves processing payments, sending statements, managing the escrow/impound account, providing collection services on delinquent loans, ensuring that insurance and property taxes are made on the property, handling pay-offs and assumptions, as well as various other services.

Loan Term Time, usually expressed in years, that a lender sets in which a buyer must pay a mortgage.

Loan-to-Value (LTV) The ratio of the amount of the loan compared to the appraised value or sales price.

Lock-Box Structure An arrangement in which the payments are sent directly from the tenant or borrower to the trustee.

Lock-In A commitment from a lender to a borrower to guarantee a given interest rate for a limited amount of time.

Lock-In Period The period of time during which the borrower is guaranteed a specified interest rate.

Lockout The period of time during which a loan may not be paid off early.

Long-Term Lease A rental agreement that will last at least three years from initial signing to the date of expiration or renewal.

Loss Severity The percentage of lost principal when a loan is foreclosed.

Lot One of several contiguous parcels of a larger piece of land.

Low-Documentation Loan A mortgage that requires only a basic verification of income and assets.

Low-Rise A building that involves fewer than four stories above the ground level.

Lump-Sum Contract A type of construction contract that requires the general contractor to complete a building project for a fixed cost that is usually established beforehand by competitive bidding.

Magic Page A story of projected growth that describes how a new REIT will achieve its future plans for funds from operations or funds available for distribution.

Maintenance Fee The charge to homeowners' association members each month for the repair and maintenance of common areas.

Maker One who issues a promissory note and commits to paying the note when it is due.

Margin A percentage that is added to the index and fixed for the mortgage term.

Mark to Market The act of changing

the original investment cost or value of a property or portfolio to the level of the current estimated market value.

Market Capitalization A measurement of a company's value that is calculated by multiplying the current share price by the current number of shares outstanding.

Market Rental Rates The rental income that a landlord could most likely ask for a property in the open market, indicated by the current rents for comparable spaces.

Market Study A forecast of the demand for a certain type of real estate project in the future that includes an estimate of the square footage that could be absorbed and the rents that could be charged.

Market Value The price a property would sell for at a particular point in time in a competitive market.

Marketable Title Title that is free of encumbrances and can be marketed immediately to a willing purchaser.

Master Lease The primary lease that controls other subsequent leases and may cover more property than all subsequent leases combined.

Master Servicer An entity that acts on behalf of a trustee for security holders' benefit in collecting funds from a borrower, advancing funds in the event of delinquencies and, in the event of

default, taking a property through foreclosure.

Maturity Date The date at which the total principal balance of a loan is due.

Mechanic's Lien A claim created for securing payment priority for the price and value of work performed and materials furnished in constructing, repairing, or improving a building or other structure.

Meeting Space The space in hotels that is made available to the public to rent for meetings, conferences, or banquets.

Merged Credit Report A report that combines information from the three primary credit-reporting agencies including: Equifax, Experian, and TransUnion.

Metes and Bounds The surveyed boundary lines of a piece of land described by listing the compass directions (bounds) and distances (metes) of the boundaries.

Mezzanine Financing A financing position somewhere between equity and debt, meaning that there are higher-priority debts above and equity below.

Mid-Rise A building which shows 4 to 8 stories above ground level. In a business district, buildings up to 25 stories may also be included.

Mixed-Use Term referring to space

within a building or project which can be used for more than one activity.

Modern Portfolio Theory (MPT) Approach of quantifying risk and return in an asset portfolio which emphasizes the portfolio rather than the individual assets and how the assets perform in relation to each other.

Modification An adjustment in the terms of a loan agreement.

Modified Annual Percentage Rate (APR) An index of the cost of a loan based on the standard APR but adjusted for the amount of time the borrower expects to hold the loan.

Monthly Association Dues A payment due each month to a homeowners' association for expenses relating to maintenance and community operations.

Mortgage An amount of money that is borrowed to purchase a property using that property as collateral.

Mortgage Acceleration Clause A provision enabling a lender to require that the rest of the loan balance is paid in a lump sum under certain circumstances.

Mortgage Banker A financial institution that provides home loans using its own resources, often selling them to investors such as insurance companies or Fannie Mae.

Mortgage Broker An individual who matches prospective borrowers with lenders that the broker is approved to deal with.

Mortgage Broker Business A company that matches prospective borrowers with lenders that the broker is approved to deal with.

Mortgage Constant A figure comparing an amortizing mortgage payment to the outstanding mortgage balance.

Mortgage Insurance (MI) A policy, required by lenders on some loans, that covers the lender against certain losses that are incurred as a result of a default on a home loan.

Mortgage Insurance Premium (MIP) The amount charged for mortgage insurance, either to a government agency or to a private MI company.

Mortgage Interest Deduction The tax write-off that the IRS allows most homeowners to deduct for annual interest payments made on real estate loans.

Mortgage Life and Disability Insurance A type of term life insurance borrowers often purchase to cover debt that is left when the borrower dies or becomes too disabled to make the mortgage payments.

Mortgagee The financial institution that lends money to the borrower.

Mortgagor The person who requests to borrow money to purchase a property.

Multi-Dwelling Units A set of properties that provide separate housing areas for more than one family but only require a single mortgage.

Multiple Listing Service A service that lists real estate offered for sale by a particular real estate agent that can be shown or sold by other real estate agents within a certain area.

National Association of Real Estate Investment Trusts (NAREIT) The national, non-profit trade organization that represents the real estate investment trust industry.

National Council of Real Estate Investment Fiduciaries (NCREIF) A group of real estate professionals who serve on committees; sponsor research articles, seminars and symposiums; and produce the NCREIF Property Index.

NCREIF Property Index (NPI) A quarterly and yearly report presenting income and appreciation components.

Negative Amortization An event that occurs when the deferred interest on an ARM is added, and the balance increases instead of decreases.

Net Asset Value (NAV) The total value of an asset or property minus leveraging or joint venture interests.

Net Asset Value Per Share The total value of a REIT's current assets divided by outstanding shares.

Net Assets The total value of assets minus total liabilities based on market value.

Net Cash Flow The total income generated by an investment property after expenses have been subtracted.

Net Investment in Real Estate Gross investment in properties minus the outstanding balance of debt.

Net Investment Income The income or loss of a portfolio or business minus all expenses, including portfolio and asset management fees, but before gains and losses on investments are considered.

Net Operating Income (NOI) The pre-tax figure of gross revenue minus operating expenses and an allowance for expected vacancy.

Net Present Value (NPV) The sum of the total current value of incremental future cash flows plus the current value of estimated sales proceeds.

Net Purchase Price The gross purchase price minus any associated financed debt.

Net Real Estate Investment Value The total market value of all real estate minus property-level debt.

Net Returns The returns paid to

investors minus fees to advisers or managers.

Net Sales Proceeds The income from the sale of an asset, or part of an asset, minus brokerage commissions, closing costs, and market expenses.

Net Square Footage The total space required for a task or staff position.

Net Worth The worth of an individual or company figured on the basis of a difference between all assets and liabilities.

No-Cash-Out Refinance Also referred to as a Rate and Term Refinance. A refinancing transaction intended only to cover the balance due on the current loan and any costs associated with obtaining the new mortgage.

No-Cost Loan A loan for which there are no costs associated with the loan that are charged by the lender, but with a slightly higher interest rate.

No-Documentation Loan A type of loan application that requires no income or asset verification, usually granted based on strong credit with a large down payment.

Nominal Yield The yield investors receive before it is adjusted for fees, inflation, or risk.

Non-Assumption Clause A provision in a loan agreement that prohibits transferring a mortgage to another

borrower without approval from the lender.

Non-Compete Clause A provision in a lease agreement that specifies that the tenant's business is the only one that may operate in the property in question, thereby preventing a competitor moving in next door.

Non-Conforming Loan Any loan that is too large or does not meet certain qualifications to be purchased by Fannie Mae or Freddie Mac.

Non-Discretionary Funds The funds that are allocated to an investment manager who must have approval from the investor for each transaction.

Non-Investment-Grade CMBS Also referred to as High-Yield CMBS. Commercial mortgage-backed securities that have ratings of BB or B.

Non-Liquid Asset A type of asset that is not turned into cash very easily.

Non-Performing Loan A loan agreement that cannot meet its contractual principal and interest payments.

Non-Recourse Debt A loan that limits the lender's options to collect on the value of the real estate in the event of a default by the borrower.

Nonrecurring Closing Costs Fees that are only paid one time in a given transaction.

Note A legal document requiring a borrower to repay a mortgage at a specified interest rate over a certain period of time.

Note Rate The interest rate that is defined in a mortgage note.

Notice of Default A formal written notification a borrower receives once the borrower is in default stating that legal action may be taken.

Offer A term that describes a specified price or spread to sell whole loans or securities.

One-Year Adjustable-Rate Mortgage ARM for which the interest rate changes annually, generally based on movements of a published index and a specified margin.

Open Space A section of land or water that has been dedicated for public or private use or enjoyment.

Open-End Fund Type of commingled fund with an infinite life, always accepting new investor capital and making new investments in property.

Operating Cost Escalation A clause that is intended to adjust rents to account for external standards such as published indexes, negotiated wage levels, or building-related expenses.

Operating Expense The regular costs associated with operating and managing a property.

Opportunistic A phrase that generally describes a strategy of holding investments in under-performing and/or under-managed assets with the expectation of increases in cash flow and/or value.

Option A condition in which the buyer pays for the right to purchase a property within a certain period of time without the obligation to buy.

Option ARM Loan A type of mortgage in which the borrower has a variety of payment options each month.

Original Principal Balance The total principal owed on a mortgage before a borrower has made a payment.

Origination Fee A fee that most lenders charge for the purpose of covering the costs associated with arranging the loan.

Originator A company that underwrites loans for commercial and/ or multi-family properties.

Out-Parcel The individual retail sites located within a shopping center.

Overallotment A practice in which the underwriters offer and sell a higher number of shares than they had planned to purchase from the issuer.

Owner Financing A transaction in which the property seller agrees to finance all or part of the amount of the purchase.

Parking Ratio A figure, generally expressed as square footage, that compares a building's total rentable square footage to its total number of parking spaces.

Partial Payment An amount paid that is not large enough to cover the normal monthly payment on a mortgage loan.

Partial Sales The act of selling a real estate interest that is smaller than the whole property.

Partial Taking The appropriating of a portion of an owner's property under the laws of Eminent Domain.

Participating Debt Financing allowing the lender to have participatory rights to equity through increased income and/or residual value over the balance of the loan or original value at the time the loan is funded.

Party in Interest Any party that may hold an interest, including employers, unions, and, sometimes, fiduciaries.

Pass-Through Certificate A document that allows the holder to receive payments of principal and interest from the underlying pool of mortgages.

Payment Cap The maximum amount a monthly payment may increase on an ARM.

Payment Change Date The date on which a new payment amount takes effect on an ARM or GPM, usually in the month directly after the adjustment date.

Payout Ratio The percentage of the primary earnings per share, excluding unusual items, that are paid to common stockholders as cash dividends during the next 12 months.

Pension Liability The full amount of capital that is required to finance vested pension fund benefits.

Percentage Rent The amount of rent that is adjusted based on the percentage of gross sales or revenues the tenant receives.

Per-Diem Interest The interest that is charged or accrued daily.

Performance Bond A bond that a contractor posts to guarantee full performance of a contract in which the proceeds will be used for completing the contract or compensating the owner for loss in the event of nonperformance.

Performance Measurement The process of measuring how well an investor's real estate has performed regarding individual assets, advisers/ managers, and portfolios.

Performance The changes each quarter in fund or account values that can be explained by investment income, realized or unrealized appreciation, and the total return to the investors before and after investment management fees.

Performance-Based Fees The fees that advisers or managers receive that are based on returns to investors.

Periodic Payment Cap The highest amount that payments can increase or decrease during a given adjustment period on an ARM.

Periodic Rate Cap The maximum amount that the interest rate can increase or decrease during a given adjustment period on an ARM.

Permanent Loan A long-term property mortgage.

Personal Property Any items belonging to a person that is not real estate.

PITI Principal, Interest, Taxes, Insurance. The items that are included in the monthly payment to the lender for an impounded loan, as well as mortgage insurance.

PITI Reserves The amount in cash that a borrower must readily have after the down payment and all closing costs are paid when purchasing a home.

Plan Assets The assets included in a pension plan.

Plan Sponsor The party that is responsible for administering an employee benefit plan.

Planned Unit Development (PUD) A type of ownership where individuals actually own the building or unit they live in, but common areas are owned jointly with the other members of the development or association. Contrast with condominium, where an individual actually owns the airspace of his unit, but the buildings and common areas are owned jointly with the others in the development or association.

Plat A chart or map of a certain area showing the boundaries of individual lots, streets, and easements.

Pledged Account Mortgage (PAM) A loan tied to a pledged savings account for which the fund and earned interest are used to gradually reduce mortgage payments.

Point Also referred to as a Discount Point. A fee a lender charges to provide a lower interest rate, equal to 1 percent of the amount of the loan.

Portfolio Management A process that involves formulating, modifying, and implementing a real estate investment strategy according to an investor's investment objectives.

Portfolio Turnover The amount of time averaged from the time an investment is funded until it is repaid or sold.

Power of Attorney A legal document that gives someone the authority to act on behalf of another party.

Power of Sale The clause included in a

mortgage or deed of trust that provides the mortgagee (or trustee) with the right and power to advertise and sell the property at public auction if the borrower is in default.

Pre-Approval The complete analysis a lender makes regarding a potential borrower's ability to pay for a home as well as a confirmation of the proposed amount to be borrowed.

Pre-Approval Letter The letter a lender presents that states the amount of money they are willing to lend a potential buyer.

Preferred Shares Certain stocks that have a prior distributions claim up to a defined amount before the common shareholders may receive anything.

Pre-Leased A certain amount of space in a proposed building that must be leased before construction may begin or a certificate of occupancy may be issued.

Prepaid Expenses The amount of money that is paid before it is due, including taxes, insurance, and/or assessments.

Prepaid Fees The charges that a borrower must pay in advance regarding certain recurring items, such as interest, property taxes, hazard insurance, and PMI, if applicable.

Prepaid Interest The amount of interest that is paid before its due date.

Prepayment The money that is paid to reduce the principal balance of a loan before the date it is due.

Prepayment Penalty A penalty that may be charged to the borrower when he pays off a loan before the planned maturity date.

Prepayment Rights The right a borrower is given to pay the total principal balance before the maturity date free of penalty.

Prequalification The initial assessment by a lender of a potential borrower's ability to pay for a home as well as an estimate of how much the lender is willing to supply to the buyer.

Price-to-Earnings Ratio The comparison that is derived by dividing the current share price by the sum of the primary earnings per share from continuing operations over the past year.

Primary Issuance The preliminary financing of an issuer.

Prime Rate The best interest rate reserved for a bank's preferred customers.

Prime Space The first-generation space that is available for lease.

Prime Tenant The largest or highest-earning tenant in a building or shopping center.

Principal The amount of money originally borrowed in a mortgage, before interest is included and with any payments subtracted.

Principal Balance The total current balance of mortgage principal not including interest.

Principal Paid over Life of Loan The final total of scheduled payments to the principal that the lender calculates to equal the face amount of the loan.

Principal Payments The lender's return of invested capital.

Principle of Conformity The concept that a property will probably increase in value if its size, age, condition, and style are similar to other properties in the immediate area.

Private Debt Mortgages or other liabilities for which an individual is responsible.

Private Equity A real estate investment that has been acquired by a noncommercial entity.

Private Mortgage Insurance (PMI) A type of policy that a lender requires when the borrower's down payment or home equity percentage is under 20 percent of the value of the property.

Private Placement The sale of a security in a way that renders it exempt from the registration rules and requirements of the SEC.

Private REIT A real estate investment company that is structured as a real estate investment trust that places and holds shares privately rather than publicly.

Pro Rata The proportionate amount of expenses per tenant for the property's maintenance and operation.

Processing Fee A fee some lenders charge for gathering the information necessary to process the loan.

Production Acres The portion of land that can be used directly in agriculture or timber activities to generate income, but not areas used for such things as machinery storage or support.

Prohibited Transaction Certain transactions that may not be performed between a pension plan and a party in interest, such as the following: the sale, exchange or lease of any property; a loan or other grant of credit; and furnishing goods or services.

Promissory Note A written agreement to repay the specific amount over a certain period of time.

Property Tax The tax that must be paid on private property.

Prudent Man Rule The standard to which ERISA holds a fiduciary accountable.

Public Auction An announced public meeting held at a specified location for the purpose of selling property to repay a mortgage in default.

Public Debt Mortgages or other liabilities for which a commercial entity is responsible.

Public Equity A real estate investment that has been acquired by REITs and other publicly traded real estate operating companies.

Punch List An itemized list that documents incomplete or unsatisfactory items after the contractor has declared the space to be mostly complete.

Purchase Agreement The written contract the buyer and seller both sign defining the terms and conditions under which a property is sold.

Purchase Money Transaction A transaction in which property is acquired through the exchange of money or something of equivalent value.

Purchase-Money Mortgage (PMM) A mortgage obtained by a borrower that serves as partial payment for a property.

Qualified Plan Any employee benefit plan that the IRS has approved as a tax-exempt plan.

Qualifying Ratio The measurement a lender uses to determine how much they are willing to lend to a potential buyer.

Quitclaim Deed A written document that releases a party from any interest they may have in a property.

Rate Cap The highest interest rate allowed on a monthly payment during an adjustment period of an ARM.

Rate Lock The commitment of a lender to a borrower that guarantees a certain interest rate for a specific amount of time.

Rate-Improvement Mortgage A loan that includes a clause that entitles a borrower to a one-time-only cut in the interest rate without having to refinance.

Rating Agencies Independent firms that are engaged to rate securities' creditworthiness on behalf of investors.

Rating A figure that represents the credit quality or creditworthiness of securities.

Raw Land A piece of property that has not been developed and remains in its natural state.

Raw Space Shell space in a building that has not yet been developed.

Real Estate Agent An individual who is licensed to negotiate and transact the real estate sales.

Real Estate Fundamentals The factors that drive the value of property.

Real Estate Settlement Procedures Act (RESPA) A legislation for consumer protection that requires lenders to notify borrowers regarding closing costs in advance.

Real Property Land and anything else of a permanent nature that is affixed to the land.

Real Rate of Return The yield given to investors minus an inflationary factor.

Realtor A real estate agent or broker who is an active member of a local real estate board affiliated with the National Association of Realtors.

Recapture The act of the IRS recovering the tax benefit of a deduction or a credit that a taxpayer has previously taken in error.

Recorder A public official who records transactions that affect real estate in the area.

Recording The documentation that the registrar's office keeps of the details of properly executed legal documents.

Recording Fee A fee real estate agents charge for moving the sale of a piece of property into the public record.

Recourse Option a lender has for recovering losses against the personal assets of a secondary party who is also liable for a debt in default.

Red Herring Early prospectus distributed to prospective investors including a note in red ink on the cover stating the SEC-approved registration statement is not yet in effect.

Refinance Transaction The act of paying off an existing loan using the funding gained from a new loan that uses the same property as security.

Regional Diversification Boundaries that are defined based on geography or economic lines.

Registration Statement The set of forms that are filed with the SEC (or the appropriate state agency) regarding a proposed offering of new securities or the listing of outstanding securities on a national exchange.

Regulation Z A federal legislation under the Truth in Lending Act that requires lenders to advise the borrower in writing of all costs that are associated with the credit portion of a financial transaction.

Rehab Short for Rehabilitation. Refers to an extensive renovation intended to extend the life of a building or project.

Rehabilitation Mortgage A loan meant to fund the repairing and improving of a resale home or building.

Real Estate Investment Trust (REIT) A trust corporation that combines the capital of several investors for the purpose of acquiring or providing funding for real estate.

Remaining Balance The amount of the principal on a home loan that has not yet been paid.

Remaining Term The original term of the loan after the number of payments made has been subtracted.

Real Estate Mortgage Investment Conduit (REMIC) An investment vehicle that is designed to hold a pool of mortgages solely to issue multiple classes of mortgage-backed securities in a way that avoids doubled corporate tax.

Renewal Option A clause in a lease agreement that allows a tenant to extend the term of a lease.

Renewal Probability The average percentage of a building's tenants who are expected to renew terms at market rental rates upon the lease expiration.

Rent Commencement Date The date at which a tenant is to begin paying rent.

Rent Loss Insurance A policy that covers loss of rent or rental value for a landlord due to any condition that renders the leased premises inhabitable, thereby excusing the tenant from paying rent.

Rent The fee paid for the occupancy and/or use of any rental property or equipment.

Rentable/Usable Ratio A total rentable area in a building divided by the area available for use.

Rental Concession See: Concessions.

Rental Growth Rate The projected trend of market rental rates over a particular period of analysis.

Rent-Up Period The period of time following completion of a new building when tenants are actively being sought and the project is stabilizing.

Real Estate Owned (REO) The real estate that a savings institution owns as a result of foreclosure on borrowers in default.

Repayment Plan An agreement made to repay late installments or advances.

Replacement Cost Projected cost by current standards of constructing a building that is equivalent to the building being appraised.

Replacement Reserve Fund Money that is set aside for replacing of common property in a condominium, PUD, or cooperative project.

Request for Proposal (RFP) A formal request that invites investment managers to submit information regarding investment strategies, historical investment performance, current investment opportunities, investment management fees, and other pension fund client relationships used by their firm.

Rescission The legal withdrawing of a contract or consent from the parties involved.

Reserve Account An account that must be funded by the borrower to protect the lender.

Resolution Trust Corp. (RTC) The congressional corporation established for containing, managing, and selling failed financial institutions, thereby recovering taxpayer funds.

Retail Investor An investor who sells interests directly to consumers.

Retention Rate The percentage of trailing year's earnings that have been dispersed into the company again. It is calculated as 100 minus the trailing 12-month payout ratio.

Return on Assets The measurement of the ability to produce net profits efficiently by making use of assets.

Return on Equity The measurement of the return on the investment in a business or property.

Return on Investments The percentage of money that has been gained as a result of certain investments.

Reverse Mortgage See: Home Equity Conversion Mortgage.

Reversion Capitalization Rate The capitalization rate that is used to derive reversion value.

Reversion Value A benefit that an investor expects to receive as a lump sum at the end of an investment.

Revolving Debt A credit arrangement that enables a customer to borrow against a predetermined line of credit when purchasing goods and services.

Revenue per Available Room (RevPAR) The total room revenue for a particular period divided by the average number of rooms available in a hospitality facility.

Right of Ingress or Egress The option to enter or to leave the premises in question.

Right of Survivorship The option that survivors have to take on the interest of a deceased joint tenant.

Right to Rescission A legal provision that enables borrowers to cancel certain loan types within three days after they sign.

Risk Management A logical approach to analyzing and defining insurable and non-insurable risks while evaluating the availability and costs of purchasing third-party insurance.

Risk-Adjusted Rate of Return A percentage that is used to identify investment options that are expected to deliver a positive premium despite their volatility.

Road Show A tour of the executives

of a company that is planning to go public, during which the executives travel to a variety of cities to make presentations to underwriters and analysts regarding their company and IPO.

Roll-Over Risk The possibility that tenants will not renew their lease.

Sale-Leaseback An arrangement in which a seller deeds a property, or part of it, to a buyer in exchange for money or the equivalent, then leases the property from the new owner.

Sales Comparison Value A value that is calculated by comparing the appraised property to similar properties in the area that have been recently sold.

Sales Contract An agreement that both the buyer and seller sign defining the terms of a property sale.

Second Mortgage A secondary loan obtained on a piece of property.

Secondary Market A market in which existing mortgages are bought and sold as part of a mortgages pool.

Secondary (Follow-On) Offering An offering of stock made by a company that is already public.

Second-Generation or Secondary Space Space that has been occupied before and becomes available for lease again, either by the landlord or as a sublease.

Secured Loan A loan that is secured by some sort of collateral.

Securities and Exchange Commission (SEC) The federal agency that oversees the issuing and exchanging of public securities.

Securitization The act of converting a non-liquid asset into a tradable form.

Security The property or other asset that will serve as a loan's collateral.

Security Deposit An amount of money a tenant gives to a landlord to secure the performance of terms in a lease agreement.

Seisen (Seizen) The ownership of real property under a claim of freehold estate.

Self-Administered REIT A REIT in which the management are employees of the REIT or similar entity.

Self-Managed REIT See: Self-Administered REIT.

Seller Carry-Back An arrangement in which the seller provides the financing to purchase a home.

Seller Financing A type of funding in which the borrower may use part of the equity in the property to finance purchase.

Senior Classes The security classes who have the highest priority for receiving payments from the underlying mortgage loans.

Separate Account A relationship in which a single pension plan sponsor is used to retain an investment manager or adviser under a stated investment policy exclusively for that sponsor.

Servicer An organization that collects principal and interest payments from borrowers and manages borrowers' escrow accounts on behalf of a trustee.

Servicing The process of collecting mortgage payments from borrowers as well as related responsibilities.

Setback The distance required from a given reference point before a structure can be built.

Settlement or Closing Fees The fees that the escrow agent receives for carrying out the written instructions in the agreement between borrower and lender and/or buyer and seller.

Settlement Statement See: HUD-1 Settlement Statement.

Shared-Appreciation Mortgage A loan that enables a lender or other party to share in the profits of the borrower when the borrower sells the home.

Shared-Equity Transaction A transaction in which two people purchase a property, one as a residence and the other as an investment.

Shares Outstanding The number of shares of outstanding common stock minus the treasury shares.

Site Analysis A determination of how suitable a specific parcel of land is for a particular use.

Site Development The implementation of all improvements that are needed for a site before construction may begin.

Site Plan A detailed description and map of the location of improvements to a parcel.

Slab The flat, exposed surface that is laid over the structural support beams to form the building's floor(s).

Social Investing A strategy in which investments are driven in partially or completely by social or non-real estate objectives.

Soft Cost The part of an equity investment, aside from the literal cost of the improvements, that could be tax-deductible in the first year.

Space Plan A chart or map of space requirements for a tenant that includes wall/door locations, room sizes, and even furniture layouts.

Special Assessment Certain charges that are levied against real estates for public improvements to benefit the property in question.

Special Servicer A company that is hired to collect on mortgages that are either delinquent or in default.

Specified Investing A strategy of investment in individually specified properties, portfolios, or commingled funds are fully or partially detailed prior to the commitment of investor capital.

Speculative Space Any space in a rental property that has not been leased prior to construction on a new building begins.

Stabilized Net Operating Income Expected income minus expenses that reflect relatively stable operations.

Stabilized Occupancy The best projected range of long-term occupancy that a piece of rental property will achieve after existing in the open market for a reasonable period of time with terms and conditions that are comparable to similar offerings.

Step-Rate Mortgage A loan that allows for a gradual interest rate increase during the first few years of the loan.

Step-Up Lease (Graded Lease) A lease agreement that specifies certain increases in rent at certain intervals during the complete term of the lease.

Straight Lease (Flat Lease) A lease agreement that specifies an amount of rent that should be paid regularly during the complete term of the lease.

Strip Center Any shopping area that is made up of a row of stores but is not large enough to be anchored by a grocery store.

Subcontractor A contractor who has been hired by the general contractor, often specializing in a certain required task for the construction project.

Subdivision The most common type of housing development created by dividing a larger tract of land into individual lots for sale or lease.

Sublessee A person or business that holds the rights of use and occupancy under a lease contract with the original lessee, who still retains primary responsibility for the lease obligations.

Subordinate Financing Any loan with a priority lower than loans that were obtained beforehand.

Subordinate Loan A second or third mortgage obtained with the same property being used as collateral.

Subordinated Classes Classes that have the lowest priority of receiving payments from underlying mortgage loans.

Subordination The act of sharing credit loss risk at varying rates among two or more classes of securities.

Subsequent Rate Adjustments The interest rate for ARMs that adjusts at regular intervals, sometimes differing from the duration period of the initial interest rate.

Subsequent Rate Cap Maximum amount the interest rate may increase at each regularly scheduled interest rate adjustment date on an ARM.

Super Jumbo Mortgage A loan that is over $650,000 for some lenders or $1,000,000 for others.

Surety A person who willingly binds himself to the debt or obligation of another party.

Surface Rights A right or easement usually granted with mineral rights that enables the holder to drill through the surface.

Survey A document or analysis containing the precise measurements of a piece of property as performed by a licensed surveyor.

Sweat Equity The non-cash improvements in value that an owner adds to a piece of property.

Synthetic Lease A transaction that is considered to be a lease by accounting standards but a loan by tax standards.

Taking Similar to condemning, or any other interference with rights to private property, but a physical seizure or appropriation is not required.

Tax Base Determined value of all property that lies within the jurisdiction of the taxing authority.

Tax Lien A type of lien placed against a property if the owner has not paid property or personal taxes.

Tax Roll Record that contains the descriptions of all land parcels and their owners that is located within the county.

Tax Service Fee A fee that is charged for the purpose of setting up monitoring of the borrower's property tax payments by a third party.

Teaser Rate A small, short-term interest rate offered on a mortgage in order to convince the potential borrower to apply.

Tenancy by the Entirety A form of ownership held by spouses in which they both hold title to the entire property with right of survivorship.

Tenancy in Common A type of ownership held by two or more owners in an undivided interest in the property with no right of survivorship.

Tenant (Lessee) A party who rents a piece of real estate from another by way of a lease agreement.

Tenant at Will A person who possesses a piece of real estate with the owner's permission.

Tenant Improvement (TI) Allowance The specified amount of money that the landlord contributes toward tenant improvements.

Tenant Improvement (TI) The upgrades or repairs that are made to the leased premises by or for a tenant.

Tenant Mix The quality of the income stream for a property.

Term The length that a loan lasts or is expected to last before it is repaid.

Third-Party Origination A process in which another party is used by the lender to originate, process, underwrite, close, fund, or package the mortgages it expects to deliver to the secondary mortgage market.

Timeshare A form of ownership involving purchasing a specific period of time or percentage of interest in a vacation property.

Time-Weighted Average Annual Rate of Return The regular yearly return over several years that would have the same return value as combining the actual annual returns for each year in the series.

Title The legal written document that provides someone ownership in a piece of real estate.

Title Company A business that determines that a property title is clear and that provides title insurance.

Title Exam An analysis of the public records in order to confirm that the seller is the legal owner, and there are no encumbrances on the property.

Title Insurance A type of policy that is issued to both lenders and buyers to cover loss due to property ownership disputes that may arise at a later date.

Title Insurance Binder A written promise from the title insurance company to insure the title to the property, based on the conditions and exclusions shown in the binder.

Title Risk The potential impediments in transferring a title from one party to another.

Title Search The process of analyzing all transactions existing in the public record in order to determine whether any title defects could interfere with the clear transfer of property ownership.

Total Acres The complete amount of land area that is contained within a real estate investment.

Total Assets The final amount of all gross investments, cash and equivalents, receivables, and other assets as they are presented on the balance sheet.

Total Commitment The complete funding amount that is promised once all specified conditions have been met.

Total Expense Ratio The comparison of monthly debt obligations to gross monthly income.

Total Inventory The total amount of square footage commanded by property within a geographical area.

Total Lender Fees Charges that the lender requires for obtaining the loan, aside from other fees associated with the transfer of a property.

Total Loan Amount The basic amount of the loan plus any additional financed closing costs.

Total Monthly Housing Costs The amount that must be paid each month to cover principal, interest, property taxes, PMI, and/or either hazard insurance or homeowners' association dues.

Total of All Payments The total cost of the loan after figuring the sum of all monthly interest payments.

Total Principal Balance The sum of all debt, including the original loan amount adjusted for subsequent payments and any unpaid items that may be included in the principal balance by the mortgage note or by law.

Total Retail Area The total floor area of a retail center that is currently leased or available for lease.

Total Return Final amount of income and appreciation returns per quarter.

Townhouse An attached home that is not considered to be a condominium.

Trade Fixtures Any personal property that is attached to a structure and used in the business but is removable once the lease is terminated.

Trading Down The act of purchasing a property that is less expensive than the one currently owned.

Trading Up The act of purchasing a property that is more expensive than the one currently owned.

Tranche A class of securities that may or may not be rated.

TransUnion Corporation One of the primary credit-reporting bureaus.

Transfer of Ownership Any process in which a property changes hands from one owner to another.

Transfer Tax An amount specified by state or local authorities when ownership in a piece of property changes hands.

Treasury Index A measurement that is used to derive interest rate changes for ARMs.

Triple Net Lease A lease that requires the tenant to pay all property expenses on top of the rental payments.

Trustee A fiduciary who oversees property or funds on behalf of another party.

Truth-in-Lending The federal legislation requiring lenders to fully disclose the terms and conditions of a mortgage in writing.

TurnKey Project A project in which

all components are within a single supplier's responsibility.

Two- to Four-Family Property A structure that provides living space for two to four families while ownership is held in a single deed.

Two-Step Mortgage An ARM with two different interest rates: one for the loan's first five or seven years and another for the remainder of the loan term.

Under Construction The time period that exists after a building's construction has started but before a certificate of occupancy has been presented.

Under Contract The period of time during which a buyer's offer to purchase a property has been accepted, and the buyer is able to finalize financing arrangements without the concern of the seller making a deal with another buyer.

Underwriter A company, usually an investment banking firm, that is involved in a guarantee that an entire issue of stocks or bonds will be purchased.

Underwriters' Knot An approved knot according to code that may be tied at the end of an electrical cord to prevent the wires from being pulled away from their connection to each other or to electrical terminals.

Underwriting The process during which lenders analyze the risks a particular borrower presents and set appropriate conditions for the loan.

Underwriting Fee A fee that mortgage lenders charge for verifying the information on the loan application and making a final decision on approving the loan.

Unencumbered A term that refers to property free of liens or other encumbrances.

Unimproved Land See: Raw Land.

Unrated Classes Usually the lowest classes of securities.

Unrecorded Deed A deed that transfers right of ownership from one owner to another without being officially documented.

Umbrella Partnership Real Estate Investment Trust (UPREIT) An organizational structure in which a REIT's assets are owned by a holding company for tax reasons.

Usable Square Footage The total area that is included within the exterior walls of the tenant's space.

Use The particular purpose for which a property is intended to be employed.

VA Loan A mortgage through the VA program in which a down payment is not necessarily required.

Vacancy Factor The percentage of gross revenue that pro-forma income statements expect to be lost due to vacancies.

Vacancy Rate The percentage of space that is available to rent.

Vacant Space Existing rental space that is presently being marketed for lease minus space that is available for sublease.

Value-Added A phrase advisers and managers generally use to describe investments in underperforming and/or under-managed assets.

Variable Rate Mortgage (VRM) A loan in which the interest rate changes according to fluctuations in particular indexes.

Variable Rate Also called adjustable rate. The interest rate on a loan that varies over the term of the loan according to a predetermined index.

Variance A permission that enables a property owner to work around a zoning ordinance's literal requirements which cause a unique hardship due to special circumstances.

Verification of Deposit (VOD) The confirmation statement a borrower's bank may be asked to sign in order to verify the borrower's account balances and history.

Verification of Employment

(VOE) The confirmation statement a borrower's employer may be asked to sign in order to verify the borrower's position and salary.

Vested Having the right to draw on a portion or on all of a pension or other retirement fund.

Veterans Affairs (VA) A federal government agency that assists veterans in purchasing a home without a down payment.

Virtual Storefront A retail business presence on the Internet.

Waiting Period The period of time between initially filing a registration statement and the date it becomes effective.

Warehouse Fee A closing cost fee that represents the lender's expense of temporarily holding a borrower's loan before it is sold on the secondary mortgage market.

Weighted-Average Coupon The average, using the balance of each mortgage as the weighting factor, of the gross interest rates of the mortgages underlying a pool as of the date of issue.

Weighted-Average Equity The part of the equation that is used to calculate investment-level income, appreciation, and total returns on a quarter-by-quarter basis.

Weighted-Average Rental Rates The average ratio of unequal rental rates across two or more buildings in a market.

Working Drawings The detailed blueprints for a construction project that comprise the contractual documents which describe the exact manner in which a project is to be built.

Workout The strategy in which a borrower negotiates with a lender to attempt to restructure the borrower's debt rather than go through the foreclosure proceedings.

Wraparound Mortgage A loan obtained by a buyer to use for the remaining balance on the seller's first mortgage, as well as an additional amount requested by the seller.

Write-Down A procedure used in accounting when an asset's book value is adjusted downward to reflect current market value more accurately.

Write-Off A procedure used in accounting when an asset is determined to be uncollectible and is therefore considered to be a loss.

Yield Maintenance Premium A penalty the borrower must pay in order to make investors whole in the event of early repayment of principal.

Yield Spread The difference in income derived from a commercial mortgage

and from a benchmark value.

Yield The actual return on an investment, usually paid in dividends or interest.

Zoning Ordinance The regulations and laws that control the use or improvement of land in a particular area or zone.

Zoning The act of dividing a city or town into particular areas and applying laws and regulations regarding the architectural design, structure, and intended uses of buildings within those areas.

INDEX

A

Afford 100
Affordable housing 79
Age 187
Agent 53, 72, 92, 142, 146, 156
Amenities 35, 37
Amenities 24–42, 31, 54, 63, 79, 80, 95, 109
Amortization 195, 211
Amortized 104
Apartment 28, 55, 73, 110, 139, 142, 171
Apartments 23, 27, 29
Appliances 30, 168
Appraisal 71
Appraisers 160
Assessment 97, 99, 107
Association 41, 110, 181
Associations 89
Attorney 72, 181
Attorneys 159

B

Bad Credit 79, 89, 99, 109, 119, 129, 139, 145, 153, 163, 171, 173, 181, 189, 193, 247
Balconies 50
Bankers 160
Borrower 101
Budget 97, 99
Builder 164, 166
Builders 169
Building 30, 191
Buy 73
Buyer 61, 69
Buyers 31, 45, 68, 161
Buying 139, 149, 164
Bylaws 61, 76, 78, 96, 181

C

Children 48, 74, 83, 141, 145, 151, 182
Closing 71-72, 148, 150
Clubhouse 109

CMA 47, 148
Common areas 34
Communities 114, 158, 172
Community 40, 50, 110, 120
Comparative market analysis 41
Complex 40, 45, 61, 92, 93, 109, 111, 115, 116, 120, 130, 145, 147, 164, 167
Compliance 185
Conditions 190
Condo 32, 33, 34, 50, 53, 54, 55, 61, 63, 73, 92, 105, 106, 110, 125, 126, 131, 171, 193
Condominium 115, 158, 181
Condos 23, 29, 43, 55, 63, 79, 83, 113, 176
Cost 131
Courtyards 45
Credit 150
Credit report 100

D

Debt-to-income ratio 100
Deck 50
Decks 61
Deed 72
Deposit 121
Developer 60, 102, 104, 165, 166, 167
Developers 166, 171
Development 165
Developments 89, 159, 163
Down payment 119
Downsizing 83
Dues 41, 106

E

Engineering 189
Equity 163
Expense 115
Exterior 29, 94, 191

F

Finance 99, 119, 122, 125, 148
Financing 99-102, 119, 149
Furnishings 44, 179
Furniture 179, 180

G

Getaway 176

H

Home 189
Home inspectors 160
Homeowner 38, 63, 66, 74, 99, 151, 158
Homeowner's association 47, 73, 86, 89, 91, 92, 94, 105, 106, 114, 118, 131, 158, 159, 164, 181
Homeowners 24, 38, 55, 81, 90, 97, 105
Homes 43
Hotel 50
Housing 46, 167, 173

I

Income 176
Inspection 71, 189, 192

Inspector 115
Insurance 65, 66, 95, 101
Interest 211, 219
Interest rate 100
Interests 166
Interior 191
Investing 109, 113
Investment 96, 101, 109, 115, 116, 124, 133, 142
Investments 139, 176
Investor 116, 172, 179
Investors 157

J

Job 45

L

Landlord 75
Lease 51, 119, 120, 121, 122, 123, 124, 125
Lender 100, 101
Lenders 160
Liability 101
Lifestyle 50, 51
Living 111
Loan 72, 104, 149
Loans 101
Location 110, 115, 117, 140, 141

M

Maintain 91
Maintenance 36, 26, 86, 94, 110, 118, 139
Manage 141
Management 76

Manager 189
Market 53, 140, 142, 157, 171
Mortgage 72, 117, 219
Moving 151

N

Negotiations 145
Neighbors 38, 91, 152
Noise 182

O

Obstructions 183
Owner 125, 139, 174
Ownership 38, 130, 172

P

Parking 174, 185
Patios 184
Payment 99, 123, 193, 195, 211
Payments 105
Pet 183
Pets 46, 75, 112, 182
Playground 117
Pool 26, 31, 35, 109, 117, 186
Pools 95
Price 40
Principal 211
Profit 28, 140, 143
Properties 90, 115, 141
Property 55, 92, 101, 117, 139, 183
Purchase 41, 65, 168
Purchases 99
Purchasing 172

R

Real estate 31, 54, 71, 146
Realtor 44
Rent-to-own 103, 122
Rent-to-own 122
Responsibilities 158
Responsibility 38
Restrictions 44
Restrictions 46, 73, 78, 175
Rule 185
Rules 181
Rules 90

S

Sale 65, 135
Schools 45, 63
Security 31, 37, 50
Sell 110
Seller 56, 67, 69, 102, 104, 119,
    125, 149
Sellers 68, 161
Selling 139, 174
Shared Housing 173
Shared Housing 119
Shared Housing 23, 31, 38, 46,
    49, 53, 61, 63, 79, 84, 85,
    99, 101, 109, 145, 152, 163,
    171, 172
Signs 184
Site 191
Storage 111
Survey 71
Surveyors 160
Swimming 30

T

Tenants 118, 142
Tennis courts 109
Timeshares 132
Townhomes 63
Townhouse 171
Townhouse 34, 50, 53, 73, 105,
    110, 130, 131, 193
Townhouses 33, 157. *townhouses* townhouse
Townhouses 23, 55, 79, 83, 84,
    176
Transactions 156
Turnaround 114

U

Unit 115, 163, 164
Units 172
Utility 191

V

Vacation 129
Vacation 130, 132, 134, 137, 138,
    163, 179, 180

W

Warranties 65, 67
Warranty 68, 69, 70, 82